W9-CFQ-347

The Golden Age of the Passenger Train

The GOLDEN AGE of the PASSENGER TRAIN

From Steam to Diesel and Beyond

C.J. Riley

MetroBooks

MetroBooks

An Imprint of Friedman/Fairfax Publishers

© 1997 by Michael Friedman Publishing Group, Inc.

All rights reserved. No part of this publication may be reproduced, stored in a retrieval system, or transmitted, in any form or by any means, electronic, mechanical, photocopying, recording, or otherwise, without prior written permission from the publisher.

Library of Congress Cataloging-in-Publication Data

Riley, C.J., 1942-
    The golden age of the passenger train : from steam to diesel and beyond / C.J. Riley.
        p.   cm.
    Includes bibliographical references and index.
    ISBN 1-56799-383-4
    1.   Railroads—History. I.   Title.
TF15.R55   1997
385'.262'09—dc20   96-38290

Editor: Nathaniel Marunas
Art Director: Kevin Ullrich
Designer: Eddy Hersche
Photography Editors: Karen L. Barr and Emilya Naymark

Color separations by Colourscan Co. Pte. Ltd.
Printed in Great Britain by Butler & Tanner Limited

1   3   5   7   9   10   8   6   4   2

For bulk purchases and special sales, please contact:
Friedman/Fairfax Publishers
Attention: Sales Department
15 West 26th Street
New York, NY 10010
212/685-6610 FAX 212/685-1307

Visit our website:
http://www.metrobooks.com

Dedication page: The *De Witt Clinton* was the third locomotive built in the United States for active service on a railroad. It was constructed by the West Point Foundry Works for the Mohawk and Hudson Railroad and put into experimental service in July 1831. The locomotive and its consist became the first passenger train ever to operate in New York State on August 9, 1831, when engineer David Matthew transported several excursionists from Albany to Schenechtady. One of the passengers on that historic trip made a sketch of the event, and from his sketch created this cut-out representation.

Contents page: As a coal-hauling railroad, the Norfolk & Western remained serious about steam power longer than any other U.S. railroad. Their magnificent 6000hp class-J 4-8-4s were built in the N&W's Roanoke shops between 1941 and 1943. The original heavyweight consist was replaced in 1949 with new smooth-side lightweight equipment. Locomotive No. 611, which at one time hauled the legendary Powhatan Arrow, was spared the scrap heap (the N&W dieselized completely by May 6, 1960) and was eventually restored. The Powhatan Arrow used to make the journey from Norfolk, Virginia, to Cincinnati, Ohio, in just under sixteen hours, regularly achieving speeds in excess of 90 mph (144kph). This elegant maroon-and-black streamliner returned to the rails for excursion service in 1981, operating until 1995, when the Norfolk Southern (a merger of the N&W with the Southern) ended its ambitious steam program and returned the locomotive to storage.

Dedication

To my most tolerant and loving wife, Denise, who has seen fit to put up
with my foibles and diversions for much longer than I probably deserve.

Acknowledgments

While the sum of my railroad ken has been augmented by various sources
and by my associations with many other knowledgeable people throughout
my life, I would particularly like to express my gratitude to the following,
whose acumen, assistance, and encouragement were crucial to the
successful completion of the book:

Anthony W. Thompson

Kalmbach Memorial Library

William Metzger

William Schaumburg

The Staff of the Michael Friedman Group, including:

Editor Nathaniel Marunas

Photo Editors Karen Barr and Emilya Naymark

Designer Kevin Ullrich

Contents

Foreword

In the early days of railways in Britain, men pushed coal-laden carts on wooden rails through the dank tunnels of mines; over time, these man-powered vehicles were replaced by swifter horse-drawn carts, which could carry more material; and eventually passenger coaches were also pulled by horses walking between the rails.

Steam-powered machinery was first installed in the British collieries to remove the water that was steadily seeping into the deep pits. After this it was only a matter of time before this wonderful new technology was applied to the propulsion of vehicles, the first of which were road vehicles. The smooth surfaces of even the earliest rails were far smoother than the rutted and muddy dirt roads of the day, making steam locomotives the next logical step in the evolution of transportation. And after all, even the earliest trains were capable of speeds in excess of 20 mph (32kph), far outpacing the 4 to 8mph (6–13kph) mean speed of a horse and carriage.

The ability of a steam-powered train to haul considerable quantities of goods cheaply and quickly provided an important impetus to the Industrial Revolution and simultaneously allowed agricultural markets to expand. The spread of rail networks allowed more convenient and faster travel for people, too, which in turn led to the quicker dissemination of news and ideas. Communities became less isolated, and businesses were no longer limited to marketplaces consisting only of nearby customers.

Without a network of rails, the populations of less developed countries of the early Industrial Revolution—such as Canada, the United States, and Australia—might have remained dependent on a limited proximity to the seacoasts or navigable waterways. Instead, the North American and Australian transcontinental railways knitted the coasts together, making it possible for populations to develop in many areas of these vast new nations.

Not surprisingly, communities raised funds, invested in railroad bonds, and lobbied furiously to insure that railroad service would be provided to them, so as to benefit from the expected commercial wealth and social benefits sure to arrive with the first trains. Cities such as Chicago and Winnipeg were minor backwater towns before becoming major rail-road centers. Other transportation industries were also affected, with many canal companies folding and others going into the railroad business themselves. Railroads soon provided the most reliable means of travel over medium and long distances, since even their modest speeds far exceeded those of foot- or horsepower, and water travel was limited to the few navigable waterways. The railroad became central to both rural and urban communities.

In North America, farmers shipped their produce to faraway markets and received farm implements and items from the Sears and Roebuck catalogue in return. And in developing countries around the world, salesmen could make personal calls to farflung customers, thereby widening their markets; draftees were sent off to and joyously returned from wars on the train; and locally unavailable medications arrived in time to cure illnesses. Indeed, there seemed to be no shortage of uses to which railroad technology could be put.

Although the earliest railway builders had considered passengers to be of secondary interest, often subcontracting that service to other companies, the pervasive human urge for mobility quickly changed rail managements' thinking, and passenger services grew into a highly competitive and important part of a railroad's business. A direct outgrowth of that was (express) mail service. The higher speed and fixed schedules of passenger trains encouraged shipments of small packages and mail, providing a source of income that was substantial enough to keep some trains running long after their appeal to human cargo had waned.

The development of more powerful and dependable internal-combustion engines had little impact on the railroads in the early twentieth century. Steam locomotives were powerful and fast, and the tremendous industry that developed in North America and Europe exported steam technology around the world. And while it took financially strong and powerful companies—such as General Motors, General Electric, Westinghouse, and Siemens—to demonstrate the practicality of diesel-electric locomotives to the world, it was the introduction of the streamliners in the late 1930s that aroused the public's passion. The custom-built Zephyr and M-10000 led to the slant-nosed E-units, GM's Electro-Motive Division's standardized line of streamlined passenger locomotives, and the fluted stainless steel lightweight passenger cars of the Budd Company.

Even as the railroads rushed to put these new streamlined trains into regular service, travelers in ever-increasing numbers were choosing other modes of transportation, particularly in North America. While the European governments were nationalizing and rebuilding the war-ravaged rail systems of the continent into a high-speed rail transportation network, the U.S. government was subsidizing the growing airline industry and building better highways. Thus it was that the preferred way of long-distance travel in the nineteenth century was eclipsed in the mid-

It is still possible to experience the golden age of the passenger train, if only in excursion service. The Chicago, Burlington & Quincy railroad (Burlington route) took delivery of sixteen E5 diesel locomotives in 1941, several of which were assigned to the Twin Zephyrs (Chicago–Minneapolis), replacing the older "shovel-nosed" locomotives from the mid-1930s. Following World War II, delivery of new Budd-built passenger cars relegated the pioneering articulated train sets to Nebraska Zephyr service (Chicago–Lincoln), where they served until 1968. E5 locomotive No. 9911A, *Silver Pilot*, was spared the scrap pile along with the "goddesses" of the train set (the cars named Venus, Vesta, Minerva, Ceres, Diana, Juno, and Psyche) and donated to the Illinois Railway Museum. Volunteers labored slowly to restore the diesel, and the train began limited operations at the museum with occasional forays onto the main line. Here, the Nebraska Zephyr rumbles across rural Wisconsin, a living reminder of the way rail travel used to be.

❖ ❖ ❖

twentieth century by the speed of modern air travel and the convenience of personal automobiles.

But are speed and convenience enough? For Edna St. Vincent Millay to have said, "Yet there isn't a plane I wouldn't take—no matter where it's going" seems most unlikely. There are clearly more intangibly appealing factors to rail travel than speed or convenience—otherwise human beings wouldn't find it so alluring.

At one time, of course, speed was a great part of the lure of passenger train travel. What travel experience could rank with the daily contests of the New York Central's Twentieth Century Limited and arch-rival Pennsylvania Railroad's Broadway Limited as they raced to be the first to reach Chicago, sixteen hours after leaving New York? Despite using quite different routes, on the final leg into the Windy City the two competitors ran on parallel tracks. Passengers and crews were passionate about the fierce rivalry and rejoiced when their train arrived first.

The New York–to–Chicago race aside, there is a pleasure and elegance in the slower pace of rail travel. The swaying cars, the clickety-clack of wheels crossing switch frogs, the pronounced Doppler effect as clanging bells change pitch when a grade crossing approaches and passes, and the "up close and personal" view of the ever-changing scenery are compelling. The inevitable conversation that results when strangers group together at a table in the dining car can be memorable, as can be the brief friendships made in the lounge. The harsh bleating of a poorly tuned air horn will never equal the plaintive wail of a steam whistle, but a good multichime horn with the proper chords can come darn close.

Riding on a passenger train is an emotional experience for many, an opportunity to stretch out and relax, read a book, escape from the hustle and bustle of normal life, perhaps even to rekindle pleasant memories of earlier trips or to fall in love. Is it possible to watch a passing train without wondering about the lives or destinations of the faces spotted in glowing windows—or to wonder likewise about the people in the ever-changing panorama seen from inside that window? A passenger train is more than a vehicle for travel—it is a way of experiencing an alternate (and often luxurious) lifestyle.

But beyond an experience to savor, a memory, or a timetable entry, a passenger train is also an ever-changing stable of locomotives, an evolving roster of passenger cars, a depot to depart from, and a crew to serve the needs of both passengers and equipment.

It is not possible to cover the complete history of every great train that deserves to be here, and the exclusion of a reader's favorite is not meant to slight. But I have tried to include examples of great trains that ran on the important routes, as well as some of the incidents and legends that helped to create the lore that makes passenger trains so fascinating.

This book tells the unique story of those trains—the history, technology, and human drama that transformed what started as a more efficient method of moving goods from place to place into the great adventure and romance that rail travel became—and after years of decline, can be once again.

C. J. Riley
Bainbridge Island, Washington

CHAPTER ONE

THE EARLY YEARS

The concept of the railway, in which wheeled vehicles are guided by a track, dates back to Babylonian times, about 2245 B.C. Parallel lines of stone blocks with grooves for wagon wheels having a gauge—the spacing between the rails—of 5 feet (1.5m) can still be found. As early as 1519, illustrators portrayed miners pushing wheeled carts along a wooden track, and a mine wagon with flanged wooden wheels, allegedly from the late sixteenth century, is preserved in a Berlin museum. The early technology was inevitably linked to mines because of the large volume of heavy material that needed to be constantly moved.

Horses succeeded men as a source of power, and iron strips topping the wooden rails improved rolling qualities, but true efficiency awaited mechanical power. The pioneers in the development of steam locomotives were simply searching for a more efficient way to move heavy loads around the slate and coal mines of the burgeoning Industrial Revolution. James Watt's successful harnessing of steam power led to Thomas Newcomen's 1705 steam pump, which was used to remove water from the deep mines. Using a piston system to drive the pump (the precursor to pistons driving a wheel), this invention demonstrated the capability of steam power to accomplish real work. William Jessop (1745–1813) developed the "fish-belly" cast-iron rail (1789), secured on stone sleepers, and the elements needed to develop a railroad were in place.

THE BRITISH PIONEERS

Locomotive design improved quickly. Richard Trevithic's (1771–1833) high-pressure steam and the refinements of Christopher Blackett and William Hedley gave *Puffing Billy* (1813) the power and reliability to trundle coal wagons around the Wylam Colliery for many years, leading to steady improvement in steam propulsion.

◆ ◆ ◆

Left: *Puffing Billy* (1813) was one of the early "grasshopper" type locomotives, named for the insect-like appearance imparted by the beam and linkages above the boiler that helped to maintain the alignment of the piston rods and the cylinders. The boiler was insulated (or lagged) with wood strips. Above: Before the invention of flanged wheels and rail, brute force and greased skids were the common way of moving heavy loads, as illustrated by this Assyrian

George Stephenson (1781–1848) was a "plugman" (steam pump tender) at Wylam when *Puffing Billy* arrived, and he quickly realized the future of steam locomotives, producing his own Blucher in 1814. Recognizing the unnecessary complexity of geared drives, Stephenson (with fellow employee Ralph Dodds) patented the Killingworth-type gearless drive, which used a chain/sprocket and crankpins and then developed the crankpin/connecting rod design that remained the standard until the end of the steam era.

Stephenson's mechanical and organizational skills won him an appointment by Quaker financier Robert Pease (1767–1858) to the important post of engineer for the Stockton & Darlington Railway. Chartered by the British Parliament in 1821 as the world's first public railway, the prime purpose of the Stockton & Darlington was to move coal some 25 miles (40km) from the Old

George Stephenson was one of the early giants of railway building. His skills in locomotive design, right-of-way engineering, bridge building, and operating concepts helped lay the foundations for modern railroading around the world.

✦ ✦ ✦

Etherly Colliery, northwest of Bishop Auckland, to tidewater at Cottage Row, Stockton. Passenger service was mentioned in the charter, but was clearly a secondary consideration and was provided via horse-drawn

When the Stockton & Darlington opened, steam power was used for coal hauling only—passengers were hauled in flange-wheeled coaches behind horses, as depicted in this John Wigton painting, *The Passing Loop*.

✦ ✦ ✦

coaches that were leased to individual toll-paying operators who were in turn responsible for collecting fares.

On the Stockton & Darlington, Stephenson oversaw the entire project, including grading and track work, drainage, rolling stock, buildings, and bridges, as well as the construction of several stationary steam engines, which hauled the primitive carriages over two ridges deemed too steep for the horses.

Stephenson's sophisticated design for the span across the river Gaunless—four elegant wrought-iron fish-belly girders—created the first iron railway bridge, a portion of which survives at the National Railway Museum, York. To provide a crossing over the river Skerne, a massive single masonry arch with elegant wing walls was erected.

During the line's construction, Pease also financed the Robert Stephenson Locomotive Works, named for Stephenson's son (1803–59) and partner, at Newcastle-upon-Tyne. Its first product was *Locomotion*, which was used on the Stockton & Darlington. The limitations of horse-drawn trains quickly became obvious, and three more locomotives—*Hope*, *Black Diamond*, and *Diligence*—soon followed.

When Timothy Hackworth (1786–1850), another mechanic from Wylam Colliery, was appointed to head the locomotive works, Stephenson was free to pursue larger projects. He took on the ambitious and difficult task of engineering the 35-mile (56km) Liverpool & Manchester Railway.

Lingering doubts about the usefulness of steam locomotives remained, despite twenty-five years of progress,

Rocket, winner of the Rainhill Trials (1829), advanced many of the concepts that would later become standard for steam power: cylinders driving the wheels via a crankpin, a multitube boiler, and a blast pipe for exhaust. The achieved speed of 29 mph (46kph) was the first noteworthy early speed record.

so the Liverpool & Manchester scheduled the 1829 Rainhill Trials, offering a prize of £500 for the locomotive that could meet the following specifications: operating with a steam pressure not to exceed 50 psi, and moving back and forth over a 1 ¾-mile (2.8km) course with a load of twenty tons (18t). The Stephensons entered the contest with *Rocket* (primarily the design of Robert), while their former superintendent Hackworth entered his own design, *Sans Pareil*. John Braithwaite (1797–1870) built *Novelty* to a design by John Ericsson (1803–1889). Timothy Birstall withdrew his *Perseverance* before the competition. *Cycloped*, a curious design by Thomas Shaw Brandreth (1788–1873), was powered by a horse walking on a treadmill, and actually achieved a speed of 15 mph (24kph).

Rocket represented a major advancement in technology, having a multiple-tube boiler, an outside water-jacketed firebox, and twin inclined cylinders that directly connected to a single pair of very large driving wheels (with a smaller pair supporting a larger firebox). The

Timothy Hackworth's *Sans Pareil* was *Rocket's* major competition at Rainhill. This locomotive exhibits early experiments with crossheads to maintain piston rod alignment, connecting rods between drivers, and a smoke box.

locomotive still lacked a smoke box (the stack remained attached directly to the front of the boiler with an elbow), but it did include a blast pipe. The blast pipe is a cone-shaped device that directs the exhaust steam through a small orifice, greatly increasing the steam's escape speed and imparting a significant draft on the fire, which improves the steaming quality of a locomotive. Because of the single driving axle, there were no connecting rods, and *Rocket* was exceptionally fast and free-running.

Hackworth's *Sans Pareil* appeared to be the chief competition to *Rocket*, but it proved to be too heavy and slow, running out of water and breaking down during the trial. *Rocket*, neither the fastest nor the most powerful of the entries, operated flawlessly and was the only one to successfully complete the requirements of the trial. Following the competition, Stephenson proceeded to pull a coach loaded with several passengers on a demonstration run, reaching a speed of 24 mph (38.5kph).

The Liverpool & Manchester made the Rocket-type its standard passenger locomotive, but adopted more powerful four-coupled designs for hauling freight. The worn-out shell of the original *Rocket* is displayed at the science museum in London, and several operating replicas still exist.

RAILROADS IN THE UNITED STATES

With gradual improvements, railroading became an important method of transport in the rest of Europe as well as Britain, where trains were quickly evolving to fill the needs in established industries or to connect existing cities. The situation in North America in the early 1800s, however, was entirely different.

With the exception of the more established eastern cities, much of the North American continent was still a lightly populated and undeveloped wilderness. Just as in Europe, the earliest North American railroads were related to a specific industry. For instance, wooden tracks were laid on Beacon Hill in Boston to carry building material for the new state house, and a railroad served a powder mill near Richmond, Virginia, in 1811.

One of the first railroad charters (1823) was granted to the Delaware & Hudson Canal Company, for a railroad connecting coal mines at Carbondale, Pennsylvania, to the end of the company's canal at Honesdale. The *Stourbridge Lion* was imported to serve the line, but proved too heavy for the strap iron–covered wooden rails. For a while the operators on the line took advantage of gravity to move the goods, letting the loaded coal cars coast downhill to the wharf, until steam power resumed in 1860. The canal was ultimately abandoned and

The earliest passenger accommodations could be very rudimentary, often foregoing a locomotive for a far more common source of power: the horse. The Baltimore & Ohio, credited as the first commercial railroad in North America (1830), began with horse-drawn coaches similar to this one.

✦ ✦ ✦

replaced by the Delaware & Hudson Railroad, which operated the line from Pennsylvania's anthracite fields to Montreal until the road became embroiled in the turmoils that followed the collapse of many northeastern railroads in the 1970s. Today, it continues to operate under the auspices of Canadian Pacific.

The first railroad to offer regular service as a common carrier was the Baltimore & Ohio, running from Pratt Street, Baltimore, to Carrollton Viaduct in then-rural Maryland, which carried its first paying passenger on January 7, 1830. The trains on the road relied on horse power until a steam locomotive called *Tom Thumb*, built by Peter Cooper (1791–1833), arrived from Britain in 1830. *Tom Thumb* was more of a scientific experiment than a railway locomotive, but its ability to pull a train encouraged the B&O to develop more powerful steam locomotives.

The Best Friend of Charleston, the first successful American-built locomotive, went into service for the South Carolina Railroad on Christmas day, 1830. Built by the West Point Foundry, New York, it operated until the following June, when it was severely damaged in a boiler explosion. (Irritated by the loud hissing of the steam escaping from the engine, the train's fireman had held down the noisy safety valve, causing the build-up—and sudden, explosive release—of a dangerous amount of steam pressure.)

By 1842—with occasional breaks in the network served by canals or ferries—railways connected Boston to the Great Lakes at Buffalo, New York, and Washington, D.C., to New York City. Although it was necessary to change trains occasionally on the journey, Chicago was connected by rail to the East Coast and the Mississippi River by 1854, and service even extended across the mighty river (via a bridge built at Davenport, Iowa, on April 21, 1856). By then, the steam locomotives *Sacramento* and *Nevada* had been transported by sailing ship around Cape Horn for service in California.

Although the construction of the transcontinental railroad was authorized by the U.S. Congress and critical funding for the project was signed into law (the Pacific Railroad Act) by President Lincoln in 1862, it wasn't until May 10, 1869, that the legendary golden spike was hammered home north of the Great Salt Lake at Promontory Point, Utah. Over the course of the next thirty years, a web of steel rails spread across the United States, linking every town of any size within a network of trains and rails that was to be the nation's primary mode of transportation until the building of the interstate highway system began in the 1950s.

CANADIAN RAILWAYS

The pattern for rail development in Canada mirrored that of many countries in Europe and the United States. The first Canadian railway was a double-tracked inclined plane in the city of Quebec, built by the Royal Engineers in 1823 to carry stone from a wharf on the Saint Lawrence River up the escarpment to the Citadel, which was under construction. While originally horse-powered, there is evidence that a steam engine was at some point installed. The operation lasted until the 1830s.

Coal transportation provided the impetus for Canadian railroading, just as it did elsewhere; horse-drawn lines were constructed in Nova Scotia at Pictou in 1827 and North Sidney in 1828. They were built to standard gauge, 4 feet 8 ½ inches (1.4m), and of iron rail—likely the first such used in North America. The Company of Proprietors of the Champlain & Saint Lawrence Rail Road operated the first steam-powered railroad in Canada, chartered in 1832. It opened on July 21, 1836, and operated between the Quebec towns of Laprairie (on the Saint Lawrence River) and Saint Jean (on the Richelieu River). Robert Stephenson & Company built the first locomotive for the line, the *Dorchester*, which served until it was demolished by a boiler explosion in 1864.

The mighty Canadian Pacific Railway (now CP Rail) was inaugurated on May 6, 1850, with the opening of the 12-mile (19.5km)-long La Compagnie du Chemin à Rails du Saint Laurent et du Village d'Industrie, which ran from Village d'Industrie (Joliette, Quebec) to Lanoraie, on the Saint Lawrence River, northeast of Montreal. Canada had built 1,882 miles (3,029km) of railroad by 1860, but the east and west coasts of the country were not united until the completion of the Canadian Pacific's transcontinental line in 1885.

Andrew Onderdonk's track-laying crews struggled though the lower Fraser Valley in British Columbia during the building of the Canadian Pacific. It took the backbreaking efforts of "iron men" such as these to force the steel rails through the vast wilderness of western Canada.

◆ ◆ ◆

The government had agreed to finance the project in the early 1870s and the push to build a transcontinental railroad began in earnest in 1875. Over the next decade, scandals rocked the government, the weather and the terrain proved to be formidable obstacles in the construction of the railroad, political infighting influenced the route the road was to take, and the original $25 million apportioned by the government

An early Canadian Pacific train pauses at the Mt. Sir Donald station, deep in Rogers Pass below the Illecillewaet Glacier. The mountain and station were named for Donald A. Smith, the former fur trader in Labrador who rose in prominence to become Chief Commissioner of Hudson's Bay Company, Member of Parliament for Selkirk, Manitoba, and a member of the CPR syndicate, as well as a major stockholder in and director of the railroad.

proved insufficient to complete the job. An uprising led by the Métis rebel Louis Riel was put down with the help of the railroad, which was used to transport troops in record time to the scene of the revolt. With their eyes opened to the military potential of a transcontinental railway, the shaken Canadian Parliament agreed to contribute further funding to the project. Thus, William Cornelius Van Horne was able to drive his plain iron final spike ("as good as any other on the line") at Craigellachie, on the Canadian Pacific on November 7, 1885.

RAILS COME TO AUSTRALASIA

Australia's railway age began in 1827 with an iron-tracked inclined tramway built by the Australian Agriculture Company to carry coal from its Newcastle mines to Port Hunter. Passenger service started in Tasmania in 1836, with the unusual Tasman Peninsula Railway, whose wooden rails enabled ship travelers to avoid the stormy Cape Raoul by taking a

Top: The interiors of early passenger cars were as ornate as the finest drawing rooms of the era. This parlor car is on the Northern Pacific's North Coast Limited of 1900, the first train in the Northwest with electric lights. Bottom: A horse-drawn car of the Dun Mountain Railway meanders down Hardy Street in Nelson, New Zealand. Soon steam would replace the horse as the motive power.

The Ghan

✦ ✦ ✦

Australia was home to one of the few mixed trains in the world to have a formal name. Far from being the crack express that is implied by such a title, the Ghan carries a mix of passengers and freight west from Adelaide over the Trans-Australian Railway to Tarcoola, after which a branch line connection runs north to Alice Springs. Serving the isolated interior of the continent, the train crosses the great Victoria desert, passes the Musgrave and MacDonnell ranges, and serves many isolated communities, following the path of the Afghan camel-drivers for which the train was named. It was a once-weekly train until the 1970s, but from 1990 to the present, the timetable shows a second train in use during the winter season (May to October).

Track workers pause in Junction Saddle on the Dun Mountain Railway on New Zealand's South Island. With a 3-foot (90cm) gauge, the mineral-hauling line was the first in the country.

✦ ✦ ✦

land shortcut across the peninsula between Hobart and Port Arthur. Convicts supplied the power for this 4.3-mile (6.9km) wooden-railed tramway, pushing the passenger's small carts uphill and climbing aboard for the free-wheeling downhill portions.

Steam power arrived in 1854 when the Melbourne & Hobson's Bay Railway opened a 5-foot-3-inch (1.6m)-gauge line connecting Flinders Street, Melbourne, with Sandridge, Victoria. The first true passenger railway was the 7-mile (11.5km) -long horse-drawn Port Elliot & Goolwa Railway, which opened in South Australia in May, 1854.

Robert Stephenson & Company shipped the region's first steam locomotives to New South Wales in 1854. They were Class 1 0-4-2s built for the Sydney & Golburn Railway to the government-adopted 4-foot-8½-inch (1.4m) standard gauge. One of these primitive locomotives has been preserved.

The growth of railroads in Australia was hampered by the gauge problem, since three primary and several secondary track widths were

adopted. South Australia adopted the 5-foot-3-inch (1.6m) as "standard" gauge, but was blessed with considerable secondary track in 3-foot-6-inch (1.1m) and was crossed by the true standard 4-foot-8½-inch gauge transcontinental main line. Remarkably, Adelaide, the capital, was not tied to the standard-gauge system until 1982.

The geography of New Zealand determined the form of its rail system. Its two islands are a total of 1500 miles (2,414km) long, north to south, and only 100 miles (161km) wide, making for a very linear railroad pattern. The

The Australian state of Victoria featured a main-line gauge of 5 feet 3 inches (1.6m), but the need to serve more sparsely settled districts led to a system of more economical 2-foot-6-inch (75cm)-gauge tracks feeding the main line. These lines were all abandoned by 1962, but the rails through Upper Ferntree Gulley were reopened as a tourist line called Puffing Billy. Here No. 4A, a locally built copy of a Baldwin 2-6-2, one of thirteen such tank locomotives built at the Victorian Railways' Newport Workshops (from originals imported from Philadelphia in 1898), sways across a trestle bridge near Belgrave, hauling a load of happy excursionists.

❖ ❖ ❖

first rails were laid in 1862 by the horse-operated, 3-foot (90cm) gauge Dun Mountain Railway, which hauled chromium ore 13 miles (21km) to Nelson, in the northwest part of the South Island.

The following year, the first steam railway opened from Christchurch to Ferrymead, also on the South Island, using 5-foot-3-inch (1.6m) gauge. This line was only temporary, until a tunnel was completed to Lyttleton, the port that served Christchurch. An ailing Robert Stephenson was asked to build the 1¾-mile (2.8km) tunnel, but turned the project over to his cousin, George Robert. When the tunnel opened in 1867, the Ferrymead branch was abandoned.

A standard-gauge line opened in 1867, connecting Invercargill to Bluff, and was the southernmost railway in Australasia. At the other extreme, the North Island's railways began with the completion in 1870 of the Bay of Islands

Coal Mining Company's standard-gauge line, used to transport coal from its mines at Kawakawa.

New Zealand learned from the Australian gauge discrepancies early enough to avoid making the same mistake. In 1870, 3 feet 6 inches (1.1m) was adopted as New Zealand's standard gauge (the Christchurch–Lyttleton section was converted in 1876). A 370-mile (595.5km) line was then built from Christchurch south to Dunedin and Invercargill (completed in 1879) and from Wellington to Auckland (completed in 1909).

Britain formed an organization known as the Gauge Commission to explore the advantages and problems of the various gauges so that a standard gauge could be determined. A number of locomotives participated in the gauge trials, including those illustrated above (clockwise from top left: *The Great A*, a Planet-type locomotive; *Engine No. 54*; narrow-gauge *Hercules*; broad-gauge *Hercules*). Differences in gauge size, however, were not the only consideration as steam power developed in the mid-nineteenth century. There was also a great divergence in approaches to engineering during this period: the location of the driving wheel in relation to nonpowered wheels, the number of driving wheels (multiple wheels being linked by a connecting rod), and frame construction.

THE GAUGE DILEMMA

One of the earliest decisions to be made by railroad builders was the matter of gauge—the spacing between the rails. In the earliest days, when rails served individual mines, the decision was simply a

THE INDIAN-PACIFIC

◆ ◆ ◆

Named for the two oceans it connects, Australia's Indian-Pacific transcontinental train rumbles across the southern part of the country between Sydney and Perth in sixty-five hours. The 2,461-mile (3,960km) route climbs several major grades and traverses the world's longest stretch of straight track—285 miles (456km) across the vast and virtually uninhabited Nullarbor Plain.

The Indian-Pacific made its historic debut on March 1, 1970—historic because the journey had only just been made possible by the rationalization of Australia's gauge problem. Prior to 1969, the Perth-Sydney journey required up to five train changes at the junctions of as many sets of tracks, each of which was of a different gauge than the next set. A massive effort to rebuild a number of 3-foot-6-inch (1.1m)- and 5-foot-3-inch (1.6m)-gauge sections (finally, they settled on British standard gauge) and the relocation of some other lines provided a connection between the original Trans-Australian Railway and the east and west coasts.

Built at the end of the streamliner-building boom in North America, the new Indian-Pacific train sets represented what might have been if another generation of streamlined equipment had rolled out of the shops of Pullman-Standard or Budd.

Following the tradition of the luxury streamliners, the gleaming stainless steel train provided roomy two-berth compartments in the first-class cars (called twinettes), each equipped with a closet, private shower, and toilet. Two adjacent twinettes could be combined by opening the separating door. Single first-class rooms were also available, but lacked the private shower. There were showers available to both first- and economy-class passengers at the ends of the sleeping cars. Compartments included ice water on tap, built-in radio, and power-operated Venetian blinds sandwiched between two glass panes. Economy-class twinette accommodations were also available, as well as coach service with reclining, aircraft-style seating.

A cafeteria/club car provided drinks and snacks for all passengers and there were organs or pianos in the first-class lounge (a unique trait of Australian passenger trains), as well as video and audio recordings for entertainment. Elegant meals were available in the diner and afternoon tea was served in the compartments. Three additional cars housed power-generating equipment, mail facilities, and dormitory space for the train staff of twenty. There was also a honeymoon suite and a fully equipped sick bay. Some trains included auto carriers so the passengers could have a personal vehicle available when they disembarked.

Electric locomotives were used on the steep climb through the scenic Blue Mountains west of Sydney, and heavy trains were sometimes hauled up in two sections before being recombined at Lithgow, the summit. A succession of diesel locomotives took over for the remainder of the route, being replaced at the junctions of the provincial systems over which the train passed with power from the appropriate regional railway.

The Indian-Pacific still treks across Australia on a twice-per-week schedule. Passing through the silver- and lead-mining area of Broken Hill, the route reaches the south coast at Adelaide, where connections can be made with The Ghan (an overnight train that courses north past the Macdonnell Range to legendary Alice Springs, deep in the outback). Skirting the coast to Port Augusta, the Indian-Pacific then turns inland again and reaches its highest speed, 70 mph (113kph), across the sunburned and treeless flatland of the Nullarbor Plain, but more typically runs at a more leisurely pace, averaging 50 mph (80kph) for the trip. After passing through the gold-mining region around Kalgoorlie, the train winds through the Darling Range before reaching the west coast at Perth.

Even in the age of air travel, the Indian-Pacific remains an important connection between two Australian coasts and is an invaluable connecting link for many isolated communities in the interior.

matter of convenience—that is, the spacing was fine as long as there was room between the rails for the miner's or horse's feet. When locomotives came into use, the choice of gauge became an engineering and cost concern. Wider gauge allowed for stability and larger- capacity rolling stock, but required more grading and track materials, making the construction cost higher. As railroads developed into transportation systems, the incompatibility of gauges at the connecting points become a growing burden. (Indeed, in some parts of the world, the issue of gauge continues to

be a problem; for instance, trains traveling across eastern Europe at this writing occasionally have to be transferred to special rails and modified before they can continue their journey on rails of different gauges.)

What was to become standard gauge in England (4 feet 8½ inches [1.4m]) evolved from the Willington Colliery wagonway system, which included the Killingworth Colliery, where George Stephenson began his work. According to legend, the gauge matched the wagon ruts made by the Roman occupiers of Britain. Stephenson chose this gauge for the

Forty J class 3-foot-6-inch (1.1m)-gauge 4-8-2s were imported from the **North British Locomotive Co.** (Glasgow) in 1939 for use on New Zealand's lighter rail sections, where the heavier 4-8-4 Ks were unsuitable. Due to maintenance problems, the streamlined "torpedo" casing was removed in 1947. J class locos survived until the end of steam in New Zealand on many trains, notably on the South Island Limited. J 1211 is seen here at Arthur's Pass in Mainline Steam Trust excursion service, restored to its 1939 streamlined trim.

Stockton & Darlington, the first chartered common carrier railway in England, and after he opened the Robert Stephenson Locomotive Works, other lines followed his pioneering lead.

Isambard Kingdom Brunel, another influential British railway engineer, was a firm believer in the advantages of 7-foot (2.1m) gauge when he began work on the Great Western Railway (GWR)—which extended from London to Bristol—in 1835, despite the fact that 4 feet 8 ½ inches was commonly accepted in England as standard gauge and 7-foot gauge was very expensive to build. Meanwhile, the Welsh slate railways had settled on an economical 2 feet (61cm). The government of Ireland formed a commission that agreed to the average of all the gauges then in use in the country, setting 5 feet 6 inches (1.7m) as Irish standard gauge. Irish engineers and navvies went around the world building railways, thus spreading their 5-foot-6-inch spacing to many other countries, including Australia, India, Spain, Portugal, and Argentina. South Africa, New Zealand, and Japan settled on 3 feet 6 inches (1.1m).

The railroad builders of the United States were heavily influenced by the British, and most of the burgeoning systems adopted the English standard gauge, although the Erie began with 6 feet (1.8m) and several others used 5 feet (1.5cm). Between 1865 and 1871, it was possible to travel from New York to Saint Louis on this "broad gauge," and as late as 1871 there were still twenty-three different gauges in use. The rail barons of the Colorado mineral hauling lines opted for economy when building in the twisting canyons of the Rockies, pushing through a 3-foot (.9m)-gauge that had a lower initial cost, while the legendarily frugal Yankees of Maine favored an even more economical 2-foot gauge for an extensive system of rails.

As railroads grew from serving a given industry to becoming regional transportation systems, webs of rails spread across countries all over the world. When systems of differing gauges met, chaos often prevailed. Passengers and freight that were scheduled to continue on the new line had to be transferred, which meant emptying an entire train, often in the middle of the night. Sleepy passengers had to gather their belongings, porters transferred trunks and express shipments from the baggage cars, and mail was shifted—usually across a crowded, narrow platform but sometimes between different depots altogether. Gloucester was a particularly congested transfer point in Britain—thus, "Lost at Gloucester" became the popular explanation for anything missing on the British rail system.

Freight transfer could also be costly, in both time and manpower. Bulk materials such as coal or cement could be unloaded into bins and chutes from an elevated track, using gravity to accomplish transfer to cars on a lower track, but boxcars were unloaded by hand, a box or a sack at a time, and reloaded in the other railroad's cars. The American Civil War proved the folly of multiple gauges. The South suffered greatly as the war dragged on because its maze of varying gauges made quick

The East Broad Top, a Pennsylvania three-foot gauge line, continued to haul coal into the 1960s, despite the gauge incompatibility problem. After that, the line was saved as a tourist hauler, but the virtually intact nineteenth-century facilities have now become endangered. The National Parks Service has been studying proposals for preservation and restoration of this "operating museum."

✦ ✦ ✦

movement of troops and materials very difficult, and the inherent delays affected the outcome of many battles.

In some instances, the differences between gauges was less problematic. The 3-foot-gauge East Broad Top (EBT), in central Pennsylvania's Allegheny Mountains, connected with the Pennsylvania Railroad main line at Mount Union. In addition to some mixed-gauge track in the yard, the EBT was blessed with generous clearances. The EBT used a track-straddling crane to lift the ends of a boxcar off its trucks so that narrow-gauge trucks could be substituted, the brakes reconnected with the help of adaptors, and the standard-gauge car hauled to its destination on the narrow-gauge rails. Since the coal mined in EBT territory was delivered to an on-line coal cleaning and preparation plant, the processed coal was simply reloaded into standard hoppers for final delivery. These atypical efficiencies allowed the EBT to remain in operation well into the 1960s, and it is still operated in excursion service.

By 1887, most of the broad-gauge railroads in the United States had been converted to standard gauge, often in massive undertakings wherein thousands of miles were overhauled over a single day. Even the legendary broad-gauge Great Western Railway built by Brunel could not last forever and was converted piecemeal, the final section in May 1892. Australia still suffers with multiple gauges, but a functioning interlocking network was in place by the 1970s.

As modern railroading has become more integrated with marine and truck shipping, using factory-loaded standardized containers, the unloading and reloading processes have become highly mechanized and efficient, canceling out some of the disadvantages of the gauge dilemma.

WELSH NARROW-GAUGE

◆ ◆ ◆

The slate-mining industry in the mountains of Wales suffered from transportation problems that were typical of the early Industrial Revolution. Heavy loads and a limited road system (which was mud for much of the year anyway) made for an intolerable situation, so development of the railroad was critical to the industry's growth.

The rugged terrain led the Welsh builders logically to choose narrow gauge for economy and practicality, since less grading on a narrower right of way would be required. What was uncommon was the choice of approximately 2 feet (61cm) as a track width, a very narrow gauge that was never widely adopted elsewhere. Soon enough, though, a network of these slim gauge rails spread over the region.

The Festiniog Railway is the world's oldest public narrow-gauge line, chartered by the act of Parliament for the Festiniog Railway in 1832. James Spooner engineered the 1-foot-11½-inch (60cm)-gauge line that ran between the coast at Portmadoc, Gwynedd, and the slate mines at Blaenau-Ffestiniog in Merioneth; the railway opened on April 30, 1836. Horses were originally used to haul the slate wagons on the upgrade and gravity took care of the rest for the journey back down. The track climbed 700 feet (213m) in 13¼ miles (21km), winding around the mountainside and finishing only 9¼ miles (15km) away from where it started (as the crow flies). A "tram" was constructed to accommodate passengers in 1850.

Following the death of Spooner, his son Charles Easton Spooner (1818–1889) assumed management. Charles was authorized to convert the line to steam power in 1863, which he did, using 0-4-0 locomotives built by George England. The world's first narrow-gauge passenger service began in 1865, and in 1869 the first double-bogie, double-boiler Fairlie locomotives became the standard power on the line. The decline of the slate industry led to the closure of the Festiniog line in 1946, but dedicated volunteers formed the Festiniog Railway Society Limited in 1954, reopening Tren Bach, "the Little Train," as a tourist attraction. The original equipment has been restored, including the much modified original Fairlies.

The Tal-y-llyn (Talyllyn) Railway, also engineered by James Spooner, opened in 1865, a year after the Festiniog, but has adopted the motto "We never closed." The 2-foot-3-inch (69cm)-gauge slate line between Tywyn and Abergynolwyn, Merioneth, had a similar history to the Festiniog line, but when the slate business faltered during World War II, the line's venerable owner Sir Hayden Jones continued operations, until his death in 1950.

The Talyllyn Railway Preservation Society was formed in 1950, keeping the line running while rebuilding and restoration efforts proceeded. The original equipment has been supplemented with three additional steamers and a diesel from other closed lines, including the Corris Railway, another Spooner project.

The narrow-gauge slate railways of Wales took advantage of early high-horsepower technology to help conquer their steep grades. British locomotive builder Robert F. Fairlie (1831–1885) made double-boilered, double-bogied locomotives with two sets of driving wheels (0-4-4-0 and 0-6-6-0 types)—including the *Merddin Emrys* (shown here), which was built in 1879 for the Festiniog Railway—that were designed with the needs of industry in mind.

Chapter Two

THE TECHNOLOGY MATURES

Once the railroad was established as a fixture in the Industrial Revolution, system growth and technological improvement were rapid. Locomotives evolved from the primitive teakettles of Stephenson and Hackworth into powerful and versatile machines, such as the 4-4-0 American, which opened up the frontier. (Indeed, it was two of these standard locomotives—the Central Pacific's Jupiter and No. 119 of the Union Pacific—that met nose to nose in the Utah desert, signifying completion of the North American continent's first coast-to-coast link, the transcontinental railroad. The planning for and completion of this monumental task is an epic tale that encompassed the breadth of the continent, involved politics at the highest level, and saw much adventure as determined men forged iron pathways across North America.)

As trains grew longer and heavier, the locomotives were fitted with larger boilers and more driving wheels to increase available power. Passenger locomotives generally had four-wheel pilot trucks, which imparted better stability at the higher speeds of passenger service, and then received two-wheel trailing trucks to support the larger fireboxes necessary to maintain steam in the ever-larger boilers. By early in the twentieth century, the 4-6-2 Pacific locomotive was becoming the standard for heavy passenger service and remained as typical power until the end of the steam era, although the heaviest trains were being powered by 4-6-4 Hudsons, 4-8-2 Mountains, and 4-8-4 Northerns (which were also called Confederation, Dixie, Golden State, Greenbrier, Niagara, Pocono, Potomac, or Wyoming depending on which railroad used the popular configuration).

As the locomotive technology matured, so did the rolling stock. The primitive lines used horses to pull carriages fitted with flanged wheels along wooden tracks, and this stagecoach quality was the norm for some time. European and North American railroads took separate paths on the way to becoming passenger cars as we know them. Individual compartments, each having an exterior door, developed on the continent, while cars of the United States tended toward parallel rows of

✦ ✦ ✦

The Union Pacific Omaha shops shrouded two steam locomotives in 1937, which were to serve primarily as relief power for the dieselized "City" streamliners. Mountain-type 7002 (4-8-2) and sister Pacific-type 2906 (4-6-2) wore the coloring of the streamliners—Armour Yellow, Leaf Brown, and Scarlet—and from 1939 to 1941 were assigned to the Forty-Niner, a five-times-per-month, all-Pullman heavyweight train that ran between Chicago and San Francisco's Golden Gate Exposition.

The 4-4-0 American was the locomotive that tamed North America. In fact, it was so widely used for both freight and passenger service that the American-type represented 85 percent of the locomotive fleet in 1870; twenty thousand were built between 1840 and 1890. The locomotive in this picture was the first of several Commodore Vanderbilts on the New York Central.

✦ ✦ ✦

seating split by an aisle, with entry from an open platform at each end. Eventually, these platforms were enclosed as vestibules to make for safer passage between cars. Overnight sleeping accommodations were begun in 1837, when Phillip Berlin of the Cumberland Valley Rail Road, which operated between the cities of Harrisburg and Chambersburg, Pennsylvania, transformed the seats of some of the train coaches into beds.

Sleeping cars improved when George Mortimer Pullman began the company that bears his name to build sleeping cars that were more comfortable than the basic accommodations then available. Georges Nagelmackers provided a similar service in Europe.

The ready availability and workability of wood determined the standard material for the first seventy-five years of train service, but there were horrible consequences to wooden cars. The coal and wood stoves used to heat the cars often overturned in even minor wrecks, converting the splintered cars into funeral pyres. Fatal accidents also occurred when the end sill of one car rode up over the adjacent one in a mishap. The wooden body construction of the cars was not strong enough to resist lateral forces, and one coach could break through the ends and slide between the walls of the adjacent car—called telescoping—with predictably deadly results.

It wasn't until the Pennsylvania and New York Central began extensive improvements, which included the construction of tunnels under the rivers and laying the underground trackage necessary to reach their Manhattan terminals, that the potential for catastrophe prompted builders to seriously explore the advantages of steel passenger cars.

Heavy steel sills and corner posts, as well as better couplers, grooved anticlimber devices, and steam heat helped to reduce the incidents of telescoping, splintering, and fire. Inevitably, the heavy riveted steel cars (known as heavyweights) quickly became the standard passenger cars.

The golden age of passenger trains arrived about the time of World War I, when the products of Pullman, American Locomotive Works (Alco), and Baldwin—the premier builders in the United States—set the standard for elegance, comfort, and dependability. Trains served all corners of the industrialized world, and considerable portions of the agrarian world as well. For twenty years, rail equipment design was relatively stable, with incremental improvements the norm, but the Great Depression of the

A three-year-old J-1-e Hudson (4-6-4) was restyled by Cleveland's Case School of Science in 1934, emerging from New York Central's Albany shops in this black Zephyr-inspired shroud. This engine, the second Commodore Vanderbilt, was North America's first streamlined steam locomotive.

Designer extraordinaire Henry Dreyfuss provided another dramatic restyling of the New York Central's workhorse as part of his work on the Twentieth Century Limited. In this 1939 view, Hudson No. 5446 storms out of Chicago with the Century in tow.

❖ ❖ ❖

1930s cast a pall over the industry. The arrival on the scene of a couple of influential designers helped revitalize the industry.

A movement that had roots in Europe found fertile ground in North America and changed the look and design of the railroads forever. Based on the principles that "form follows function," that manufactured products should look good as well as work properly, the industrial design movement took hold in the States in the late 1930s/early 1940s. Visionary designers Raymond Loewy and Henry Dreyfuss came to the attention of the railroad magnates. Loewy was hired by the Pennsy (the nickname for the Pennsylvania Railroad) after a varied career designing everything from a Macy's window to streamlined steam boats, and Dreyfuss was engaged by rival New York Central. Because of the efforts of these men U.S. railroad design was transformed.

The idea of streamlining—shaping products to move smoothly through air—began to be applied to everything from toasters to steam engines. In the end, perhaps, speed was less important than looks: the Puget Sound ferry Kalakala, which never exceeded 15 mph (24kph), received the streamlining treatment, and of course toasters never had to contend with the principles of fluid dynamics in the least. While locomotives rarely achieved 100 mph (161kph), they were the most obvious moving symbol of industrial might and they became a logical target for such updating.

Newly streamlined trains included the German Fliegende ("Flying") Hamburger and the British Coronation Scot, while the United States saw the construction of the Loewy-styled GG1 and K-4 on the Pennsy and the Commodore Vanderbilt and the Dreyfuss-styled Hudson on the New

York Central. All through the mid- to late 1930s, railroads found ways to add rounded noses, skyline casings, smoke deflectors, wings, and fins to smooth out the rough-hewn steam locomotive. But the railroads did not stop at streamlining locomotives in their efforts to further the advantages of passenger train service.

In 1934, General Motors' fledgling Electro-Motive Division (EMD) joined with the Budd Company of Philadelphia to produce the shovel-nosed stainless steel Zephyr, North America's first diesel-powered streamliner. The Union Pacific's sleek yellow-and-brown M-10000 arrived from the Pullman Company at the same time, and the smooth steam-powered

flyers of the time were eclipsed by the streamlined internal combustion products of EMD.

These early trains were composed of semipermanently coupled units arranged as a fixed train set. Their light weight and streamlining contributed to efficient operation and high speeds. But because they were unique trains, they could not be blended easily into the railroad's fleets. In addition, the entire train had to be removed from service whenever maintenance was necessary on any portion of it, and cars could not be added when traffic warranted. EMD took the lead in applying the lessons of automobile assembly lines, which relied on standard parts, quickly

Pioneer Zephyr, the Chicago, Burlington & Quincy streamliner that began the revolution in passenger trains, poses beside younger sister Kansas City Zephyr, which was made up of lightweight, Budd-built cars pulled by standardized EMD E Units, the ubiquitous combination that quickly became synonymous with the term "streamliner."

❖ ❖ ❖

putting an end to the production of custom-built locomotives. The "E" series of passenger diesels was developed in careful steps from the 1,800hp EA to the 2,000hp E6; EMD produced two hundred E Units by the beginning of World War II.

The passenger-car builders followed suit, producing a new generation of streamlined cars for the new trains. The Budd Company, a newcomer to the car-building business, patented its "shotwelding" process, which enabled stronger and thinner (and thus lighter) stainless steel panels to be fastened invisibly onto the car frames. The lighter weight of the cars, the absence of rivets and overlapping plates that were common on the traditional heavyweights, and the polished silvery finish that eliminated the need for painting provided the extra sparkle that helped to promote the new streamliner image. The gleaming, "fluted-side" Budd cars became the symbol of streamlined elegance (although it should be noted that Pullman and the American Car & Foundry produced colorful "smooth-side" cars that were the equal in comfort and stylishness of those produced at Budd).

The railroads clamored for new cars and locomotives with which to reequip older "name trains" or to begin brand-new services in an attempt to break the malaise of the depression. The builders naturally struggled to keep up with the orders, and outdid themselves trying to create new and more exciting concepts.

With the attack on Pearl Harborin 1941, equipment purchases were severely curtailed as the factories geared up for war production. The development of steam locomotives stalled during the war, but diesel power plants (important to tanks, trucks, and ships) greatly benefited from major wartime research and development programs.

The immediate postwar years found the railroads of the United States and Canada rundown from the tremendous traffic of the war effort, and those of Europe ravaged by the war itself. This gave progressive-thinking railroad management the perfect opportunity to improve the quality of the rolling stock and locomotives. The diesel had already come of age in North America, the defense demands having proven the advantages of

the growler (as the diesel plants were called) in freight and passenger service alike. Europe took the opportunity to rebuild its devastated rail systems with massive installations of overhead catenary and electric locomotives, although the lower cost of operating diesel trains was not overlooked in the rebuilding of some secondary lines.

The pioneer trains Zephyr, M-10000, and Super Chief had proven the speed and comfort advantages of the streamliner, so the U.S. railroads embraced the concept of the streamlined diesel-powered passenger train enthusiastically. The Santa Fe's El Capitan, an all-coach streamliner, had also shown the way to attract the economy-minded traveler. The car and locomotive builders were swamped with orders for new equipment as the railroads scrambled to secure passengers who were becoming increasingly attracted to the speed of the airplane and personalized convenience of the automobile.

Though the Budd Company of Philadelphia was only a beginner in the car-building business, it was immediately distinguished because of its patented "shotwelding" process. It should be noted, however, that all the builders of the period were caught up in the need for innovation in the rapidly changing times. Other companies turned to alternative high-strength steel alloys that lightened the weight of the cars and made them more economical to operate. Air conditioning allowed for the installation

The Pennsylvania Railroad's experiments with advanced steam concepts included this S-1 6-4-4-6 duplex, which was built in the Altoona shops in 1939.

of smooth, round-cornered, fixed, insulated glass in the windows. The builders also discarded the traditional olive green of the trains and painted the steel exteriors in bright, bold colors that immediately set the streamliners apart from the run-of-the-mill trains.

A number of other innovations emerged at this time: dome cars; full-length domes; double-deck coaches, sleepers, and diners; roomier forty-eight-seat coaches instead of the seventy- or eighty-seat cars that formerly were the norm; and numerous exotic experiments with parlor, lounge, and observation cars.

POSTWAR MOTIVE POWER DEVELOPMENT

Steam power in North America was not completely abandoned following World War II. The Union Pacific built a number of steam-turbine-electrics for freight service, and the Chesapeake & Ohio (C&O) joined with General Electric and Baldwin to build three spectacular M-1 steam-turbine-electric locomotives for its stillborn Chessie streamliner. Perhaps even more out of character for the normally conservative C&O was the 1946–1947 rebuilding of five twenty-year-old F-19 Pacifics into class L-1 Hudsons. These 4-6-4s were as modern as steam could be, with poppet valves, a booster engine on the trailing truck, and Timken roller bearings on all axles and rods. They were encased in a bright orange and stainless steel shroud with corrugated stainless on the tender, intended to blend in with the new steam-turbine-electrics and the luxurious cars that had been built for the Chessie.

The Norfolk & Western built the elegant maroon-and-black class J streamlined 4-8-4s for the equally elegant smooth-side Powhatan Arrow, and tried mightily to extend the life of steam with the 1954 experimental 4,500hp steam-turbine-electric that they dubbed Jawn Henry, after the legendary "steel drivin' man" of folk song. Unlike the bright colors of the C&O turbine, Jawn Henry's color was traditional black, befitting its intended use for freight service.

The Pennsylvania Railroad also dabbled in experimental locomotives. The shark-nosed 4-4-4-4 T1s and "Buck Rogers"–styled 6-4-4-6 S1s were both prewar duplex designs, with two sets of cylinders improving driver balance and speed. Fifty more T1s were built in 1946 and 1947, but the S1 was not replicated.

These noble experiments to keep steam alive were ultimately doomed. The final attempt to keep steam on the Pennsy was the 6-8-6 S2 turbine. Unlike the C&O and N&W steam-turbine-electrics, the S2 used a turbine to drive the drivers directly through a gearbox and connecting rods. It looked much like a large conventional steamer without the cylinders and valve gear. The swoosh-swoosh sound the power plant made (as opposed to the conventional chuffing heard from most steam engines) announced the presence of the 6,000hp S2 streaking across the flatlands of Ohio and Indiana at the head of a fast freight or passenger train. But even this high-performance behemoth had succumbed to the economics of dieselization by 1950. Despite the increases in efficiency, speed, and horsepower of these new steam engines, the maintenance requirements of steam power remained high, in part because one locomotive (particularly among custom-built machines) quite often needed parts or tools that were quite different from those needed to repair another steamer (not to mention the new diesels).

The diesel-electric concept had been considerably refined during the course of World War II, encouraged by the government's huge investment in diesel-powered machinery at the very time when wartime restricitions were stifling the development of steam. The diesel manufacturers were eager to fill the railroads' needs for new locomotives to replace those ravaged by heavy wartime service. These manufacturers also wanted to provide the sleek, streamlined designs that promoted the image of modernism so desired by their customers.

The bulldog-nosed F Units from General Motors' Electro-Motive Division, the square-jawed PAs from the American Locomotive Works (Alco), and the Loewy-styled C-Liners and Erie-builts from Fairbanks-

Chesapeake & Ohio's steam-turbine-electric (1947) was a bold attempt at reversing the trend toward dieselization. Built for a new streamliner, the Chessie, the bright yellow, light gray, dark blue, and aluminum coal burner was capable of 6,000hp. Three such locomotives were built, along with a number of passenger cars, but the Chessie never entered service and the ambitious locos were scrapped in 1950.

Morse competed with the somewhat less successful Baldwin Centipedes, Sharks, and Babyfaces for the attention of railroad managements. Numerous orders flowed to Baldwin and Alco because of relationships that had been developed during the steam age, while rumors circulated that General Motors was applying its ample muscle to the railroads in an effort to coerce orders for GM product.

In addition to producing very reliable locomotives, General Motors was one of the largest originators and receivers of rail shipments of many kinds, as well as a heavy investor in railroad securities. GM executives sat on several railroad boards and as a result had considerable clout in the industry. By early 1949, the Electro-Motive Division of GM had sold three thousand F Units (primarily for freight service) and seven hundred passenger-hauling E Units to American railroads. This complete domination of the market sparked a Congressional investigation—in order to determine whether the situation constituted a monopoly on GM's part—that tried to make

The Pennsylvania Railroad's experiments with advanced steam concepts included the T-1 4-4-4-4 duplex, which featured streamlined "shark-nosed" styling by Raymond Loewy. The design was developed in 1942, but World War II delayed production of the locomotives until 1946, when fifty were built, some by Baldwin and the others by the Pennsy's Altoona shops.

✦ ✦ ✦

sense of vague statistics and circumstantial evidence, but finally determined that there was insufficient evidence against GM. Electro-Motive continued to dominate the North American locomotive business as the competition faded away, until General Electric, which had specialized in foreign markets for many years, struck back in the 1980s with its fuel-efficient Dash 8 models and took over the sales lead.

The postwar years saw great changes in passenger cars as well. The streamlined passenger train had toddled out of infancy and was quickly striding toward maturity. Railroads around the world were exploring the efficiencies of new diesel or electric locomotives and luxuriously appointed lightweight cars as they battled the airlines for passenger traffic.

The airline industry had benefited from the war years even more than had the locomotive industry. Vast manufacturing plants were built, work forces

When the American Locomotive Works switched from the production of steam locomotives to diesels, beginning in earnest during World War II, their handsome square-jawed PA and FA locomotives enjoyed modest success. PA-1 No. 1776, shown here at Philadelphia's Broad Street Station, toured the United States with the first American Freedom Train, celebrating the 150th anniversary of the American Revolution. With Pullman cars filled with original historic documents, including the Bill of Rights and a draft of the Constitution, and a complement of U.S. Marines, the train covered 33,000 miles (52,800km) on fifty-two railroads in 493 days.

gained invaluable experience with design and production, and after the war the airlines could draw on a freshly retired cadre of seasoned pilots and mechanics. Every town now wanted an airport to gain economic advantage over its neighbors, just as they once had fought over rail service. The railroads knew that they could only offer comfort and service against the speed of the airplane and the convenience offered by the automobiles streaming out of postwar factories. In competing with cars and planes, the railroads looked to develop new ideas that would make rail travel more appealing to the consumer.

The mass-produced diesel locomotives already allowed for much higher speeds with fewer servicing stops and didn't require locomotive changes for varying terrain. Hotel-like amenities had long been featured on special first-class trains, but such attractions as cocktail lounges, observation cars, and comfortable sleeping quarters were becoming the norm on every long-distance train. The Burlington added the final touch of spice into the mix by improving on an old freight-train concept—the caboose cupola.

THE DOME CAR

Long established as a convenient way for the conductor to keep tabs on his train from end to end, the cupola's airy lookout had inspired the Canadian Pacific in 1890 to modify some observation cars, adding a pair of viewing cupolas to cars in service through the Canadian Rockies. These cars were retired after three years, and the idea lay dormant until July 1944, when Cyrus R. Osborn, a General Motors vice president, took a freight diesel cab ride on the Denver & Rio Grande's spectacular route through Colorado's Glenwood Canyon. Bowled over by the view from up high at the front of the train, he mused that some people would pay $500 extra for such a ride, rather than settle for the limited view available through the train's side windows. His hastily drawn sketches intrigued GM management, and a refined design for the projected "Astra Liner" was exhibited to railroad executives in the spring of 1945.

Meanwhile, the perceptive president of the Burlington had seen the early sketches. He immediately ordered his own shops to convert an existing Budd-built stainless steel coach into the first Vista-Dome, which entered service in 1945. This prototype car, christened Silver Dome, dazzled passengers with its raised lounge encased in a large, glazed "cupola," which allowed expansive views in all directions, including skyward. By the end of the year, forty dome cars were on order with various car builders, but the Burlington had the lead with the coaches and parlor-lounge-observations built by Budd; these luxurious cars entered Twin Cities Zephyr service in the fall of 1947. (Today, a monument adjacent to

Above: The Milwaukee Road Super Domes, the first full-length domes, were first put into service on January 1, 1953. Comfortable seating surrounded by glass added to the enjoyment of any rail journey. Below: The patch on the steward's shoulder identifies this elegant car as the Dome-Diner on the City of Los Angeles.

Designer Brooks Stevens styled the famous Sky Top Lounge observation cars for the Hiawatha streamliners of the Milwaukee Road (Chicago, Milwaukee, St. Paul & Pacific). These wonderful cars were eventually sold to the Canadian National.

✦ ✦ ✦

the tracks at Greeley, Colorado, honors the Vista-Dome's contribution to modern railroading. The monument, a stone cairn topped by a scale-model Vista-Dome car, sits amid the inspiring scenery where the awe-struck Osborn riding in the fireman's seat had first conceived of the car.)

General Motors joined with Pullman-Standard to build the four-car experimental Train of Tomorrow, which included a dome diner, dome sleeper, dome chair car, and dome tavern-observation. This concept train toured the nation from 1947 to 1950, eventually settling down in Union Pacific's Portland-to-Seattle service from 1950 to 1958. These domes were glazed with separate flat glass panels on the sides and in the roof, whereas those built by Budd and, later, American Car & Foundry (ACF) used curved glass that wrapped from the sides of the car onto the roof.

Other railroads scrambled to keep up with the Burlington, making a ride in the dome an attractive perquisite on a variety of long-distance train rides. While the early dome cars featured a short dome over the center of a car with seating located below, several railroads built full-length domes—called Big Domes on the Santa Fe, Great Domes on the Great Northern, and Super Domes on the Milwaukee Road. These cars featured raised seating over most of the car, which gave more passengers a bird's-eye view. However, there were drawbacks to the full-length domes. These cars were difficult to keep cool because of the huge glass area, the view to the front was more limited for those who were seated further back, and some of the cars (the Milwaukee Road cars at least) were notoriously bouncy.

SHOTWELDING

✦ ✦ ✦

Apart from the Electro-Motive Corporation's E Unit passenger diesel, the most important development in the streamliner era was the Budd Company's shotwelding process, which was patented and invented by Budd's chief engineer, Colonel E.J.W. Ragsdale. Shotwelding made possible the gleaming, fluted, stainless steel exteriors that are so closely associated with streamlining that it is all too easy to slight the beautifully finished, smooth-side cars of the Pullman Company and American Car & Foundry.

Shotwelding involves the passage of a measured "shot" of electricity through two pieces of stainless steel, melting the adjoining surfaces together without marring the exterior. The strong current and short time, monitored by an electronic weld recorder, preserves the strength of the material and avoids harmful carbide precipitation. A warning alarm signals an improper weld, allowing for immediate correction. Ragsdale summed up the virtues of stainless steel in the Santa Fe employees magazine: "These cars not only have a bright, enduring finish, but they are lighter, stronger, and more economical of operation. For once, a brilliant appearance can be combined with a definite utility."

The new process was introduced with the Chicago, Burlington & Quincy's Zephyr, the 1934 semipermanently coupled train set that used smaller cars than the typical heavyweight. Budd delivered the first standard-sized stainless steel passenger car, Santa Fe's No. 3070, in 1936. The car proved the value and durability of the design and paved the way for the 1937 Super Chief and the huge fleets that would crisscross the United States until the present day. Distinguished by its fluted stainless steel exterior and large, sealed double-pane windows, the car weighed just 83,000 pounds (37,649kg), compared to the 160,000 pounds (72,576kg) of a conventional heavyweight, but was more spacious inside. The heavily insulated interior featured elegant wood-veneer finishes and was air-conditioned. An unqualified success, No. 3070 remained in regular service into the 1980s, ending its days in commuter service for New Jersey Transit.

The splendid fluted stainless steel Budd-built cars of the Rio Grande Zephyr, with dome lounge Silver Sky "carrying the markers," waits for the highball at Denver Union Station. The sleek and shiny finish of such cars was made possible by the shotwelding process. The Denver & Rio Grande Western resisted Amtrak's overtures to absorb the line, but finally turned over operation of this remnant of the golden age in 1983.

Southern Pacific built low-profile three-quarter-length domes for the Daylight, using older cars as a base and adding glazing to the roof, while the Baltimore & Ohio built lower Strata-Domes for its Capitol Limited and Columbian. These were the only dome cars to operate in the East, because of restricted clearances under bridges and tunnels, not to mention the high-voltage overhead wiring in the electrified districts.

Other railroads tried to achieve some of the ambience of the domes by wrapping the side glass up and over the roof in the lounge portions of single-level cars: for instance, the Seaboard built three Sun-Lounge Cars for its Silver Meteor service to Florida. By far the most elegant of this type, however, were the Milwaukee Road Skytop Lounge cars. These delightful cars considerably advanced the traditional open-platform observation concept. Noted industrial designer Brooks Stevens created the plans for a glass enclosure at the rear of the observation lounge that wrapped up over the roof, as well as around the end. These cars operated on the rear of the speedy Hiawathas that traveled between Milwaukee and Chicago, and the cross-country Olympian Hiawatha, which went to Seattle.

The Santa Fe took its Big Domes a step further when two experimental Hi-Level coaches were added to the consist of El Capitan in July 1954 for extended testing. These revolutionary cars differed from the dome cars in that all seating was on the upper level, separated from the noise and vibration of steel wheels on rail, while the lower level was devoted to luggage storage and rest rooms. The elimination of storage space and toilets from the seating area resulted in an increase in coach seating to sixty-seven passengers, a substantial increase from the standard forty-four- to forty-eight-person capacity previously available. To make room for the additional seating, the air-conditioners and other mechanical equipment were also moved to the lower level, which enabled the equipment to be serviced while the train was moving. This was an important factor for the Santa Fe (and every other railroad, for that matter), which wrestled with the economics of providing attractive service while maintaining low operating costs in the tough postwar market.

The cars were a hit with both passengers and the railroad, so the Santa Fe ordered a fleet of Hi-Levels to reequip El Capitan completely: twenty-five seventy-two-passenger chair cars; ten sixty-eight-passenger chair cars (which had stairs to the lower level at one end so that the Hi-Level consists could be mated with conventional equipment); six eighty-eight-passenger dome lounges (called Top of the Cap); and six eighty-seat diner cars. Six baggage-dormitory cars were fitted with Hi-Level adaptors—an airfoil device designed to blend the two types of equipment. The new cars allowed a seven-coach train to carry 496 passengers, compared with 350 in eight coaches on the conventional El Capitan.

The "Doodle-bug," a self-propelled car (also known in Budd Company terminology as a Rail Diesel Car, or RDC), was the result of an ongoing effort to hold down costs that goes all the way back to the wooden-car era. The Reading Company used this fluted stainless steel version to maintain a sense of the modern while holding down costs on lightly used lines.

EXPERIMENTS IN EFFICIENCY

Other attempts at reducing losses with more efficient equipment were less successful. General Motors followed its Train of Tomorrow with the 1956 lightweight Aerotrain, made of GM bus bodies mounted on single-axle trucks. Powered by a turret-cabbed 1,200hp locomotive designated EP-12, it was a reminder of the early days of integrated train sets with powered cars.

Two ten-car demonstrators operated on the Pennsylvania, New York Central, Union Pacific, and Santa Fe, but the extremely rough-riding cars did not satisfy the railroads. The Aerotrain demonstrator sets 1000 and 1001, along with one additional train set, were sold to the Rock Island Line.

Financier Robert R. Young cooperated with Baldwin Lima Hamilton on the low-slung Train X, which operated for a while on Young's New York Central as the Xplorer, but failed to spark much enthusiasm.

GEORGE MORTIMER PULLMAN
(1831–1897)

✦ ✦ ✦

A cabinetmaker by trade, George Pullman moved to Chicago from Brocton, New York, and began a construction business. There was clearly room for improvement in the rudimentary railway sleeping accommodations of the day, and in 1854 Pullman and his friend Benjamin Field received a patent for a folding upper berth. Pullman soon contracted with the Chicago & Alton Railroad to rebuild two coaches into more comfortable sleeping cars, using the railroad's own shops; the cars were completed in 1859.

The first new car, Pioneer, went into service in 1865 and featured an innovative (and patented) concept—facing seats that extended and slid together to form a comfortable lower berth. The Pullman reputation was boosted considerably when Mrs. Abraham Lincoln chose Pioneer as her car in the slain president's funeral train.

The success of this new car encouraged Pullman to incorporate the Pullman's (later Pullman) Palace Car Company, in 1867. Within eight years, the Pullman Company was producing the majority of sleeping cars in North America. Pullman took the burden of providing first-class accommodations (sleepers, as well as some diners and parlor cars) off the shoulders of the railroads. As a result, Pullman was able to have his cars (which were entirely built, serviced, and staffed by his employees) hauled in the railroad's regularly scheduled passenger trains. The almost universal acceptance of this practice made the name Pullman synonymous with first-class rail travel (to the extent that it became common practice to refer to all Pullman porters as "George").

The Pullman Company constantly innovated, introducing Hotel Cars (sleepers that included kitchen and dining-car facilities) in 1867, a full dining car (Delmonico) in 1868, the first vestibule train in 1887, and an air-conditioned car in 1927 (showing that Pullman's death did not slow the wheels of progressive design).

The Pullman heavyweight sleeper Australia, built in 1892, provided a comfortable ride for those with sufficient funds for first-class travel.

The level of comfort of the Pullmans made a deep impression on James Allport, General Manager of Britain's Midland Railway, as he traveled 6,000 miles (9,656km) around the United States in Pullman's parlor and sleeper cars. Allport invited Pullman to Britain in 1873, but the Midland Railway's directors remained skeptical until the carbuilder offered to build diners and sleepers and parlor cars to the British loading gauge, ship them to England, and operate them at his expense. In order to maintain the homogeneity of the train, the railroad agreed to order similar coaches with traditional British-style accommodations. The cars were fabricated as kits at Pullman's Chicago works and shipped to Derby for final assembly.

The imported Pullmans' American parentage was obvious, with their four-wheeled trucks (bogies), clerestory roofs, and open platforms—not to mention that they were built entirely of wood. The sleepers were a success, but the British coach passengers disliked the "American-style" reversible back seating and avoided the cars. Even so, the Pullman concepts spread across Britain, particularly after British newspaper magnate Davison Dalziel (1854–1928) purchased the British operations from Pullman in 1907.

The Pullman empire grew to include both freight and passenger-car building shops, a company town (Pullman, Illinois), and the operation of almost ten thousand passenger cars across North America. This almost complete dominance of the market led to antitrust action in 1947, which split the car-building and operations portions of the company into separate entities. Passenger services continued until January 1, 1969, when responsibility was returned to the railroads. The car-building segment continues to produce freight cars as Pullman-Standard, but passenger-car building was discontinued.

While General Motors' Electro-Motive Division produced the wildly successful E and F series of locomotives, their futuristic Aerotrain was a dismal failure. A bold response to declining passenger train revenue, GM's Aerotrain offered a consist of relatively inexpensive lightweight equipment (based on GM bus bodies). Unfortunately, the train proved to be extremely rough-riding and unpopular with passengers. Following unspectacular demonstrations of the Aerotrain on the Union Pacific, New York Central, and Pennsylvania railroads, the less fussy Rock Island became the only road to purchase the train, acquiring the two demonstrators and even ordering one more train set (one of which is shown here in Chicago during the final week of its service, in May 1965).

❖ ❖ ❖

In the end, these specialized train sets suffered from many of the same problems as the steam turbines and other experiments—the maintenance departments were not really prepared for handling these oddballs, which affected operational readiness and costs—and these negative experiences early on stifled further development. Additionally, the lack of flexibility of these fixed sets (the "shopping" of one car removed the whole train from service) affected dependability.

More successful was the Rail Diesel Car (RDC), a self-propelled passenger car. The Budd Company married its stainless steel passenger-car technology to the old railroad standby, the Doodle-bug, variations of which had been operating over lightly traveled branch lines for several decades. Although specialized cars, the Doodle-bugs did not suffer from the disadvantages of the fixed dedicated train-sets, as they could be coupled together in any configuration, and with each unit self-propelled, the total power was always equal to the load.

Budd sold the first RDCs to the New York Central on April 19, 1950. The power plant grew out of GM's wartime diesel-engine development efforts. A 275hp, relatively flat V-twin developed for tanks fit nicely under the RDC floor, allowing for easy access and a ninety-minute change-out time for a replacement engine, so damaged engines could be serviced while the car continued to operate.

The lightweight, fluted, stainless steel RDCs operated at a top speed of 83 mph (133.5kph), accelerated from 0 to 60 in two minutes, and were able to maintain a speed of 25 mph (40kph) on an uphill grade of 3 percent. They required only a two-man crew—an operator and conductor—and their resemblance to a Budd coach (with a roof-top bulge to accommodate the radiator) enabled them to blend with streamliner fleets. They were offered in five versions: RDC-1 was a ninety-seat coach; RDC-2 was a coach-baggage combination; RDC-3 was a coach-baggage-Railway Post Office; RDC-4 was a combination baggage-RPO; and the RDC-9 was a coach unit with no controls, which needed to be coupled to another car to operate. It was common to see "trains" of RDCs on some more heavily traveled routes.

The early success of the RDCs inspired additional experimentation. The New Haven road's Hot Rod was a five-unit train with an F

Unit–like streamlined nose and a top speed of 110 mph (177kph). The New York Central mounted two J47 jet engines in a roof-mounted streamlined pod and added a smooth shovel-nose to a single RDC. On a closed section of straight track, a speed of 185 mph (297.5kph) was attained, but no further development was done.

By the time the final twelve units were delivered to the Reading Railroad in 1962, 398 units had been built. Even the efficiencies of the RDC failed to save the American passenger train, but the RDCs still operate in Cuba, Saudi Arabia, Brazil, and Australia. The last units built are still running on the British Columbia Railway.

THE AMTRAK ERA

The founding of Amtrak, in 1971, resulted in additional development of equipment. Congress formed the quasi-public National Railroad Passenger Corporation to try to solve the "long-distance passenger-train problem." The rapid development of an interstate highway system had done further damage to the railroads' business: the highways not only enabled people to drive directly to their destination, thus hurting passenger rail service; they also enabled trucks to provide door-to-door delivery service. This meant that manufacturers could locate on cheap suburban

or rural land without concern for proximity to rail sidings, putting a dent in the freight business. Many of the North American railroads were struggling for survival, and the government, recognizing their value to the economy, was trying to maintain a viable system without nationalization.

The price for divestiture of passenger trains was steep. Railroads were required to donate passenger cars and locomotives into an Amtrak pool, as well as pay millions of dollars each for several years to aid in the transition. While twenty-two railroads chose to pay the price, the Southern Railroad, Denver & Rio Grande Western, and the Chicago, Rock Island & Pacific declined, electing to continue passenger service on their own. In the end, even these diehards gave up, with SRR and D&RGW joining Amtrak after another decade of independence, while the Rock Island fell victim to bankruptcy and was abandoned.

From its beginning, Amtrak faced serious equipment problems. Anticipating an end to passenger service, many railroads transferred their newest locomotives to freight service. Innovation in passenger train development trailed off. In fact, EMD's E9, the most modern passenger-locomotive design, was first produced in 1954—the last in 1963. A few FP45s, a passenger version of a freight locomotive, were in the Amtrak pool, but they proved to be no bargains and were disposed of after several inexplicable, disastrous derailments.

While the new managers wrestled with schedules and train consolidations, they also struggled to collect enough dependable equipment to operate the trains that they intended to keep. Fortunately for the new service, several railroads, including Santa Fe, Union Pacific, and Burlington, had done a credible job of maintaining certain standards in the waning years, so Amtrak did glean some gems from the junk. In 1977, for example, an Empire Builder included cars from five railroads: Atchison, Topeka & Santa Fe (AT&SF), Northern Pacific (NP), Chicago, Burlington & Quincy (CB&Q), Union Pacific (UP), and Southern Pacific (SP). The oldest was an ex–Santa Fe lounge car built by Budd in 1938 (meaning it had seen thirty-nine years of service), while the newest was an ex–UP 11 double-bedroom sleeper built by Pullman-Standard in 1956. The three major car builders were represented in the Amtrak mix (Pullman-Standard, Budd, and American Car & Foundry), but there were no cars from the old Great Northern Empire Builder. There were, however, a pair of domes from the Northern Pacific's North Coast Limited.

The age of this distinguished fleet posed a serious problem, which Amtrak immediately addressed. It developed the stainless steel Amfleet equipment for shorter runs, while the Santa Fe Hi-Level cars were used as the basis for Amtrak's highly successful collaboration with Pullman-Standard on the Superliner cars that continue to dominate the long-distance trains of the West today.

Amfleet cars are somewhat spartan on the inside, and much like a stainless steel tube on the outside. They ride on inside-bearing trucks, so the wheels are fully exposed, and the windows, although enlarged after the early deliveries, are still on the small side. They do ride comfortably, though—even at the high speeds of the Northeast Corridor—and the snack cars (Amcafes) and club cars provide a relief from the coaches.

The Superliners were built as coaches, sleepers, diners, and "Sightseer" lounge cars. Seven and a half inches (19cm) higher above the rail than the Santa Fe cars, Superliners ride smoothly at 120 mph (193kph) on air-cushion trucks of German design. Electric power for lights, heating, and air-conditioning is drawn from the locomotives, eliminating the onboard generators of the Hi-Level cars and thereby allowing

seating for handicapped passengers on the lower level (there are small elevators up to the main levels).

The Sightseer cars include snack and bar service on the lower level, with the upper floor devoted to swiveling chairs and fixed couches for easy viewing of the scenery through glass that wraps up onto the roof, much like in a dome car. The diners are also on the upper level, with the cooking done on the lower floor. Dumbwaiters transfer the meals and dirty dishes between levels.

The Superliner cars are now in the second generation of development, and their acceptance seems to guarantee that they will remain as the standard rolling stock on the Western trains for the foreseeable future. Unfortunately, tighter clearances in tunnels and under bridges have kept these new cars from Eastern operations, except on the Sunset Limited (Florida–California) route.

In 1983, Amtrak took over the hauling of passengers and their automobiles from suburban Washington to Florida, following the Autotrain Corporation's 1981 shutdown (several disastrous derailments and an ill-fated attempt to operate a train to the Midwest brought about Autotrain's downfall, despite high patronage). Autotrain service began in 1971 with covered auto racks carrying the cars, while the passengers rode in conventional coaches and sleepers. Amtrak was prohibited from carrying "freight," but had the exclusive right to carry passengers on its routes, so the private Autotrain contracted for trackage rights on routes that were roughly parallel to Amtrak's. The Autotrain featured the ex–Santa Fe full-length domes and extensive evening entertainment, and the service remains very popular under Amtrak's management.

Recent years have seen numerous Amtrak experiments with equipment that may signal the future. The sleek General Electric Genesis locomotives could be the replacement for the venerable F40PHs and Dash 8s, a leased European Inter City Express (ICE) train toured the United States in 1993, and a Talgo train was operating between Seattle and Vancouver in 1995.

It is obvious that as long as passenger trains are still running in the United States, equipment will continue to evolve in unexpected ways. Dreamers in the U.S. Congress and the private sector still envision high-speed trains in the United States; and maybe there is a Bullet Train or TGV in the future.

❖ ❖ ❖

Opposite top: Perhaps the most glamorous development of the golden age of the passenger train was the creation of the Budd Company's full-length dome cars, called Big Domes on the Santa Fe. When passenger service was turned over to Amtrak, one of these superb cars was retained for company use, for instance on directors' specials (unique trains reserved for transporting railroad officials on occasional tours of inspection). Opposite bottom: Modifying existing Pullman-built cars with the addition to the roof of low-profile three-quarter-length domes, the Southern Pacific was a relative latecomer to dome-car operation, putting their domes into service beginning in 1955.

CHAPTER THREE

GREAT TRAINS OF THE NORTHEASTERN UNITED STATES

The golden era of passenger trains, roughly the first half of the twentieth century, produced many superb trains in the United States. It is not possible to provide substantial details on all of them, but those included here represent a variety of designs or routes and defined the epitome of passenger-train travel of the day. They are all first-class trains, with the best equipment and service their owners could provide, and it is fitting that we begin with the New York Central's Twentieth Century Limited, whose very name derived from the hope and expectations of a new age of travel. While more space is devoted to the Century, Pennsylvania's Broadway Limited, and the Santa Fe's Super Chief (in Chapter Four) than to some other equally deserving trains, it is only because they represent typical examples of histories, equipment, and services.

✦ ✦ ✦

Several adventurous high-rollers enjoy the passing scenery from the rear platform of the heavyweight Twentieth Century Limited. The open-veranda observation car is one of the most enduring images of the classic era of passenger trains, an image reinforced by the parade of politicians that took advantage of the observation car to deliver hundreds of speeches during their so-called whistle-stop campaigns.

THE TWENTIETH CENTURY LIMITED, NEW YORK CENTRAL RAILROAD

George H. Daniels, a marketing genius and a former patent-medicine salesman, ran the passenger business of the New York Central Railroad from 1889 to 1907. His understanding of the value of marketing and advertising was decades ahead of his time. He was already respected for his invention of the free redcap baggage-handling service for rail passengers when the 1893 Columbian Exhibition presented a golden opportunity for him to try out some new ideas.

To accommodate the anticipated hordes of visitors to the exhibition, a handsome new train had been built by the Wagner Palace Car Company for temporary New York to Chicago service during the summer and autumn of the event. Daniels' Exposition Flyer made the 980-mile (1,577km) journey in twenty hours, an amazing schedule for the time. The commercial success of the Flyer enabled Daniels to begin a permanent deluxe service between the Windy City and Gotham in November 1897.

The New York Central Railroad again turned to the Wagner firm to produce two seven-car train sets for the new train to Chicago, to be called The Lakeshore Limited (the precursor to the Century). Three cars of each train were sleepers, one of them scheduled through between Chicago and Boston, with a parlor car, club car, diner, and observation car filling out the luxurious consist. The club car was a businessman's sanctuary, with buffet, cigar, and wine service, and stock market quotes delivered at each station stop, hot off the wire. A barbershop and white-tiled bathroom were also available. Women and children passengers could find refuge in the parlor car, complete with its own buffet, a library, and a private sitting room. Another buffet was available in the sleeping cars, in addition to the full meal service offered in the superbly finished diner, which was decorated in opulent carved oak and had heavy curtains to close off two private dining rooms. The observation car combined eight private staterooms with the observation lounge, and included another library complete with available stenographer. Such a serious train demanded first-class service, and the Wagner company was as meticulous as Pullman in supplying highly trained staff equal to the superb equipment.

The Lakeshore Limited traveled from New York to Chicago in twenty-four hours, but Daniels was not satisfied and pushed for a twenty-hour timetable. In the predawn of the twentieth century, the marketing genius coined the name destined to become legendary—The Twentieth Century Limited—to describe the train that was to usher in a new era in fast luxury travel.

The first Century had just five cars and accommodated only forty-two passengers when service began on June 15, 1902. In addition to the normal extra fares paid for first-class and sleeper service, a premium was added for the pure speed and comfort of the Twentieth Century Limited, a fee paid by the passengers of very few other prestigious trains (the Pennsylvania Railroad's Broadway Limited, Santa Fe's Chiefs, and the New Haven's Merchants Limited and Yankee Clipper among them). Even given the extra fees, the early Century was hard-pressed to cover its expenses with the revenue. Many also doubted its technical ability to maintain such a tight schedule, and predicted the abandonment of both the luxury and schedule.

The venture did succeed, ultimately becoming the New York Central's flagship train, although it must have cost the railroad dearly to maintain this prestigious service. Operating personnel were ordered to give the train absolute priority over other traffic, and back-up locomotives were kept under steam along the route to cover any mechanical failure. For many years, passengers were offered a one dollar refund for each hour the train was late. The railroad was able to trim the twenty-hour schedule a bit at a time (even during the steam era), eventually reducing it to sixteen hours by converting to diesel power.

EXTRACTS FROM THE WAGNER PALACE CAR COMPANY STAFF MANUAL OF 1898

◆ ◆ ◆

Personal Appearance: Avoid putting hands in pockets in tails of uniform over-coats in cold weather, giving employee a rather loafering appearance, as well as spreading the tail of the coats and getting them out of shape.

Collars and cuffs: White linen only—celluloid are prohibited.

Maids: Will wear the prescribed uniform while on duty, and must at all times carry sufficient linen for the round trip. They must also have the following equipment: Book of Rules, set of keys, bottle of smelling salts, liquid camphor, black and white thread, package of needles, and box of assorted pins for ladies' use. Maids must be extremely careful to maintain a proper deportment while on duty. Under no circumstances will they allow any familiarity on the part of the crew or passengers, and they should at all times avoid even the appearance of it. No excuse will be accepted for any violation of this rule.

In the streamliner era, many trains, including the Twentieth Century Limited (seen here in 1948), dispensed with the drafty and cindery open rear platform; in its place, the trains provided fully enclosed rear lounges (called observation cars) that offered wide views through glass windows—as well as heating, air-conditioning, and attentive waiters who would supply passengers with beverages and snacks—to a greater number of people.

✦ ✦ ✦

All of this luxury was overwhelming to visiting Europeans, who suffered (by comparison) with Continental passenger service, which was still very early in its development. The Century's lavish equipment and staffing (including porters, maids, valets, barber, and stenographer) made for an unparalleled traveling experience that was by all reports reflected (if not magnified) by the opulence of the meals that were served. The diner was a glorious extravaganza in carved mahogany, stained glass, and leather. Potted plants were placed between the windows, and fresh flowers graced each table, set with specially commissioned linens, silver, crystal, and fine china. Passengers were overwhelmed and awed even before they read the extensive menu, which touted a sumptuous multicourse repast equal to the finest nonmobile restaurant. The price of such a rewarding meal was just one dollar, an incredible bargain even in those days, and made for a standard item of conversation among railroad

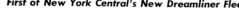

World Premiere!
the New 20th Century Limited
First of New York Central's New Dreamliner Fleet

New **Lookout Lounge**—Modern setting for the club-like sociability that's long been a *Century* tradition.

New — from its streamlined Diesel to its raised "Lookout Lounge"...

New **King-Size Diner**—So spacious it needs a separate kitchen car! Smart designing gives each table privacy plus a perfect outlook. There's a festive feel about the *Century* dinner hour and a sense of being served with distinction.

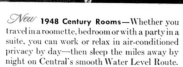

New **1948 Century Rooms**—Whether you travel in a roomette, bedroom or with a party in a suite, you can work or relax in air-conditioned privacy by day—then sleep the miles away by night on Central's smooth Water Level Route.

NEW YORK CENTRAL
The Water Level Route — You Can Sleep

NEW YORK CENTRAL SYSTEM

BETWEEN THE HEART OF CHICAGO AND THE HEART OF NEW YORK
Vacation overnight aboard the new Century. Arrive refreshed—with no business time lost.

travelers throughout the eastern United States in the early part of the twentieth century.

The long-simmering rivalry between the New York Central and Pennsylvania railroads, competing fiercely for the lucrative New York-to-Chicago passenger traffic, intensified when the Pennsy chose the very day of the Twentieth Century's first run to announce that it was cutting eight hours off its own schedule (to match the Century's twenty-hour timing) with a lightweight new train, the Pennsylvania Special. The two giants battled head to head, constantly trimming minutes off their schedules to stay competitive. The Pennsy's 908-mile (1,453km) route ran south to Philadelphia before turning west for the tough climb over the Allegheny Mountains while NYC's longer, but lower grade, "water level" route followed the Hudson River north before turning west along the Great Lakes. In November 1912, Pennsy dumped the Special in favor of a new,

Left: The introduction of brand-new streamlined equipment on the Twentieth Century Limited in 1948 rated full-page advertisements in national magazines. **Above:** In their decor and service, the early dining cars clearly reflected the opulent tastes of the wealthy patrons who liked to travel by rail in style. **Opposite:** While the menus changed over the years, it was always imperative that the food offered be the best possible.

The train usually ran in two or more sections (complete trains following the same timetable a few minutes apart), requiring a dedicated pool of equipment totaling twenty-four locomotives and 122 Pullmans.

On January 7, 1929, the eastbound Twentieth Century Limited set a traffic record, running in seven sections and carrying a total of 822 paying passengers, each one paying ten dollars extra over the regular fare for riding this train. The supplementary fee seems minor today, but in 1929 a dollar would still buy a good meal on the train. The well-heeled traveler gladly paid ten times that amount for the pleasure and prestige of riding the Century.

The railroad took its crack train quite seriously. Each morning, the New York Central's president arrived at his office to a report on the previous day's Century, detailing the loadings, gross revenue, schedule performance, and a list of notable personalities (from the business, political, or stage and screen worlds) on board. In keeping with the exclusive nature of the Century's wealthy and famous clientele, a 260-foot (79m)-long, 6-foot (1.8m)-wide maroon carpet embellished with the Twentieth Century Limited art deco logo was ceremoniously rolled out the length of the departing train's platform at Grand Central Terminal. This practice began in 1922 and continued, with the exception of the World War II years, until the demise of the train under Amtrak sometime during the early 1970s.

Like all business, the Century suffered through the Great Depression, but, as prosperity beckoned, the New York Central decided to reequip its flagship from end to end. Noted industrial designer Henry Dreyfuss (who had previously applied an "inverted bathtub" shroud to a NYC 4-6-2 Pacific for the Cleveland–Detroit Mercury) was engaged to handle the work, competing with his rival Raymond Loewy, who had been assigned the same task for the Pennsylvania Railroad's rival train, the Broadway Limited. Dreyfuss completely redid the train, from the locomotive to the upholstery in the observation car. As a result, the 1938 Twentieth Century Limited was one of the finest trains yet seen, setting the standard for years to come.

Dreyfuss revised the entire concept of the Century. The classic Pullman upper- and lower-berth sections were eliminated and replaced with private rooms of various sizes. The new car sides were smooth-welded steel, eliminating the characteristic pattern of rivets on the classic Pullmans. The New York Central produced its workhorse passenger locomotive, the fabled 4-6-4 Hudson, in a new variation, the ten-loco class J-3a. Dreyfuss applied an elegant streamlined styling compatible with the cars—a smooth "skyline" casing and a rounded and finned "bullet nose" over a fared and smoothed flush pilot and deck with skirting along the running boards. The tender was generously rounded along the top and bottom corners, and the entire train was painted an elegant two-tone gray with silver stripes.

heavyweight steel Broadway Limited (originally Broad Way, for the six-track-wide raceway between New York and Philadelphia) and retreated to the earlier twenty-hour timetable. New York Central, well aware of the excessive cost of maintaining the tight schedule, quickly followed suit, and the schedules for both trains remained fixed until 1932.

With the development of the more spacious and smooth-riding, all-steel heavyweight Pullman cars, the New York Central's passenger business flourished, particularly on the all-Pullman, extra-fare Twentieth Century Limited. In the late 1920s, just before the onset of the Great Depression, the Century alone grossed in excess of $10 million per year.

The Henry Dreyfuss–styled Hudsons powered the New York Central's Twentieth Century Limited throughout the war years.

✦ ✦ ✦

The interiors lacked the traditional ornate woodwork, brocaded furniture, and brass fixtures, but were dressed in simple elegance. Soft fluorescent lighting glowed from indirect sources, illuminating such materials as cork, leather, and Formica. Venetian blinds controlled the outside light more subtly than the earlier cloth blinds had. Amenities such as secretarial and Dictaphone services were included, with freshly typed documents mailed by railroad personnel at appropriate stops. Dreyfuss' designs minimized the corridor-like feeling inherent in passenger cars by dividing large spaces such as the diner and lounge into more intimate groupings of tables, chairs, and built-in banquette sofas. His services also included such details as the china and menus in the diner.

Perhaps as significant as the new equipment was the accelerated schedule. The Century was assigned sixteen hours, including stops, to cover the 980 miles (1,577km) and five states (New York, Pennsylvania, Ohio, Indiana, and Illinois) from New York to Chicago. The high level of personal service was maintained as well. At one point, a traveler stepping off the Century could expect as many as sixty-five redcaps to be waiting to assist with the luggage.

As fine a train as this Twentieth Century Limited was, the heavy traffic of wartime took a toll; a new train was put into service in 1948. By this time, the handsomely shrouded Hudsons had been replaced by sleek streamlined E-7 diesel locomotives from General Motors' Electro-Motive

HORSESHOE CURVE

✦ ✦ ✦

While there are railroads tracks throughout the world that make a dramatic horseshoe-shaped curve around the end of a valley, there is only one Horseshoe Curve, the grand engineering achievement that, since January 1854, has made it possible for the Pennsylvania Railroad climb to the summit of the Alleghenies on a .85 percent grade.

Altoona, Pennsylvania, was a company town, home of the massive Pennsy locomotive shops, where the leaves were always black, making it impossible to tell if it was spring or fall. The porches were washed every morning and the curtains once a month. The climb began on the edge of town and ended 12 twisting miles (19.5km) later at AR tower in Gallitzin. Part-way up, the track folded back on itself in a huge sweeping curve around the Altoona reservoirs and provided a panoramic view back down to the valley. The grade took a toll on both men and machine (the Pennsy resisted installing mechanical stokers until late in the steam era), but there was no way around it.

Don Ball, in his book *The Pennsylvania Railroad, 1940s–1950s*, eloquently described his experiences riding in the cab of a 575,880-pound (261,219kg) J-1 class 2-10-4 Texas locomotive with two helpers on the rear of the freight train:

The engineer on 6423 glances at the steam pressure sitting at 265 pounds [per square foot], eyes the water glass, and yells over to the fireman, "This is where friendship ceases!" A little further up the Railroad, things get rougher; the hogger is heard to say, "I got the sand under her. . . come to me, baby." He's serious, almost grim. The fireman works the stoker [the J-1s had them], pays absolute attention to the job. This is teamwork between engineer, fireman, and machine. The engineer feels the hard-working engine through his gloved hands on the throttle and sander valve; he listens to each boom of the stack. Gauges jiggle; water spurts from pipes on the backhead; the thrust of rods and pistons heaves through the cab. Up on the mountain, they pass through the 6° Wilkes curve. The fireman looks down from his cab at the long shadow of the great engine cast over six ribbons of rail. On the engineer's side, the nearby rocks threaten to tumble onto the tracks from the thunderous booming of the stack. "You don't have to shake it [the grates]. I'll clean it up for you!" yells the engineer. They steadily blast up grade, through the 6° McGarvys Run curve to the left. Shortly they head into Miller's curve, 6° back to the right. The big 2-10-4 raises incredible hell through the nearby woods and mountains. Steam is still up around 255 pounds, "with a feather in her cap" [meaning the light plume of steam from the safety valves]. She hammers hard into the heavily ballasted 9° curve to the left at Baker's Run. "You put it in, I'll burn it!" shouts the engineer. The big engine is steady, into a 2°45' curve to the right, and then around the wall of Kittanning Point. The railroad can be seen high up on the mountain to the left. Horseshoe's great 9°30' curve comes into view. In a minute, they are into the apex of Horseshoe, "puttin' 300 feet into the air and not a kink in it no place."

"Look her over. See if it's black [see if the train's alright]," the engineer tells the student fireman who is with them today. The great mountainous amphitheater spreads out ahead and to the left over the reservoir. Eastbound general merchandise is coming down the railroad, high over Sugar Run. . . heading down No. 1 track, back toward Altoona. [The operating pattern established by president J. Edgar Thomson in 1854 remains in place today, although the four tracks are now just three.]

The strategic importance of Horseshoe Curve in U.S. railroading is illustrated by an event that took place in the early days of World War II. At midnight on June 13, 1942, the German submarine U202 silently surfaced off the foggy coast of Long Island and deployed a rubber raft that included four men and a huge crate of supplies. As the submarine slipped away, the men paddled ashore, changed into civilian clothes, and buried the crate. When challenged by a frightened and unarmed Coast Guardsman, the four German soldiers replied in unaccented English, stating that they were fishermen from nearby Southampton. Boarding Long Island Rail Road No. 21 out of Amagansett, they arrived in New York City with fifty thousand dollars in cash and directions, orders, and contacts printed on their handkerchiefs.

They intended to detonate nuisance bombs in the Penn Stations of New York and Philadelphia, before destroying a Philadelphia aluminum plant. Proceeding west, their targets were key interlocking plants on the Pennsylvania Railroad, and the Gallitzin tunnels at the summit of Horseshoe Curve. Fortunately, they were caught before they could embark on their explosive rampage, and the Pennsy's trains continued to thunder over Horseshoe Curve until supplanted by Penn Central and Conrail.

Amtrak experimented with special extra-fare first-class service by offering passage in a leased private car attached to the back of the Pennsylvanian, a daytime Pittsburgh–Harrisburg–New York Amfleet-equipped train. Here, the open-platform heavyweight Cannon Ball trails the Pennsylvanian on Horseshoe Curve in 1995, before the service was dropped.

Division, dressed in the extremely elegant "lightning stripe" two-tone gray scheme. Dreyfuss was still involved in the $4-million project, which was intended to regain the traffic of the prewar years. Alas, intercity passengers were already transferring their allegiance to the airplane and automobile; even so, during its final golden years, the Century was able to stem the tide a little longer.

Even in its decline, a ride on the Twentieth Century Limited was an experience to cherish. The doors of Grand Central Terminal, a great beaux-arts cathedral, opened into a hubbub of tens of thousands of long-distance travelers and commuters swirling through the vast concourse. A virtual army of mop men, squeegee men, and gum scrapers had worked through the night to keep the marble sparkling. As the passengers embarked, dozens of redcaps hustled baggage down the red carpet to the

Century, where white-coated porters waited to escort passengers to their Pullmans. There might be eight to eleven sleeping cars—the number varied with the season.

Accommodations varied considerably, even within the first-class Pullman cars. The least expensive were roomettes, small single rooms arranged along both sides of a corridor (a refinement of the open-section Pullman berth), which provided a sitting room by day and, at bedtime, an already-made-up bed folded down from the wall. The single and double bedrooms, arranged along one side of a corridor, were slightly roomier, and the double bedroom included its own private toilet. A still more luxurious space was the drawing room, which had two berths along one wall (with small windows set above the regular windows, so that passengers in the upper berths would be able to see out), with the

The slick and modern interiors of the later-model dining cars were very different from the mahogany and brass of earlier cars. While the 1948 Century featured generous helpings of stainless steel and fluorescent lights, the quality of the food and the level of service remained constant nonetheless.

HENRY DREYFUSS

♦ ♦ ♦

Henry Dreyfuss, along with his major rival, Raymond Loewy, was a founder of the American industrial design profession. He was born in New York City on March 3, 1904, and by the age of seventeen he was working as a set designer on Broadway.

Dreyfuss took his first steps toward his future profession in 1927, when he was hired to do store design work. The store owner asked for suggestions on how to improve the appearance of some of his products. Dreyfuss resigned, stating that such work needed to be done by the manufacturer, early on in the product-development process.

Dreyfuss acted on these words and opened his first product-design office in 1929. He quickly attracted the attention of Bell Laboratories, which hired him to design telephone equipment. The New York Central Railroad hired him for its second experiment with streamlining a steam locomotive, and Dreyfuss applied a "bathtub" shroud and "white-wall tires" to a single 4-6-2 Pacific for the Cleveland–Detroit Mercury. The success of that venture encouraged the NYC to commission Dreyfuss to do an entire train, the 1938 Twentieth Century Limited, flagship of the railroad's Great Steel Fleet. His work also included the 1948 reequip-ping of the Century as well as the design of the streamlined locomotive for the James Whitcomb Riley. Other of Dreyfuss' major projects included the interiors for Lockheed's Super G Constellation airplane and the interiors for the ocean liner *Independence*.

Dreyfuss' philosophy was to concentrate on the end user of his designs. He stated, "When the point of contact between the product and people becomes a point of friction, then the Industrial Designer has failed." He detailed this philosophy in his books, *The Measure of Man* (1960), which clearly defined all dimensional aspects of a human being so that designers could properly size their products, and *Designing for People* (1965). He taught at the University of California, Los Angeles, from 1963 to 1970. Sadly, Dreyfuss died, along with his wife, from car-bon monoxide poisoning at his home in Pasadena, California, on March 5, 1972.

Henry Dreyfuss admires the results of his streamlined restyling of the New York Central's 4-6-4 Hudson locomotives that were to haul the 1938 Twentieth Century Limited. This was the first all–private room train in the United States and one of many Dreyfuss designs for the New York Central.

rest of the area set aside for a roomy lounge area containing individual chairs. At the top-of-the-line were the master bedrooms, suites that included a double-bedroom with private shower and lavatory adjacent to a handsome lounge with four armchairs.

Once aboard, a passenger found a brochure listing the array of avail-able onboard services—valet, an electric razor, or a Dictaphone on loan, complimentary newspaper delivered with your freshly shined shoes in the morning, and light refreshments at any time. A bedside telephone con-nected a passenger with service personnel, and a radio telephone con-nected to the outside world.

Departure time from Grand Central was 6:00 P.M. daily, with an elec-tric locomotive assigned for the 34 miles (54.5km) to Harmon, freeing the extensive tunnels from noxious fumes (and complying with smoke-abatement laws) while exiting New York. Then the new diesel-electrics took over, and the train swept along the scenic bank of the majestic Hudson River until the climb to Albany, where the train crew changed (additional crew-change points were Syracuse and Buffalo, New York; Cleveland and Toledo, Ohio; and Elkhart, Indiana).

Once the traveler had settled in, it was time for dinner. The train carried two diners, set back to back, and Dreyfuss had cleverly arranged the seating into three separate areas. Two eight-seat dinettes with four-seat tables on each side of the aisle flanked a central twenty-two-seat space ingeniously arranged with different-sized tables, some placed laterally, some longitudinally. Along the walls stood uphol-stered banquette sofas as well as individual chairs. Leather covered the walls and seats, accented with walnut pan-eling and a gray-and-rust color scheme. Fluorescent panels provided soft lighting.

In the evening, a dinner-jacketed stew-ard presented each woman with a compli-mentary orchid (and a boutonniere for the gentlemen the following morning), and regu-lars on the train were typically addressed by name. During the golden age, one famous steward claimed to be able to identify fifteen thousand passengers by name and identify three-quarters of the passengers on any trip. Additionally, stewards frequently kept note-books listing the preferences and peculiari-ties of the regulars. For example, Marshall Field, the Chicago department-store mag-nate, was known to expect the makings of two dry martinis in the cocktail shaker, even though he always ordered only one, and Bing Crosby preferred to begin his day with a 6:00 A.M. breakfast of wheatcakes.

Following a dinner that was priced at $1.75 (even as late as 1948), the crisp white

linens were replaced with soft rose-colored cloths, the lighting was dimmed, and the recorded big-band music of Tommy Dorsey or Glenn Miller transformed the diner into a sophisticated nightspot.

Alternate rolling entertain-ment was provided in the club car or the observation lounge. The former was entered through a cir-cular foyer containing large-scale models of early New York Central steam locomotives in recessed cases. Once again, Dreyfuss mini-mized the tunnel effect of the car with a serpentine arrangement of leather settees and individual arm-chairs set around low tables. The color scheme here was the famil-iar gray and rust, but the walls were covered in cork. At the far end of the lounge was a well-stocked bar, the barbershop was beyond that, and the crew quarters (with showers and bunks for eighteen) occupied the end of the car. The observation lounge was quite similar in decor, but included a speedometer mounted on the wall for the passengers' amusement.

For the entire length of its run, the Twentieth Century Limited carried a mini-mum staff of forty: the Pullman conductor; a Pullman porter in each sleeping car; the train secretary and a railroad passenger–department representative; a barber and a ladies' maid; and the catering

◆ ◆ ◆

Above: The Pullman Company continually experi-mented with increasing the comfort of overnight passengers at economy rates. This 1940 photo is of a room (in its daytime configuration) aboard the company's recently introduced coach-sleeper. These cars provided berths at half the cost of a first-class ticket for forty-five passengers in five three-person compartments and five six-person compartments. Left: This advertisement, which probably dates from the early 1940s, illustrates several configurations of Pullman's economy-class sleeping arrangements.

staff—two chief stewards, two chefs, six cooks, fourteen waiters, and two bartenders. This was to service a passenger load of 150 on a train with eight sleepers and did not include the operating crew: conductor, baggage man, and two brakemen (who were relieved at Buffalo and Toledo); and the locomotive crews (who were replaced seven times). All totaled, more than sixty personnel were required for the sixteen-hour trip.

The Century was synonymous with first-class service. But the high labor cost associated with such service doomed it in the face of the business travelers' defections to the airlines. By 1958, satisfactory extra-fare loadings of an all-Pullman train could no longer be maintained and, on April 27, 1958, the Twentieth Century Limited was demoted to ordinary coach-sleeper service, the first of the great New York–Chicago luxury trains to be curtailed.

The New York Central continued to run the reduced-status train under the Century name, but the legendary train made its last run when Amtrak took over North American intercity passenger service in 1971, choosing to keep the workaday Lakeshore Limited on that route.

THE BROADWAY LIMITED, PENNSYLVANIA RAILROAD

The Pennsylvania Railroad operated a vast rail system, moving passengers and freight from New York, Philadelphia, Baltimore, and Washington, to Chicago and St. Louis. Hundreds of trains per day funneled through Pittsburgh, across the industrial belt of northern Ohio and Indiana, until they reached the Windy City (described as "Where the West Begins!" in the line's advertising literature). As "The Standard

The lounge car aboard the great trains provided an opportunity for passengers to wander through the train and socialize. It was the preferred location for smoking, eating snacks, or consuming alcoholic beverages, enabling travelers to relax away from their compartments or seats.

✦ ✦ ✦

Railroad of the World," its influence was immense. In the predepression Philadelphia business community, if someone mentioned the "President," he had to clarify whether it was the man in charge of the United States or the head of the Pennsy. The railroad always paid a dividend to its stockholders, even during the Great Depression, and its cash reserves were sufficient to embark on numerous $100 million-engineering projects (which would be the equivalent of billions in today's dollars). The employees were rightfully proud of the Pennsy, and the pride of the railroad was its premier passenger train—the Broadway Limited.

Designed to compete with rival New York Central's crack Twentieth Century Limited for the lucrative New York–Chicago traffic, the Broadway began life as the Twenty Hour Special. On June 2, 1902, the very day of the Century's debut, the Pennsy announced that this new all-Pullman and extra-fare lightweight train would slash the previous New York–Chicago schedule of twenty-eight hours and match its rival's timetable. The train was quickly rechristened the Pennsylvania Special to avoid any confusion with its rival, although the new name was just as confusing because the Pennsy was already operating a New York–Chicago train called the Pennsylvania Limited. Designed to make a splash, the new train was painted a flamboyant yellow, and was known as The Yellow Kid. Delays caused by severe freight-train congestion at Pittsburgh required the schedule to be abandoned after eighteen months, but, after new construction eased the bottlenecks, a new Special was announced in June 1905—now with an eighteen-hour schedule. The New York Central immediately trimmed the schedule of the Century to match.

In an era obsessed with speed, this high-speed passenger train and its race with rival Twentieth Century Limited captured the public's imagination (as well as newspaper headlines across the country). It was advertised as The Fastest Long Distance Train in the World and inspired

THE PORTER AND THE TRAVELING SALESMAN

◆ ◆ ◆

A salesman summoned a porter before retiring for the night, and requested that he be awoken and put off the train when it arrived in Buffalo in the wee hours of the morning. "I'm very grumpy when I wake up, and I'll probably resist. Here's ten bucks to pay for your trouble. I've an important meeting early in the morning, so don't listen to my complaints—just put me off in Buffalo."

The next morning, when the eastbound train stopped in Schenectady, the furious passenger found the porter and began shouting at him. After the enraged man hurried away, a bewildered fellow porter asked, "Why was that man shouting? He sure was mad as a hornet!"

The first porter rolled his eyes, shrugged, and said, "But not nearly as mad as that man I put off the train in Buffalo."

Porters and redcaps (station porters identifiable by their red headgear) provided important services to travelers.

earnest tributes of many kinds, including a two-step march penned by bandmaster Innes of the New York Orchestral Band called The Pennsylvania Special.

In November 1912, the Specials were retired in favor of a new, but slower, heavyweight train named the Broad Way Limited (quickly becoming Broadway). The name derived from the Pennsy's six-track main line between New York and Philadelphia, called the Great Broad Way. The all-steel train was entirely Pullman-serviced and was, by all measures, a match for the Twentieth Century Limited.

The Broadway Limited was a first-class train, providing a "ladies' maid," manicurist, barber, and secretary for the passengers' convenience. The tables in the diner were set with china and silver, with a morning newspaper from the destination city available at breakfast. Mahogany paneling graced the walls, the stewards wore dinner jackets in the evening and striped morning trousers at breakfast and lunch, and the waiters dressed in tan mess jackets and wing collars. In 1925, the Broadway's diner served a full prime-rib dinner for $1.25 or a Kansas City sirloin (for two) for $2.50.

The more sedate Broadway lacked the Century's red-carpeted platform, celebrity interviews, and press photographers' flashbulbs at departure time, but it took advantage of its dignified and businesslike air to imply that the Century was vulgar and ostentatious. The Pennsy also had the visual advantage, after the 1930s, of the streamlined GG1 electric locomotive at the point of the train in New York, while the Central settled for one of its functional but homely box cabs for the initial part of the run, from Grand Central to Harmon.

Even though the origination and destination cities and departure/arrival times of the two rivals remained identical through much of their histories, their routes were quite different. Both left New York with electric power because of the extensive tunneling under the city, but the Pennsy's 908-mile (1,461km) route ran southwest from New York to Philadelphia before turning west for the steep climb to Horseshoe Curve and Pittsburgh, then diagonally across Ohio and Indiana to Chicago. The Central's route was longer, at 980 miles (1,568km), running north along the Hudson River and turning northwest to Albany before following the Great Lakes west to the Windy City, but the easy grades of its water-level route eliminated the slow going on the Alleghenies' steep slopes.

The GG1 hauled the Broadway through the New York tunnels, under the Hudson River, and across New Jersey to the west end of the electrified district at Harrisburg, Pennsylvania. There, the elegant Tuscan red–and-gold train was turned over to the Pennsy's classic K-4s Pacifics, designed for both power and speed, which were capable of charging up the Allegheny grades or racing across the farm fields of Indiana, although they were frequently doubleheaded on heavy trains. (The New York Central preferred to use just a single locomotive.) Between Englewood

The lounge car on the Pennsylvania Railroad's crack Broadway Limited was an ideal place for strangers to meet and socialize, an activity that was part of the romance of rail travel. The designers of the great trains lavished considerable time and money on these traveling hotel lobbies.

◆ ◆ ◆

and Chicago, the two trains converged, running on parallel tracks and, if they were both on time (and they damn well better have been), raced the final miles to and from Chicago side by side (the Century touched down at La Salle Street Depot and the Broadway in Union Station).

In 1938, the Pennsylvania's management, perhaps sensing an end to the Great Depression, boldly decided to completely reequip the Broadway. Raymond Loewy, having successfully collaborated with the Altoona shops in the styling of the railroad's new GG1 electric locomotive, was retained for the new project. This put Loewy directly in competition with Henry Dreyfuss, who was commissioned to design a new Twentieth Century Limited for the New York Central.

Loewy responded with the elegant "Fleet of Modernism"—new streamlined train sets from Pullman and an elegant, "Buck Rogers"-inspired, streamlined shroud for the K4s (turned out by the Altoona shops). The 142 painted smooth-side cars (not the fluted stainless steel used by the Zephyr and other Pioneers) were assigned to four east–west

trains: the Broadway Limited, the General (New York–Chicago), the Liberty Limited (Washington–Chicago), and the Spirit of Saint Louis (New York–Saint Louis). Simultaneously, the Broadway's schedule was squeezed to sixteen hours—the fastest ever.

The exteriors of the new trains retained the traditional Tuscan red of the Pennsy fleet, but Loewy added a darker red window band and a series of continuous horizontal gold stripes. Round-end observation lounges replaced the traditional brass-railed veranda cars, and the interiors matched those of Dreyfuss' Century for comfort and luxury. Gone were the traditional Pullman upper and lower berths, replaced by an all-compartment layout. The public lounges were divided into smaller, more intimate spaces, and interiors featured fluorescent lighting, formed plywood, cork, aluminum trim, and other elegant contemporary materials and detailing, also similar to the Century. The master bedroom included a radio.

The Broadway Limited, like the rest of the United States' passenger trains, operated at full capacity through the duration of World War II, usually warranting multiple sections. Doubleheaded K4s were frequently seen at the front end of passenger trains, along with even bigger locomotives, such as Loewy's streamlined S-1 4-4-4-6 duplex, his shark-nosed T-1 4-4-4-4 duplex, or the experimental S-2 6-8-8-6 turbine. By the time hostilities ended in 1945, the railroads' noble contributions to "The Arsenal of Democracy" had taken a terrible toll—they were thoroughly worn out.

Following the war, the Pennsylvania Railroad tried to secure its postwar passenger traffic by rebuilding tracks, the locomotives, and freight-

THE PROPOSED MERGER OF TWO GREAT TRAINS

◆ ◆ ◆

In the early days of the discussions regarding the merger of the New York Central with arch-rival Pennsylvania Railroad, some thought was given to combining the two flagship passenger trains as well. The two trains—the Twentieth Century Limited and the Broadway Limited—both ran from New York to Chicago on identical schedules, although on quite different routes, and it would not be logical to keep both money-losing trains operating. In the spirit of the proposed new name of the combined railroads—Penn Central—an irreverent story made the rounds at both headquarters that the combined train would be christened "the Twenty Cent Broad."

RAYMOND LOEWY
(1893–1986)

✦ ✦ ✦

Raymond Loewy's notable relationship with the Pennsylvania Railroad grew from the simple assignment of redesigning the trash cans in New York's Pennsylvania Station. Legend has it that Raymond Loewy was such a pest at Pennsylvania Railroad headquarters that he was given the contract to get rid of him. By the time Loewy's relationship with the railroad ended, he had been credited with some of the most important of the classic designs of railroading's golden age (and in other industries as well).

One of the founders of the profession of industrial design, Loewy began his career in France, where at age fifteen he designed and patented a model airplane, formed the Ayrel Corporation to manufacture it, and hired a salesman to sell it. He then designed an award-winning three-foot (90cm)-long speedboat model before serving with the French army in World War I. After emigrating to the United States in 1919, the fledgling designer was fired from his first job as a window designer for Macy's because his employer found his spare, uncluttered look unsatisfactory. Loewy turned to illustrating department-store ads and designing costumes for Florenz Ziegfeld, and considered returning to Paris before launching a "one-man industrial crusade under the aegis of good taste." He became a naturalized U.S. citizen in 1938.

Successful designs for Gestetner duplicating machines and the Hupmobile (an automobile) solidified his reputation, but Loewy was obsessed with transportation design and aggressively pursued the Pennsy. Following the trash-can commission, he was invited to submit a proposal for the styling of a newly engineered electric locomotive, the GG1. The Pennsy, in collaboration with Westinghouse Electric, had already distinguished the prototype locomotive (designated No. 4800) from its previous box-cab electrics by giving it a new streamlined center-cab design, but railroad officials were still shocked when Loewy presented a clay model and sketches of a radically new approach to locomotive building.

Drawing upon his experience in the automotive field, Loewy proposed welding the entire body shell rather than the railroads' usual process of riveting overlapping steel panels. This would eliminate the rough texture of the rivets and joints. Loewy also proposed a number of contour and detailing changes that refined the already-built prototype into a smooth and sleek classic, finished off in the almost-black Brunswick green paint with an elegant five-stripe, gold "cat-whisker" paint scheme that converged on the front and rear pilots. The design was practical as well as aesthetic. "I decided to put gold stripes in front in a noticeable pattern so that people working on the tracks would see that gold on dark green, which would stand out very well in critical light situations," according to Loewy. The word Pennsylvania was stretched out across most of the locomotive's flank "to visually extend the length of the engine." Thus, with Raymond Loewy's help, an engineering success was transformed into one of the truly great locomotive designs.

Following the tremendous success of the GG1, the railroad continued to work with Loewy. An already-operational steam locomotive, the legendary K-4 Pacific, was fitted with a streamlined shrouding after wind-tunnel testing on clay models showed the design's aerodynmaic advantages. It was assigned to the new Broadway Limited train set of 1938, the flagship of the Loewy-designed "Fleet of Modernism." He assisted with the styling of a single S-1 6-4-4-6 Duplex in 1939, which was displayed under steam at the New York World's Fair: the radically experimental train sat on a large fixture with its seven-foot (2.1m) drivers slowly turning on rollers. This was followed by the design of the T-1 4-4-4-4 Duplex of 1942, built by the Baldwin Locomotive Works and adorned with a handsome shark-nose styling by Loewy. Fifty more were built with a simplified version of the styling, and these hauled Pennsylvania varnish at speeds of 100 mph (160kph) for a brief while.

The skilled Loewy also restyled some diesel locomotives. The shark-nose treatment of the T-1 was also applied to Baldwin passenger and freight locomotives, a most notable visual success, while Fairbanks-Morse H-10-44 switchers and their handsome 2,000hp Erie-built streamlined cab units were considerably enhanced by his refinements.

Raymond Loewy frequently competed with Henry Dreyfuss, co-founder of the industrial design profession, for clients, and the two men went head-to-head numerous times as Dreyfuss produced new locomotive and train set designs for the New York Central at the same time that Loew worked for arch-rival Pennsylvania. Loewy went on to design other things, including ships, cars (notably the Studebaker Avanti), and *Air Force One* and other aircraft (Loewy also undertook projects for NASA).

✦ ✦ ✦

Raymond Loewy stands proudly on the pilot deck of a Pennsylvania Railroad K4s Pacific that was streamlined according to his design; the standard version of the locomotive can be seen in the background.

Lucius Beebe (left) and Charles M. Clegg Jr. were noted rail enthusiasts and raconteurs who produced several books of railroad prose and photography. Here the two celebrities enjoy a meal in the dining room of Clegg's private car, Virginia City.

LUCIUS BEEBE AND THE BROADWAY LIMITED

◆ ◆ ◆

Lucius Beebe, the legendary rail traveler and irascible raconteur, described the Broadway Limited in his book, *The Trains We Rode* (1966):

> The Broadway Limited was a wonder and a glory of the railroad world. The peer in every aspect of equipment, services, cuisine and operational technique of the direct competition in the form of the New York Central's Twentieth Century Limited, it glittered from locomotive pilot beam to the brass railed platform of its observation lounge as the showcase of its owner's wares, a paradigm of elegance and superb promotion. Just as The Century was an essentially Chicago train in the character of its patronage, so The Broadway was the quintessence of Old Philadelphia and the grandeurs of the Main Line inherited from the era of Alexander Cassatt, a magnifico in whose presidency of the carrier it had been inaugurated. Its style was that of Rittenhouse Square. . . . Aboard it on their upholstered occasions in Chicago, rode Morrises, Biddles, Reeves and Cadwalladers, Penroses and Lippincotts, and it was no error in judgment on the part of the management that there was scrapple on the breakfast menu and Chesapeake Bay oysters at dinner. . . . Specially assigned K-4s Pacifics bore the train's name on their smokebox and its conductors were aristocrats.

The Pennsy dieselized quickly following World War II, and the staccato exhaust of the K4s was replaced by the growl of a General Motors-built 567B, the prime mover in EMD E8 locomotives.

◆ ◆ ◆

car fleets. The company also invested in a new Broadway Limited in 1948. The new train's interior, once again designed by Raymond Loewy, clearly reflected the epitome of design for that time, but the train's exterior appearance was little changed, save for one factor. Despite heavy investment in sophisticated experiments with advanced steam concepts, the PRR quickly dieselized in the postwar years. The new Broadway was led by streamlined diesel locomotives, but the railroad again resisted the fluted stainless steel cars created by the Budd company, retaining the two-tone red, smooth-sided design accented with multiple gold stripes. As could be expected, the New York Central came out with a new Dreyfuss-designed Twentieth Century Limited the same year, and the two premier trains continued their head-to-head rivalry for another decade.

On April 27, 1958, the New York Central gave up the financially exhausting race. The speed of air travel and the convenience of interstate highways had bled away passengers willing to pay an extra fare for the first-class Pullmans, so the Central reduced the train's status to standard coach-and-sleeper service. The Broadway Limited rolled on, although as

A character played by noted Hollywood and stage actor Jose Ferrer (in the robe) is restrained in a compartment of the Twentieth Century Limited in this scene from the play *Twentieth Century*.

THE CENTURY AND THE BROADWAY COMPETE AS STAGE PLAYS

◆ ◆ ◆

the fortunes of the railroads declined across the country, the equipment became somewhat shopworn, the schedules tenuous, and passengers scarce. The shutdown of Pullman's train service operations was another blow, but the PRR nonetheless struggled on with the Broadway Limited.

When the government relieved the struggling railroads of their passenger services with the formation of Amtrak on May 1, 1971, the Broadway Limited was retained to make the run from New York to Chicago. Amtrak pooled the equipment supplied by the railroads, and the smooth Tuscan disappeared in a hodgepodge of stainless steel mixed with the colors of America's railroads. Amtrak rebuilt its Heritage Fleet (as its classic equipment was called), bought new locomotives, and slowly rebuilt passenger service, but the era of the great trains was gone forever—in 1993, the schedule once again called for almost twenty hours to complete the Broadway route.

When the U.S. Congress' attention shifted to deficit cutting in the early 1990s, Amtrak's budget was a natural target. Forced by these cuts in funding to consolidate trains, Amtrak elected to retain the already reequipped Washington–Chicago Capitol Limited (which also stopped in Pittsburgh), adding a new train for the connection to New York City. On September 9, 1995, the Broadway Limited made its final run, almost a full century after entering service.

The sustained and bitter rivalry for supremacy on the New York–Chicago run continued for fifty-five years and usually focused on service, speed, luxury, and cuisine, but the oddest example of this competition occurred on the Broadway stage.

In 1932, playwrights Ben Hecht and Charles MacArthur wrote a comedy called *Twentieth Century*, which was produced on Broadway by George Abbott. A sensational hit, even in the depths of the Depression, the play featured Moffat Johnson, Bill Frawley, and Eugenie Leontovich cavorting zanily among the drawing rooms and lounges of the eastbound No. 26. Hollywood could not ignore the opportunity to cash in on such a sensation, and had equal success with a movie version of *Twentieth Century*.

A severe case of jealousy overwhelmed the Pennsy management, which observed the mountains of free publicity garnered by its rival. The Pennsy negotiated with Hal Roach and convinced him to participate in the production of a new screen comedy called *The Broadway Limited*. The film, featuring Marjory Woodworth, was not particularly successful, either as a film or as a publicity generator.

CHAPTER FOUR

GREAT TRAINS OF THE SOUTHEASTERN UNITED STATES

Long before the concrete ribbons of interstate highway and the vapor trails from Boeing 707s crossed the United States from top to bottom—making it possible for nearly every U.S. citizen to travel to warmer climes at the drop of a hat—hordes of frozen folks of the North fled the ice and snow of winter and sought comfort among the palm trees and beaches of Florida. Most of these sun-starved masses arrived by train.

THE FLORIDA TRAINS: CHAMPION, FLORIDA SPECIAL, ORANGE BLOSSOM SPECIAL, SILVER METEOR, SILVER STAR

Without the vision of some early sun-seeking pioneers, that exodus would not have been possible. The most important of the early visitors may well have been Henry Flagler, partner with John D. Rockefeller in Standard Oil. Flagler retired at the age of sixty with a massive fortune, and took his

◆ ◆ ◆

The railroads' publicity departments arranged an impressive lineup of early Electro-Motive Division E units at rest in 1940 or 1941. The locomotives represent the following railroads that served Washington, D.C. (left to right): Atlantic Coast Line E3, Florida East Coast Railway E3, Seaboard Railway E4, Southern Railway E6, and the Baltimore & Ohio Railroad E6 (the only non-Southerner in the group).

The Florida East Coast's April 1896 arrival in sleepy Miami was the beginning of the village's transformation into an important city, a center of commerce and the destination of millions of travelers in search of a little fun in the sun.

❖ ❖ ❖

ailing wife to the warmth and charm of Saint Augustine, Florida, then a sleepy town of twenty-five hundred. Appalled by the lack of appropriate hotels, he spent $1.5 million building the opulent Hotel Ponce de Leon, patterning it after a Moorish palace. The hotel opened in 1888 as one of the most lavish resorts in the world.

Knowing that luring patrons to his hotel would require comfortable travel accommodations, Flagler began his railroad empire with the 1885 purchase of the narrow-gauge Jacksonville, Saint Augustine & Halifax. In 1890, a new bridge across the Saint Johns River completed the rail connection from Saint Augustine to Jacksonville, and the entire line was converted to standard gauge, becoming the Florida East Coast Railway (FEC). Through-car service from the New York City area to Florida began in 1884, when the Atlantic Coast Line (ACL) extended its Jersey City–Waycross, Georgia, sleeper to Jacksonville. A joint Jersey City–Tampa sleeper was inaugurated with ACL in 1886.

The burgeoning Florida market justified deluxe service, so a new through-train, the Florida Special, was instituted on January 9, 1888. The Pennsylvania Railroad was responsi-

ble for the new train from Jersey City to Washington, D.C., where the Richmond, Fredericksburg & Potomac took over, hauling it until Richmond. The Atlantic Coast Line then carried the Special on to Jacksonville and the FEC.

The Florida Special was made up of six wooden Pullman Palace cars, including a baggage car that contained a dynamo to provide electric lighting to the train, and full vestibules—among the first examples of such advances. Also included were a smoking-library-refreshment car, a diner, and three ten-section, two-drawing-room sleeping cars.

Aboard the first run was the train's builder, George M. Pullman himself, and the passengers dined on delicacies that included roast antelope. The plush Victorian elegance was typical of the era, with chandeliers, French glass windows, and Spanish mahogany to comfort the riders on the 31¼-hour journey.

Florida was booming, and Flagler took full advantage, building a string of world-class hotels as he extended the railroad of the FEC to the south, reaching Miami in 1896. At the same time, Henry B. Plant, owner of the Southern Express Company, was extending his own railroad, the Plant System, through northern Florida and down the Gulf Coast to Tampa. In 1884, he opened the Tampa Bay Hotel, a proper rival to the Ponce de Leon. By 1902, the newly formed Seaboard Air Line (SAL, a railroad despite its misleading name) had purchased the Florida Central

Henry M. Flagler (circled) was eighty-two years old when he arrived on the first passenger train to reach Key West (on January 22, 1912), fulfilling his dream of building the Overseas Railroad, "the railroad that went to sea."

Above: Florida East Coast's brand-new Henry M. Flagler train set poses at Stuart, Florida, behind an EMD E3A diesel-electric locomotive in characteristic trim.
Below: The Orange Blossom Special receives a gala champagne christening in Pennsylvania Station, New York, prior to its inaugural run in 1935.

& Peninsular, gaining entrance to Tampa, and ACL had absorbed the Plant System. With another connection between Richmond and Florida, the Seaboard flourished. SAL's first winter season all-Pullman train, the Seaboard Florida Limited, began service in 1903, beginning a rivalry with the Florida Special that would last until the debut of the fabled Orange Blossom Special (1925).

By 1902, the Plant System had been absorbed by the Coast Line, and the Florida rail network was all but complete. Flagler was not yet finished, however, and began an eight-year project to extend the FEC 100 miles (161km) into the Gulf of Mexico, bridging the Florida Keys all the way to Key West. The goal was to carry freight and passengers as far south as possible, before transfers to steamship for the final leg to Latin America.

The Key West extension was one of the great engineering feats of the day, hopping from island to island to bridge 26 miles (42km) of open ocean. Knights Key was reached in 1908, and the Florida Special was extended to Palm Beach, with cars to West Palm Beach and Knights Key, for the following winter season. The train made a 3:20 A.M. stop at the then-sleepy little town of Miami, the site of Flagler's under-construction Royal Palm Hotel. Completion of the 7-mile-long (11km) Knights Key–Little Duck Viaduct enabled the rails to reach Key West; the first train to "America's Gibraltar" arrived on January 22, 1912.

In the 1920s, the Havana Special, descendant of the 1878 New York & West Indian Limited, routinely thrilled passengers on the open observation platform. The pink dawn illuminated the dramatic ride across the 2¼-mile (3.6km)- long Key Viaduct—nothing was visible but the sky, sea, and a narrow band of receding track. The Special was reequipped for the 1926–1927 season, and the new train included separate men's and women's lounges, a soda fountain, a bath and shower, valet service, and a ladies' maid.

The Roaring Twenties fueled Florida's explosive growth, and passenger traffic peaked in the winter of 1924–1925. Jacksonville was the state's revolving door, with 750,000 passengers arriving from as far away as Montreal. One postcard boasted, "More millionaires passed through the terminal than any other in the world" (it might have added "more fast-buck artists" as well).

THE HIJACKING PROBLEM

✦ ✦ ✦

During the late 1960s, the airlines operating to Florida cities faced a particularly vexing problem. In the days before the stringent airport security efforts that are now taken for granted, passengers and their luggage passed freely onto planes, making it easy to carry on weapons and explosives. It became almost common during this period for criminals or mentally unbalanced persons to escape the country by forcing an air crew to fly to Havana, where prosecution was impossible, given the nonexistent relations between the United States and Cuba.

The Seaboard Air Line railroad took advantage of this unfortunate situation, poking fun at its airborne competition at the same time that it offered an alternative. Print ads gleefully announced: "If you want to go to Miami without a stopover in Havana, call us."

Florida East Coast responded with its own building boom. The crush of traffic encouraged the FEC to double-track the main line, and Seaboard affiliate Florida Western & Northern began a new 204-mile (328.5km) connection between Coleman (northeast of Tampa) diagonally across the state to West Palm Beach. By 1927, Seaboard had also reached Miami.

Seaboard debuted a future legend in 1925, inaugurating a brand-new winter-season heavyweight Pullman train, the Orange Blossom Special. The New York train's first run was on November 21, with cars for Saint Petersburg and West Palm Beach, and was equipped with a women's lounge, baths, maids, and "unrivaled service." Unfortunately for the Orange Blossom, the Florida boom collapsed almost immediately, tourism lagged, and then the Great Depression struck. By 1930, Pullman traffic was down by half, freight traffic had plummeted, and Seaboard Air Line entered receivership.

By the mid-1930s, Pullman traffic had rebounded sufficiently for the Florida Special routinely to require multiple sections, peaking at seven sections on February 29, 1936. The nation's passenger revenues were still running at half those of the boom years, however, and America's railroads were looking for something other than traditional marketing techniques to entice travelers back to the rails. In May 1934, a shovel-nosed stainless

A lingering remnant of the long-gone connection to Key West, Atlantic Coast Line's Havana Special passes through Fayetteville, North Carolina, in August 1961. The United States' difficulties with the Castro regime eventually resulted in the cancellation of the historic name, which had long outlasted the boat connection to Cuba.

Above: The Gulf Mobile & Ohio's sleek new lightweight Rebel train set (built in 1935 by American Car & Foundry) helped to nudge the Florida lines toward the streamliner era. Below: The comfortable interior of the "boat-tailed" observation car provided sweeping views for the passengers aboard the Rebel.

steel apparition had streaked across the American plains at record-breaking speed—the Zephyr arrived at the Century of Progress Exposition in Chicago, and the railroad industry was changed forever.

Eager to bring the new streamliner technology to Florida, the Miami News kicked off an editorial campaign in March 1938, calling the campaign "Streamliners for Miami." The editors pointed out that the old heavyweight fleets that brought the tourists south were not running at capacity, and that tourism, the essential business of the area, was still lagging in general. The cost of a Florida vacation was beyond the reach of most families, while gleaming lightweight streamliners bearing the names of other tourist destinations competing for the nation's vacation dollars skimmed across the country leaving clouds of free publicity in their wakes.

With the backing of the business community and public support, the newspaper sent a writer to Denver and Chicago to report on the wonders of these new trains. Along with "puff pieces"—actors and chamber of

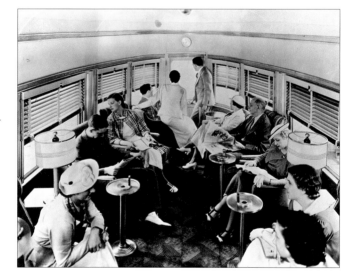

commerce representatives talking about speed and comfort—the *Herald* featured interviews with Chicago, Burlington & Quincy president Ralph Budd on the efficiency of diesel-electric power and with Rock Island's J.D. Farrington on the profitability of the new streamliners. The Rock Island Line had joined many other railroads in receivership during the depression, and had begged for funding for six new streamliners to boost income from passenger service. Reluctant creditors agreed, and the new Rockets were turning a substantial profit within three months of their 1937 delivery.

The conservative Atlantic Coast Line brushed off these articles, claiming that diesels were only practical in the open expanses of the West and would not be efficient in Florida, where the stops were frequent and close. As late as 1938, the ACL ordered new heavyweight day coaches. The newspaper pointed out the efficiency of the Chicago–Des Moines Rocket, which in the course of one day operated a daily round-trip of the same distance that a steam-hauled FEC local covered one-way.

The Auto-Train Experiment

✦ ✦ ✦

In 1966, the Atlantic Coast Line joined the Federal Department of Transportation to explore the feasibility of a new service—hauling both people and their cars to Florida vacations on the same train. Shipping passengers' cars to the South had been a regular part of the Coast Line and Seaboard freight rail business for many years. The years 1939 and 1940 saw nine thousand cars shipped on the ACL alone.

This new service would be more like a ferry, however, since the passengers would ride inside their vehicles (though the people were free to move around on the train), which would be loaded on specially built, air-conditioned, two-level cars with windows. Passengers were allowed to roam the train, and had access to dining and lounge cars located at each end of the ten-car string of auto carriers.

Testing was done using Pennsy's Class B70A theatrical-scenery cars, which had large end doors designed for loading the sets of traveling Broadway shows. The cars were attached to the tail end of the speedy Champion. Coast Line brass, riding in automobiles in these cars, pronounced the ride to be satisfactory. A similar trial run using rougher-riding auto racks did not meet with the same approval.

The success of this new concept depended upon the (unlikely) willingness of passengers to remain inside their cars for most of a twelve-hour trip. The basic idea of bringing people and their cars to the same destination was solid, however, and the Auto-Train began service in 1969, operated by a private corporation on Seaboard Coast Line rails. On the Auto-Train, automobiles were loaded onto auto racks and the passengers stayed in sleepers, with access to the traditional dining and lounge cars. A fleet of 182 passenger cars and 315 auto-carriers whisked passengers to Florida vacations until the company fell victim to several disastrous derailments and general economic woes, shutting down in 1981. Amtrak absorbed the service two years later, and still operates the popular Auto-Train from outside Washington to Sanford, Florida.

Rock Island

TIME FLIES WITH THE ROCKETS

streamliner market with a 1936 order for lightweight cars—six coaches and four combines from Pullman's Osgood-Bradley plant. The sleek turtle-roofed cars were based on a pioneering design for the New Haven, and were put into service on the Orange Blossom Special.

A shortage of cash forced the Seaboard, much as it had the Rock Island, into decisive action. The railroad ran losses as high as $8 million (in 1934) and not under $4 million annually during the next three years, despite an increase in passenger revenues. In 1938, even that encouraging development had vanished as passenger revenues dropped by over 10 percent from 1937.

The Seaboard Air Line (SAL) purchased nine Electro-Motive E4 diesel passenger locomotives in three A-B-B-A sets for the Orange Blossom Special, the lower operating costs justifying the purchase. Reduced maintenance costs (and time) and the higher speeds of the diesels, as well as the completion of the New York tunnels, allowed for a shorter schedule, so through-cars from Boston were added. Realizing that the secret to real passenger growth was tapping the market that could not normally afford a Florida vacation, the Seaboard Air Line began planning an all-coach train that could run year-round and thereby attract econ-

Despite this resistance on the Florida roads' part, streamliners were penetrating the South at this time. The Rebel, an experimental non-articulated three-car streamliner built by American Car & Foundry, went into service between Jackson, Tennessee, and New Orleans on the Gulf, Mobile & Northern in July 1935. The Seaboard dipped a toe into the

This is an artist's impression of the 1937 Rock Island Rockets, which were custom-built streamlined train sets powered by General Motors' TA diesel-electric locomotive. The TA had the first carbody built at GM's new Electro-Motive Division (EMD) plant in La Grange, Illinois, and was the precursor to the legendary E series of passenger-hauling locomotives.

✦ ✦ ✦

THE FLORIDA BLACK MARKET

✦ ✦ ✦

Demand for tickets during the height of the Florida tourist season in the heyday of rail travel in that region was so great that trains were usually sold out well in advance. Hotel guests who decided to prolong their vacations were therefore sometimes caught in a bind, since they could not book new travel dates with the railroads. It was typical for hotel employees to "handle" the problem for the guests, exchanging the useless tickets for new ones while accepting a five-dollar gratuity for the service.

The reality was there was a thriving black market in place that allowed the hotel staffs to collect and rotate the railroad tickets constantly, acting as an informal clearing house that solved the travel problems for tourists while making a tidy profit in the process. In light of the New York–Miami one-way fare of $22.40, the five-dollar premium clearly provided substantial under-the-table income for the employees.

omy-minded holiday travelers during Florida's off-season, when hotel rates were lower.

All-coach trains were generally more profitable to run than all-Pullman or mixed service trains because of their higher capacity and broader market. A year-round train would also make more efficient use of both equipment and train staff since the Florida lines were often forced to lease dining cars and hire off-line crews to accommodate the winter traffic spurt. The Santa Fe's highly successful El Capitan served as an excellent model, as the five-coach train and its "affordable luxury" service had attracted considerable ridership from the same market that interested the Seaboard. In a departure from its first experiment with lightweight cars, SAL turned to the Budd Company of Philadelphia. The unpainted, gleaming fluted-side car bodies (made by shotwelding)

reduced the need for maintenance and weighed the same as those built from the Cor-Ten steel alloy favored by Pullman-Standard in the construction of its lightweight cars, and likewise further reduced operating costs by ¼ cent per mile.

Once the major northern connection with the Seaboard's route, the Pennsylvania Railroad, had formally agreed to the idea of assembling and operating such a train over the line, SAL placed an order with Budd on October 12, 1938, for a single set of the lightweight streamlined cars. The railroads held a contest to name the new train, offering a five-hundred-dollar prize that attracted more than seventy-six thousand entries. "Silver Meteor" was the winning name, and on January 25, 1939, the new train had its first outing, on a 30-mile (48.5km) shakedown run from the Budd plant to Downingtown, Pennsylvania.

Five days later, the Meteor hustled two hundred invited guests of the Budd Company from Philadelphia's Broad Street Station to Pennsylvania Station in New York, where it was put on public display. On February 5, ninety-five hundred curious onlookers passed through palm trees and other seductive Florida decor at Gate 3 to visit the shimmering six-car air-conditioned train. The first car was baggage-dormitory-chair car 6000, with twenty-two seats reserved for "colored" passengers in this pre-Civil Rights era. Crew accommodations for twelve and a steward's room were also included in car 6000 (called the "green car" due to its decor, which featured blue ceilings, brown walls, and blue-green pin-

As much as the stainless steel exteriors of the new streamliners differed from the riveted plates and double-hung windows of the older heavyweight cars, the interiors moved even further from the often ornate "drawing room" aesthetic of the traditional Pullman era. The lounge of the Silver Meteor, pictured here, reflects the trend toward spare and clean design that began during the 1930s and permeated the streamlined age.

✦ ✦ ✦

striped seating). All coach seating areas were floored with rubber, which in the case of the coaches was a dark oak color, with striping in the aisles.

Coach 6200 contained sixty reclining seats that were alternately upholstered in fawn or rust with coral pinstripes. Walls were brown; ceilings were tan, brown, and coral; and the rubber flooring was striped in red, gold, black, and coral.

A chair-tavern car, No. 6300, seated thirty passengers and had an additional thirty lounge seats. In the center of the car was a room for the hostess, who was also a registered nurse. An orchid-gray ceiling and Tuscan-rose walls contrasted with the coach seating, which sported brown pencil stripes alternating with patterned chamois. Red leather with tan piping covered the lounge seating, and the oval tables were robin's-egg blue. Red-and-gray striped draperies covered the windows. The bar front reflected the Seaboard's Florida-inspired diesel colors: stainless steel with stripes of green, orange, yellow, and mustard. The entire car was carpeted in apple green, with a brown pattern.

Adjacent to the lounge was the twelve-table dining car, No. 6100, with olive-gray walls and a three-toned ceiling of sand, stone, and Tuscan

rose. Beige window curtains were framed by patterned drapes in gray and rose. A rust-colored carpet lay under the gray and maroon chairs, which were covered with raisin-striped upholstery. A walnut veneer buffet stood adjacent to the stainless steel kitchen.

Two more sixty-seat coaches followed: the "brown car" (No. 6201), so-called for its oyster-white ceiling, gray walls, and seating decorated in brown floral with fawn pinstripes; and the "blue car" (No. 6202), with blue pinstripe/blue floral seating, blue walls, and lemon cream–colored ceiling.

Bringing up the rear was the chair-observation car, No. 6400, with a yellow-and-turquoise interior and coach seats covered with brown or turquoise stripes. The observation area contained seventeen movable chairs, three love seats, and a writing desk in rose, green, or gray. The carpet was mahogany with taupe accents. A glass partition, etched with images of game fish to reiterate the Florida theme, divided the sections.

The day following the public display, a Long Island DD1 hauled the Silver Meteor, a load of dignitaries aboard, through the East River Tunnel to Flushing Meadows, site of the New York World's Fair, for a

General Motors' Train of Tomorrow demonstrator toured the country from 1947 to 1950. Hauled behind a specially (some might say gaudily) tricked-out stainless steel E Unit, the Pullman Standard–built train of dome cars helped to prompt many reluctant railroads to enter the streamliner age.

✦ ✦ ✦

dedication ceremony broadcast on the radio. Following short speeches by the fair's design chairman, SAL's receivers, Edward G. Budd, and a representative from EMD, fair employee Ruth Francis Schmitt christened the train "Silver Meteor, the 'Train of Tomorrow'," and proclaimed, "Godspeed on your inaugural trip to Florida."

After a quick trip back to Penn Station, and the attachment of a sparkling GG1 on the head end, the first Silver Meteor departed at 3:30 P.M. with a full load of VIPs and paying passengers. Emerging from the Hudson tubes into a mixture of blowing rain and snow, the train turned south, heading for the warm and sunny climes of the Sunshine State.

At Washington Union Station, the Seaboard's own power took over—a new 2,000hp E4 diesel in green, orange, yellow, and silver built specifically for the Meteor—for the run over the Richmond, Fredericksburg & Potomac line to the home rails at Richmond, Virginia. After a stop at Petersburg, Virginia, the train sped nonstop through rolling Appalachian foothills to Hamlet, North Carolina, the hub of SAL's spoked system. The speedy schedule of both the Meteor and the Orange Blossom Special precluded a stop at Raleigh, the state capital, until 1942, when a new depot eliminated what had been a time-consuming backup move into the former stub-end terminal.

By the time the train reached Savannah, Georgia, the aromas of a southern breakfast filled the diner or dining car. The fifty-cent meal

included a choice of ham and scrambled eggs, corned beef hash with eggs, or cereal, all served with citrus fruits (available as marmalade, juice, or whole).

At Jacksonville, press representatives from that city, Palm Beach, and Miami all climbed aboard for the final leg of the new train's journey. The residents of the area had been well primed about the importance of the new streamliner with its unsurpassed speed and comfort, and gathered along the track to watch it pass—a thousand onlookers gathered at West Palm Beach, two thousand at Fort Lauderdale, and countless others at every grade crossing. The Meteor rolled into Miami's pink stucco depot under sunny blue skies and 76-degree F (24°C) temperatures to be greeted by the Miami Drum & Bugle Corps, radio station WQAM, and seventy-five hundred cheering Miamians. Mr. Budd stated the case most eloquently when he told the crowd, "The Silver Meteor speaks for itself."

The Silver Meteor departed the next morning on the return trip to New York. Upon its arrival, the train was turned and cleaned the same day for an afternoon departure on its alternate route south to Tampa and Saint Petersburg, where it was mobbed by crowds and feted by dignitaries once again. This alternating schedule continued until June 5, when the single train was split at Wildwood, Florida. The three Tampa–Saint Petersburg-bound cars proceeded southwest behind an EMC motorcar painted in the matching "citrus scheme," and the remainder of the train turned eastward

THE KEY WEST EXTENSION
(THE RAILROAD THAT DIED AT SEA)

✦ ✦ ✦

When Henry Morrison Flagler was asked about the difficulties that he expected in building the island-hopping Key West Extension of his Florida East Coast Railway, he overconfidently replied: "It is perfectly simple. All you have to do is build one concrete arch, and then another, and pretty soon you will find yourself in Key West." Beyond the technical challenges, many questioned the logic of the endeavor, since the traffic base was not obvious. Key West's population was seventeen thousand in 1904, and only a few pioneer families eked out a living on the string of twenty-nine islands.

But Key West was only 90 miles (145km) from Havana, and the War of 1898 had cemented a good relationship between Cuba and the United States. It was also 300 miles (483km) closer to the soon-to-be Panama Canal than any other Gulf port. Flagler foresaw profits in bringing sugar, pineapples, bananas, and oranges by ferry from all of the countries in the region to Key West for transfer to the North American rail network. He also expected to carry passengers destined for exotic Havana, known for its wild nightlife, gambling, and magnificent music.

Flagler had retired as John D. Rockefeller's partner at Standard Oil with a virtually endless supply of money, vast sums of which he was willing to spend to achieve his dreams. In 1904, he hired Chief Engineer J.C. Meredith, an expert in reinforced concrete, to oversee the construction of Flagler's "simple" concrete arches as well as the many miles of rock fill across the shallow inlets. Virtually all of the building was done from a huge fleet of shallow draft boats. Said one engineer, "It was a web-footed job all the way," and one frustrated skipper (after running aground once too often) bellowed that the Keys had "not quite enough water for swimming and too damned much for farming."

Flagler wanted the bridge to be completed by 1913. In order to maintain momentum on the project, work continued right through the September/October hurricane season of 1906. The advance camp on Long Key was too remote to depend on the weather forecasts from Miami or Key West, so the foremen depended on crude barometers that they checked almost as often as their watches. A major storm hit in October, devastating the camp with 100 mph (161kph) winds. Rain-soaked gasoline motors wouldn't start, so escape was impossible. Much equipment was lost, construction was washed away, and at least 120 men died.

Meredith's reaction was simple: "No man has any business connected with this work who can't stand grief." Flagler's terse message was, "Go ahead." One lesson learned was to eliminate houseboats, so all workers moved into island camps. Even so, the conditions were severe, and the rate of worker turnover was extremely high.

Long Key Viaduct, consisting of 186 concrete arches spanning 2.2 miles (3.5km) of water, was completed in 1907 despite the hurricane damage. Trains were now hauling material to the rail head, and work began on a 7-mile (11km) bridge at Knight's Key, where the main channel was bridged with 210 concrete arches and a steel swing bridge to maintain navigation. Three shorter approach bridges were built of steel deck girders on concrete piers. A 1908 hurricane blew five not-yet-anchored steel spans into the water, yet left a keg of nails standing on another.

Despite the difficulties presented by location, labor problems, hurricanes, and a forest fire on Big Pine Key, the railroad pushed ever southward until another large storm struck in 1910, pounding the lower Keys for thirty hours. Miles of rock fill were washed away, and an entire shipload of material that had been anchored as the foundation for the Bahia Honda Bridge's center span was dislodged and had to be replaced.

Although the target for completion was 1913, Flagler's failing health forced a promised completion by January 1912. On January 22, the Extension Special left Miami with the ailing Henry Flagler on board his private car, Rambler, along with four coaches filled with various notables. The trip was smooth and uneventful, and the train rolled over vast expanses of a calm sea on a trip that was interrupted only by the crossings of the beautiful emerald-green Keys. Upon the train's arrival at Key West, bands played, politicians rambled, and ships in the harbor blew their whistles. School children tossed roses in Flagler's path, and his words were typically direct: "We have been trying to anchor Key West to the mainland. . . and anchor it we have done." A crowd estimated at ten thousand, many of whom had never seen a train, strained for a view. Then the entire island kicked off a three-day fiesta.

Flagler, too fragile to participate in the frenzied festivities, boarded a ferry for Havana. In May 1913, he was dead, his will designating his old friend J.R. Parrott as president of the Florida East Coast Railway, but

Parrott also was gone only five months later. The massive project had also claimed Meredith and seven hundred others before completion.

Despite the heavy cost in human life, the railroad had achieved its builder's purpose, hauling countless carloads from the Key West wharf to markets across the United States. By 1934, thirty-five hundred cars of pineapples alone passed through the islands annually. And passenger service on the Havana Limited proved popular. The trip between Cuba and New York took only two nights and required no car changes. The trains also carried away many Key residents, who expected to find greener pastures on the mainland, and transported many northern hoboes to the sunny warmth of Key West in the winter.

The Extension went into receivership during the Great Depression, having never really earned its keep despite the countless carloads of produce and half a million passengers carried during its existence. Then, on September 2, 1935, the morning sky turned ominously leaden as a giant hurricane roared toward the Keys. The Florida East Coast called for a train to evacuate residents as well as a crew of highway workers who were camped directly in the path of the storm at Islamorada, where the track was only seven feet (2.1m) above sea level.

The relief train, delayed several hours by equipment problems, finally arrived at 8:20 P.M., when the barometric pressure read 26.35 and falling, the lowest ever recorded in this hemisphere. As frightened men, women, and children desperately struggled through the storm to reach the coaches, the sea suddenly receded—only to return as a seventeen-foot (5.2m) tidal wave that swept across the island, engulfing everything in its path.

The hurricane's eye passed directly over the island, and the devastation was complete. Islamorada was cleared of structures and the train had rolled over on its side, but the 106-ton (95.5t) No. 447 and its tender had remained upright and saved the lives of the engineer, the fireman, and the conductor. There were pitifully few other survivors—the bodies of 288 highway workers were recovered along with some two hundred residents of the Keys.

The Key West Extension had also perished. Forty-two miles (67.5km) of fill were washed out, and a train marooned in Key West had to be barged to Miami, accompanied by the sarcastic headline: "FEC's Havana Special Arrives from Key West Months Late."

The Depression left FEC officials wary of reinvesting in the line, so they sold the remains for just $640,000. It was a bargain indeed, since the concrete viaducts were still standing, and are used to this day as support for a two-lane highway, still linking Key West and the string of emerald Keys to the mainland.

The first of the Florida streamliners, Seaboard's Silver Meteor, crashes through a banner celebrating the train's millionth mile of service on November 15, 1940. The Meteor pioneered the streamliner boom that carried shivering passengers from the North to the Sunshine State.

✦ ✦ ✦

toward West Palm Beach. This arrangement allowed for service every third day to both Saint Petersburg and Miami.

Despite the considerable initial investment, the Silver Meteor was an unqualified success. Seaboard ran the first advertising for it in the January 15, 1939, issue of *The New York Times* and was inundated with twenty-five hundred inquiries in forty-eight hours. Four trips of 280 passengers each were sold out by January 18. Clearly, the Seaboard had attracted a great deal of attention that normally was focused on the rival Atlantic Coast Line's heavyweight trains (the ACL overall had a more aggressive PR department), and net revenue for the first five months of operation was a healthy $1.98 per train mile. This accomplishment was duly noted by the Florida East Coast and Atlantic Coast Line, which proceeded with its own streamliner, to be called the Champion, while Seaboard ordered more equipment so that the Meteor could operate daily to Miami (Saint Petersburg remained on the third-day schedule).

There were other Seaboard trains still operating to Florida, including the Orange Blossom Special, Southern States, and the New York–Florida Limited, an accommodation train whose leisurely pace required two nights on the road. The Blossom's twenty-nine-hour schedule was no match for the Meteor's 26½ hours, and even that would be cut to further outpace the competition.

The Atlantic Coast Line was slow to invest in streamliners. While the until-recently bankrupt upstart Seaboard was ordering E4 passenger diesels and lightweight cars for the Orange Blossom Special, along with the brand-new Silver Meteor, the ACL was air-conditioning its heavyweights (while continuing to order new ones) and buying twelve new Baldwin 4-8-4 steam locomotives. It had introduced its own Vacationer, the first deluxe coach service from New York to both coasts of Florida, in 1938, and just wasn't interested in either the lightweights or diesels.

The attention given to the Silver Meteor completely overshadowed the ACL's efforts, and was reflected in the ridership and revenue figures, both of which were rising on the Seaboard and falling on the Coast Line, whose trains left from across the same platform in Penn Station. The ACL finally reacted in June 1939 by placing an order for two E3A diesels with EMD and going to Budd for two seven-car train sets. Its New York–Miami partner (south of Jacksonville) was the Florida East Coast, which also ordered two E3s and a pair of similar train sets. One set was for the New York pool, and the other was needed for its own new train, the Jacksonville-to-Miami Henry Flagler.

The new ACL equipment was virtually identical to that of the Silver Meteor, differing primarily in the method of air-conditioning (steam ejector versus electro-mechanical) and the inclusion of full tavern-lounge cars, which required an additional coach to maintain capacity, rather than the Seaboard's half coach, half lounge. As with the Meteor, a contest was held to name the train and, from 101,000 entries vying for the three-hundred-dollar prize, the name "Champion" was chosen.

The public got to view the finished Champion at Penn Station on December 1, 1939. The interior colors of blue, rose, brown, pink, and green were reminiscent of the Meteor, reflecting the trends in the marketing of warm-weather vacations. What was different was the tavern-lounge-observation car, called Bay Biscayne, which was dedicated entirely to entertainment. The two seating areas were divided by a bar—the large-windowed rear lounge was nestled at the teardrop-shaped end of the car and fitted with comfortable upholstered seating, and the front portion's curving divans and booths accommodated thirty-six passengers.

The sold-out Champion departed New York behind a Pennsylvania Railroad GG1, carrying the obligatory officials from the railroads and building companies, and arrived in Washington for the dedication. There, the striking red-and-yellow Florida East Coast E3 1002 (temporarily wearing an ACL herald) took over for the run south on Coast Line rails. The warm light of dawn reflected off the silver train as it arrived in Jacksonville and transferred onto FEC trackage for the remainder of the route through Florida's beach communities.

At Fort Lauderdale, the Champion was met by its near-twin, Henry Flagler, waiting

Ex-Atlantic Coast Line E6 No. 501, which hauled the Champion, rolls through Belleville, Wisconsin, in excursion service in 1983, resplendent in its classic purple-and-silver paint scheme.

on what was normally the northbound track. The two brand-new trains paraded south side-by-side on the double-track main line to a spectacular greeting at Miami's modest depot. The University of Miami Band played, a squadron of biplanes trailing smoke buzzed overhead, and a crowd of five thousand cheered.

Once again, Edward G. Budd spoke at the celebration, and his words were prophetic: "Few people realize it, but thirty million persons reside in the eastern section radiant from New York. Only 2 percent of them have ever come to Florida. We feel that with the advent of streamlined service into Florida, at least nine more persons will be added to that two out of every hundred to come to this state every winter."

Budd was not far wrong: 1939 turned out to be one of the busiest travel seasons ever. The uncertainties caused by the hostilities in Europe encouraged domestic vacations, and the Atlantic Coast Line/Florida East Coast combine was prepared: twenty new all-room heavyweight sleepers were added to the pool; a West Coast section was added to the all-Pullman Florida Special in December; the Vacationer was reequipped; and a second all-Pullman train to Miami, the Miamian, was added to the schedule. Even the slower and less glamorous Havana Special and Florida Mail carried their own share of the load. When the inevitable slowdown arrived in the spring, the Vacationer, Miamian, and Florida Special were eliminated from the schedule. At the same time, the Atlantic Coast Line added connections in New York to the northern vacation land of Maine in order to help make up for the decrease in traffic.

The heavy loads that prompted the Seaboard to order additional equipment for the Silver Meteor also affected the Champion, so Atlantic Coast Line followed suit with an order to Budd that doubled the size of its flagship train. The December 1939–December 1940 season had chalked up average loads of two hundred passengers per trip for a gross revenue of seventy-two hundred dollars daily for the two trains. The new fourteen-car trains averaged 362 passengers daily between January and May, 1941, doubling the revenue-per-train-mile to $5.34 and proving the economics of the longer train.

The disparity between winter and summer loads continued to vex the Florida railroads, but the expansion and contraction of the ACL schedules was the worst. In the summer lull of 1940, only seventeen diners (and crews) were required, but that number skyrocketed to sixty-eight during the follow-

In 1935, the Seaboard provided a preview of the sun-drenched pleasures that lay ahead for passengers by staging a fashion show—featuring the latest creations in beach wear—in the lounge car of the southbound Orange Blossom Special.

✦ ✦ ✦

ing winter. Partners RF&P and FEC supplied seventeen cars, while leases with northern roads provided another eighteen to supplement the ACL's own fleet of thirty-three. Of the 917 dining department employees rostered during that winter, more than seven hundred were seasonal only.

When the summer season heavyweight Tamiami was merged with the Champion in 1941, the new train ran in two sections (one serving each coast) with a mixture of heavyweight Pullmans and lightweight cars. A unique Pullman paint scheme highlighted the Tamiami Champion's premier status. Its "special streamlined colors" are thought to have been aluminum with black trucks, purple letter boards, and gold Pullman lettering to match the ACL's lightweight equipment—but there is no definitive documentation to verify this assertion.

The onset of the Second World War affected all North American railroads, but threatened the Florida lines more than most. Since a major part of the prewar traffic had been tourism, which conflicted with the war effort's requirement that all transportation concerns focus on military-related travel, the management of the newly created Office of Defense Transportation froze the passenger systems in the autumn of 1942. Multiple

sections and new trains were prohibited, as the cars of the Pullman pool were needed elsewhere. The Florida tourist industry was devastated, but troop traffic kept the Florida trains sold out for the duration of the war. In August of 1943, for instance, just under one million troops were carried by America's railroads, and the crush of soldiers heading home at the close of the war rode in everything that could roll, including baggage cars.

The 1945 surrender of Japan marked a new beginning for the Florida railroads. The overworked physical plants and equipment, unattended to during the war, began to recover slowly. Tracks and roadbeds were rebuilt, and orders for new locomotives and cars backed up at the factories of the swamped builders. Seaboard emerged from the war financially solvent, but had "run the wheels off" the streamliners that had been brand-new when the war had begun. Equipment that had been purchased with an expected life span of twenty-five years had deteriorated enough after just seven to be demoted to secondary service.

In April 1945, SAL ordered thirty new cars from Budd, complemented by an additional eighteen ordered by RF&P and PRR for Florida service. Later in the year, the three railroads jointly purchased thirty-one sleeping

SEGREGATION ON NORTH AMERICAN RAILROADS

✦ ✦ ✦

In the years before the American Civil War, segregation of black and white passengers was the norm in both the North and the South. The practice was as old as railroading itself, and curiously, the rules were often more rigid in the North. In an early look at railroading in the 1800s, Austrian engineer F.A. Ritter Von Gestner wrote that while blacks in the North were required to ride in a separate car, many Southern railroads accommodated black passengers in the baggage car for half fare; furthermore, the black riders were allowed to travel in the coaches with white passengers if they paid full fare.

Whether on a train or at the station, service as a porter on the railroads—and in particular Pullman service—was a stepping-stone to the middle class for many struggling African-American families who were willing to put up with dad's long absences.

Separation of the races, including freedmen, was general policy until Lincoln's Emancipation Proclamation promoted more liberal attitudes toward African Americans, particularly in the North. Throughout the South, however, state laws mandated separation, which was commonly referred to as Jim Crow legislation. In accordance with these laws, many southern depots maintained separate waiting rooms and facilities for "colored" passengers. The adherence on the part of the railroads to Jim Crow policies meant that coaches and combines (cars that were part coach area, part baggage car area) were also segregated, a practice that continued well into the streamliner era.

The original Silver Meteor and Champion each carried a baggage-dormitory-coach for "colored" passengers, and the seat identification coupons for the Silver Meteor were punched not only with the destination but also with the passenger's race and gender as well.

In 1941, the practice of segregation on U.S. railroads was dealt the first blow by a Supreme Court decision (Mitchell vs. U.S.A.) that ruled the Interstate Commerce Act required the Pullman Company to provide equal facilities for blacks and whites. This racist "separate but equal" solution was terminated by President Truman's 1950 directive to the Interstate Commerce Commission prohibiting segregation in dining cars.

On the southern railroads, the difficulty of balancing management's need to comply with these directives and the laws of multiple states while coping with the resistance of their customer base is illustrated by the instructions in a Seaboard Air Line dining car department manual of 1944, several years before Truman's edict:

Serving Meals to Colored Persons

Portieres are to be hung between stations "One" and "Two" at all times between 6 A.M. and 10 P.M. These curtains are to be pushed back against the wall until occasion arises for use of same.

You are provided with a "Reserved" placard, which is to be placed on the two stations nearest the buffet at the beginning of each meal. These two tables are to be reserved for colored passengers until all other seats in the dining room have been occupied. If no colored passengers have presented themselves, the "Reserved" cards may be removed and the tables used for white passengers.

No white passengers are to be allowed in the space reserved while colored passengers are being served therein. This also means that no white persons will be seated in this space while colored persons are waiting to be assigned seats therein.

If while the first two tables are occupied by white passengers, a colored person should present himself and request service, he is to be informed that he will be called as soon as seats reserved for colored passengers are vacated. When such seats are vacated, the colored persons will be called and served in the space set apart for them. No white persons are to be allowed in such space while colored persons are being served therein.

If colored passengers present themselves while this reserved space is occupied, the steward will also offer to serve them in the coach or the Pullman, as the case may be, promptly, in the event they do not wish to wait until the space which has been reserved for them is available.

Colored nurses accompanying white families may be seated in the dining car at the table with such white families for the purpose of taking care of children, such nurses to be allowed to have their own meals at the same time. It is understood that in such cases, no other person (other than the family the nurse is accompanying) are to be seated at the table with the colored nurse.

The crushing irony of this situation, of course, was that the majority of the passenger train service personnel, particularly in the diner and Pullman cars,

Starched and fresh, dining-car waiters stand at the ready on the New York Central's Twentieth Century Limited. These employees were critical to the comfort of passengers and the image of the train.

◆ ◆ ◆

were themselves black, and thus responsible for enforcing the patently unjust rules of segregation.

While by today's standards such work might seem menial and undignified, Pullman service was one of the few means by which black men in the first half of the twentieth century could break the chains of poverty. The basic pay was quite poor (relatively speaking), but the exposure to so many business travelers and people of means often resulted in generous tips and, in some cases, even investment advice. A well-spoken and attentive Pullman porter could earn a comfortable living; accordingly, many black families found their way into the middle class thanks to Pullman employment at a time when advancement for African Americans was almost nonexistent. This is not to say life on the railroads was easy—porters suffered many hardships, not the least of which were enduring racism and constant separation from their families.

During the 1960s, the declining number of passenger trains roughly coincided with the aging of the service staff, so retirements or contract buyouts conveniently eased the overstaffing created by reductions in the number of trains in service and provided for the departing employees. By the time Amtrak was up and operating, the number of trains had stabilized somewhat and active recruitment of on-board personnel again became necessary. With modern civil rights laws now in force, the service staff on Amtrak trains (including operating crews) has become fully integrated both in terms of race and gender—very different from the state of affairs during the oft-lamented golden age of the passenger train.

cars from Pullman, responding to the antitrust problems that Pullman had encountered, which allowed Pullman to continue to operate the now railroad-owned cars. Atlantic Coast Line and its partners PRR, RF&P, and FEC added eighty-six cars to their unfilled order for thirty that had been placed with Budd in 1941. While cars from the early order arrived in 1946–1947, Coast Line grew extremely frustrated by delays with Budd, which deferred delivery of the postwar order until 1949–1950. The ACL partnership also absorbed a portion of the Pullman fleet, purchasing fifty-five heavyweight sleepers of various types in 1948.

Motive power needs were not ignored either. Seaboard had received nineteen E7As from EMD by the end of 1946, and Atlantic Coast Line, with the largest fleet of passenger diesels in the country, was bragging that all of its New York–Florida trains were diesel-powered south of Richmond.

While waiting for new rolling stock, the railroads sent crews back to school to polish their war-worn skills. In 1944, the ACL had served four times as many meals as in 1939, which ultimately forced the spit-and-polish service to give way to efficiency. At the same time, if the new trains were to retain patronage in the postwar years, courtesy and service would have to continue to be a priority.

The seasonal nature of the Florida service continued to have an impact on both the equipment orders and train schedules. The loss of cost-efficient leases from the pool of heavyweight sleepers of the Pullman era meant that the railroads had to purchase their own sleeping cars. A new 1949 Florida Special debuted as a streamliner for the winter season as an all-Pullman, all-room (no sections) train and included what were to become the standard features of the postwar era. All rooms contained their own toilet facilities, individual heating controls, and piped-in music. In deference to the need for year-round flexibility, this luxury train was heavily supplied with roomettes and had no observation car, both deci-

For a great many travelers in the United States in the early postwar years, over-crowded troop trains and older equipment were their only rail travel experience. With wartime restrictions curtailing luxury travel, the Florida trains were particularly hard-hit, though heavy troop traffic made up for lost fares. These soldiers are headed for a training facility in the Arizona desert in June of 1943; it is unlikely that they later looked back on their travels by train as a wonderful experience once they had been mustered out. Unfortunately, such negative experiences contributed to the precipitous drop in rail traffic following the war.

✦ ✦ ✦

sions flying in the face of the traditional first-class Florida vacation trains. The West Coast Champion was also reequipped with new lightweight coaches, diners, and lounges.

These dramatic changes in the service and the $14-million investment in new equipment proved to be wise decisions. The Florida Special was popular even before streamlining, and now began to siphon customers from the Seaboard's Orange Blossom Special. The phenomenally successful Champions fared even better, becoming the Coast Line's most profitable train. For the year ending May 31, 1949, the East Coast Champion posted revenue-per-train-mile of $8.85 southbound and $8.99 northbound.

The future looked very bright as the Atlantic Coast Line began an extensive upgrade of its older equipment, rebuilding twenty-two head-end cars and fifty-six coaches in its Emerson Shops. The complete modernization of these cars made them fully equal to the streamlined products of the major car builders, the most striking difference being a new paint scheme using the ACL colors—solid purple body, silver letter board, yellow striping, and a black roof. This exotic scheme was also applied to some standard heavyweights and the railroad-owned heavyweight sleepers, as well.

As the decade of the 1950s matured, so did the Coast Line's passenger services. The Florida Special operated as an all-Pullman lightweight to Miami; the East Coast Champion was the Special's all-coach counterpart; the West Coast Champion remained all-coach; and the mixed equipment Miamian and all-Pullman Vacationer picked up some of the heavy wintertime loads. The Vacationer also included a group of through-sleepers from Boston, via the New Haven.

Although by the standards of the Interstate Commerce Commission's "fully allocated" accounting formula, the Coast Line's passenger trains were costing $1.28 for each dollar collected, the railroad preferred to look at "avoidable costs," which assumed that such overhead expenses as real estate taxes on rights of way and track maintenance costs would still pertain even if just freight trains were operated. By using "avoidable costs" accounting, passenger trains were in the black, although most of the income came from the long-haul trains—75 percent in 1953.

As residential air-conditioning became more common in Florida, summertime traffic also began to grow. By 1950, the five months of winter provided only 54 percent of local income, down from 64 percent in 1940, and this trend continued. In the right place at the right time, Coast Line had by 1953 captured 67 percent of the Florida-bound traffic (including the growing number of summer sojourners), and the East Coast Champion might run with thirteen cars even in the autumn off-season.

Unfortunately, the ACL's partners were not as optimistic about the viability of passenger service, and in 1955 the trustees of the Florida East Coast demanded that the Miamian be scaled back to winter-only service as a way of cutting costs. The Vacationer was dropped in the same year, when the New Haven opted out. All of the Florida lines also began to scale back their local service, concentrating on the more profitable long-haul trains. By the middle of the decade, Coast Line's reliance on the outdated heavyweight sleepers at the same time that Seaboard was receiving new lightweight sleepers was having an effect on bookings. While the ACL grumbled that a Pullman room was a Pullman room and that its heavyweights were perfectly fine accommodations, Seaboard's revenues remained steady through the remainder of the 1950s and into the 1960s while those of the Coast Line dropped.

Despite a reluctance to invest in equipment, however, the Coast Line steadily upgraded its main-line track work and signaling, until speed limits of 100 mph (161kph) were possible on the basically flat route by October 1955. New York-to-Miami times were reduced to twenty-four hours, and thirty-five minutes were knocked off the Saint Petersburg schedule. Continued purchases of EMD E Units meant that the ACL was fully dieselized by this time.

But the end was near. Automobiles had become readily available and affordable for most people by the 1950s and the growing Federal Defense Highway System (that is to say, the interstates) only served to facilitate the siphoning of traffic from the railroads, although the Florida lines fought their demise longer than most. The final blow came on December 10, 1958, when National Airlines began the first regularly scheduled jet airliner service on the New York-to-Miami route.

Valiantly fighting back with an increase in amenities, "travel now, pay later" credit plans, and onboard fashion shows—as well as reconfiguring trains and using simpler paint schemes to save money—the railroads could do little to stem the slow downward slide. The Florida Special, an all-Pullman train since 1888 and equal in stature to such trains as the Twentieth Century Limited, became a coach/sleeper operation for the 1959–1960 winter season.

On July 22, 1960, the Interstate Commerce Commission received a merger proposal—the Atlantic Coast Line and Seaboard Air Line would become the Seaboard Coast Line. Putting the long-time rivalry behind them, the two lines realized their merger would result in cost savings estimated at thirty-eight million dollars per year, eliminate duplicated routes, and make for a leaner, more efficient operation. Unfortunately, litigation delayed the ICC's approval for several years.

Still confident enough to continue rebuilding section sleepers into more appropriate bedroom cars through 1961 and 1962, the Coast Line also began planning for the seventy-fifth Anniversary of the Florida Special. Equipment was shuffled so that a uniform consist of this historic train could be assembled. The purple paint had been dropped in the spirit of cost-saving, so the entire train was to be stainless steel, with black roofs and lettering. Several Pennsy sleepers assigned to the train were repainted silver for the occasion (although they were replaced before the celebration began).

The Coast Line advertised the Florida Special winter season of 1962–1963 to be a once-in-a-lifetime opportunity to witness what a railroad could still do with a first-class train, even in the twilight of the golden age. An extra fare of $5 per Pullman and $2.50 per coach was levied, and was well worth it. Amenities included reserved-seat dining, complimentary champagne, hostesses, and the return of the recreation car (although it was missing the swimming pool and gym that had been a highlight of the 1932–1933 train). Taking a cue from the hyperactivity of cruise ships, the recreation car was used for movies, bingo, horse-racing games, sing-alongs, fashion shows, and even radio and telephone service.

The marketing efforts paid off, with such luminaries as Art Buchwald and representatives of the Today Show covering the festivities. Passengers raved about the train, and patronage was high, even in an era of declining ridership. Other railroad revivals sprang up, too, and

The run to the sun began in New York on the Pennsylvania Railroad. A GG1, still handsome in the later-generation paint scheme (a solid buff band replacing the gold "cat whiskers," with a large keystone added) heads south under singing catenary. The train will be turned over to one of the Florida Railroads at Washington.

The widespread rail mergers of the 1960s, brought on by changes in the ways North Americans traveled, affected the Florida lines as much as any other. Accordingly, the Atlantic Coast Line and the Seaboard joined and became the Seaboard Coast Line, publishing the first joint timetable on July 1, 1967. Here, triple-headed E Units are at the head of a still-lengthy Florida Special sometime following the merger.

this trend continued into the 1960s, though for most of the organizations in the railroad industry this only served to reduce losses rather than turn the roads around.

On January 23, 1963, the Coast Line's hard work began to unravel when the Florida East Coast refused to go along with a national labor agreement for eleven non-operating unions signed by 192 other roads. The FEC operating unions honored the picket lines, and this important southern link in ACL's Florida route was shut down over a matter of ten cents per hour. Management began operating trains without union personnel, instigating a level of violence not seen since the early years of the North American labor movement. More than two hundred bombing and dynamiting incidents were reported, and five trains were wrecked by vandals.

This was not the environment in which to be operating trains loaded with passengers, so the Florida liners were rerouted during the strike, using Seaboard tracks to Miami and buses from the ACL Sanford depot to points on the FEC. Ultimately, the Florida East Coast emerged from the strike as a pared-down, non-union, freight-only operation—the seventy-five-year history of passenger service on the FEC had ended.

Although passenger revenues were increasing from 1961 through 1963, buoying the Coast Line's hopes for the future, the Florida lines continued to trim consists and implement other savings measures. In 1964, the political situation in Cuba was at last formally recognized by

the transportation concerns and the Havana Special was renamed the Gulf Coast Special—by then, the steamship connection to Havana was long gone.

For 1965, budget-minded travelers on the East Coast Champion were offered space in all-roomette cars (redesignated Budget Room Coach) for only fifteen dollars more than coach fare. Previously, these lesser-quality cars had been declared unsuitable for the Florida market and were usually farmed out to other railroads. Three former Baltimore & Ohio Strata Dome sleepers from the Capitol Limited were added to the Florida Special, although tunnel clearances in Washington, D.C., kept the domes south of Richmond.

The cautiously rosy outlook for the Florida trains did not apply to railroads elsewhere, including the ACL's northern partners. While Coast Line and Seaboard were breaking even with their passenger operations, the critical link to New York (via Pennsy) and Midwest (via B&O and C&O) connections at Washington, D.C., were becoming undependable because of resistance by the partner lines to instituting operational changes that were needed to achieve better efficiency. Such overtures by the Florida roads were met with a lack of cooperation by the northern railroads, which were losing money. Time was running out even for the Atlantic Coast Line. In the twenty years following the war, ACL's passenger revenues had been cut in half despite inflation and a huge investment in new equipment. But the railroad didn't give up.

On July 1, 1967, the merger proposal between the Atlantic Coast Line and Seaboard that had simmered for over seven years finally won ICC approval, allowing for the merger of the two formerly fierce competitors. The new Seaboard Coast Line initially made very few changes to the combined passenger services, although name changes to some individual cars were necessary to avoid duplication (and confusion): the Seaboard Sun Lounge sleepers formerly known as Hollywood Beach, Miami Beach, and Palm Beach became Sun View, Sun Ray, and Sun Beam, for example. But the summer schedules for 1967 featured the original Silver Fleet and Champions running on traditional routes with normal consists.

More substantial changes were made, however, by the winter of 1967. The dwindling use of the rails by the United States Post Office doomed most secondary trains, which had survived only because of the mail contracts. Even the name trains were affected. The East and West Coast Champions were combined into a single Champion serving the Gulf Coast. The Silver Meteor, Silver Star, and Florida Special returned, but were heavily sprinkled with Tuscan-red cars from the Pennsy and the blue-and-yellow of the Chesapeake & Ohio.

As the SCL was grappling with these consolidations, the New York Central merged with the Pennsylvania, the two mighty giants embarking on what would become one of North America's biggest business disasters—the Penn Central. The loss of SCL's critical northern partner (the Pennsy) doomed any attempts to maintain regular service from the Northeast to the South. The merger forced a number of cost-saving measures on the parts of the New York Central and Pennsy, leaving little money for cooperation with the passenger-friendly SCL.

Consolidation of trains continued until, by the end of 1968, SCL operated twenty-one fewer passenger trains than it had the previous year. Then the legendary Pullman Company, the operator of sleeping-car services for more than a century, accepted its fate. Already suffering as railroads tried to economize by operating (or even abandoning) their own sleeper services (by 1968 only six sleeper carriers remained), the company was hit by further defections as Penn Central canceled its contracts and tried to coerce other railroads operating in Penn Station and Grand Central Terminal on Penn Central trackage to do likewise. At midnight on New Year's Eve, 1968, this North American institution ceased all sleeping-car operations in the United States, and then dropped all mainte-

nance of sleepers on August 1, 1969. The company that George Pullman had founded, which had provided shelter for and fed as many as one hundred thousand passengers a night during the peak years of the 1920s, was gone, leaving only the freight car–building business (which had divested during the 1947 antitrust litigation) to carry the Pullman name.

Once again, the management of Seaboard Coast Line reacted aggressively, taking over the operation of the sleeping cars that previously had been managed by Pullman, offering free champagne with candlelight dinners, movies, television, and telephone service. But when partners PC and RF&P canceled the Silver Comet between New York and Richmond in May 1969, Seaboard lost 69 percent of the train's ridership. With mail and express service also reduced, management predicted a loss of $350,000, and the Comet was dropped in June. Other trains followed suit, for similar reasons.

In an effort to reduce costs, the entire operation of the sleeping-car fleet was transferred to Hamburg Industries of Augusta, Georgia, and leased back by SCL. SCL somehow persuaded Hamburg to purchase eight additional secondhand sleepers from the B&O, including three domes. No other U.S. railroad was adding sleepers as late as 1969.

By this time, the passenger-train problem was a national issue in the United States, as railroads begged Congress and the Department of Transportation to stop the cash hemorrhage that was financially crippling them. In 1968, SCL (doing better than many) took in revenues of twenty-two million dollars but still suffered a devastating nineteen million dollar deficit. The government responded with "Railpax," which was signed into law on October 30, 1970; consequently, Amtrak began operation the following April. Until then, SCL continued to operate its top trains in a first-class manner, even successfully fighting back when Penn Central announced that it would not operate the famous Florida Special for the 1970 winter season.

In the spring of 1971, SCL announced that the new National Rail Passenger Corporation (Amtrak) would be assuming responsibility for operating New York–Miami, New York–Tampa–Saint Petersburg, and Chicago–Florida trains. Amtrak faced the unenviable task of creating trains from a hodgepodge of equipment, much of it run-down, that the nineteen participating railroads donated to the pool (along with substantial cash) in order to be relieved of passenger-hauling duties. Railroads that had always taken passenger traffic seriously—such as Seaboard Coast Line, Santa Fe, Union Pacific, and Burlington Northern—provided the majority of the usable equipment.

The final Seaboard Coast Line passenger train departed New York on April 30, 1971, as it had for many years—behind a GG1 electric locomotive on the point and with a Budd fluted-stainless steel round-end observation on the tail end, the glowing red markers fading into the darkness of the subterranean tunnels for the last time.

Chapter Five

GREAT TRAINS OF THE MIDWESTERN UNITED STATES

The city of Chicago was critical to the youthful North American railroads, first as a destination and then—after railroads crossed the continent—as a junction, where the eastern railroads exchanged passengers and freight with the railroads of the West. Most of the westbound travelers from the northeastern United States—whether destined for Los Angeles, San Francisco, Portland, or Seattle—left from Chicago. As the steam era segued into the era of the diesel-powered streamliner, Chicago proved to be a vital hub in the national network of rails.

THE CITY TRAINS: CITY OF LOS ANGELES, CITY OF DENVER, CITY OF SAN FRANCISCO

The Union Pacific scheduled many legendary name trains out of Chicago during the steam era. Stalwarts such as the San Francisco Overland Limited (which showed the new talking films in the

◆ ◆ ◆

The Budd Company brought the brand-new Zephyr to Philadelphia for a formal christening on April, 18, 1934. Ralph Budd, president of the Burlington (in front of the locomotive, standing on the left), joins Edward Budd (no relation, second from left), the builder, at the ceremony. The event was of sufficient interest to bring out a field representative from NBC radio.

The original custom-built locomotives that hauled the **City of San Francisco** and **City of Los Angeles** trains resembled the styling of the M-10000; the locomotives that replaced them in 1937 (such as the E2 pictured here) already exhibited the styling traits that would culminate in the classic look of the later E Units. The 1800hp E2 LA-1, a three-unit locomotive, exhibits on its chrome-bedecked nose the heralds of its two operators: **Chicago & North Western** and the **Union Pacific**. Below: In a reversion to times past, the interior of the **City of Los Angeles** club car featured the **Little Nugget Bar**, modeled after a prosperous hostelry from California's gold-rush days.

✦ ✦ ✦

dining car), Fast Mail, Pony Express, Columbine, and Portland Rose, were joined in 1935 by the all-coach Challenger, the marketing of which was aimed at cost-conscious family travelers.

With the advent of diesel power, Union Pacific (UP) jumped headlong into the streamliner business with the flashy brown-and-yellow M-10000, a fixed train set introduced in 1934 that joined the Burlington's stainless steel Pioneer Zephyr. UP then replaced the long-running, steam-powered Los Angeles Limited in 1936 with the new streamliner City of Los Angeles, another custom-built train set intended to attract attention and entice the traveling public. With eleven cars, this was the longest streamliner in the world, and it clipped fourteen hours off the fifty-to-sixty-hour journey from Chicago to Los Angeles. It was soon followed by the City of San Francisco, running five round-trips per month, and the City of Denver, which was billed as the world's fastest train when it averaged 75.5 mph (121kph) between Omaha and Denver.

While new dedicated locomotives were built especially for these trains, the early streamliner days were a time of experimentation, with such exotic developments as a General Electric steam-electric locomotive and the porthole windows of the Copper King observation car.

The Union Pacific retained just two of its fleet of bright-yellow E Units at the dawn of the Amtrak era. Fully restored and used for excursions and special trains, E9As Nos. 949 and 952 along with booster No. 963 lead a string of lightweight coaches through Emkay, Wyoming, in 1984—a lingering remnant of "Uncle Pete's" former glory.

✦ ✦ ✦

The Chicago-to-California routes of these haughty grandes dames was more than one railroad could handle, and the Union Pacific joined with the Chicago & North Western (and later the Milwaukee Road) to reach Chicago from Omaha, Nebraska, and with the Southern Pacific to complete the San Francisco run from Ogden, Utah. The instant success of these trains encouraged the UP to order two more sets of state-of-the-art replacement equipment. The seventeen new cars were wider, the compartment interiors were altered, and a new car type (the roomette) was provided.

The City of San Francisco was to the rails what the Titanic had been to the sea: the fastest, largest, most modern, most elegant, and perhaps the most beautiful, example of the blossoming new technology (it was also presumed to be equally immune to the forces of nature). While the City of Los Angeles featured a throwback to Victorian elegance in its Little Nugget Bar, the COSF was pure Bauhaus-in-motion. Velour love seats, bevel-edged mirrors, and Gay Nineties attire for the bartenders were replaced with spare, elegant interiors that could have been used as a movie set for Fred Astaire to dance through.

Powered by six 900hp, 12-cylinder diesel engines set in a three-unit locomotive and capable of achieving speeds up to 110 mph (177kph), the bright-yellow seventeen-car train could make the run from Chicago to San Francisco in thirty-nine hours—just one full night. Its cars bore the names of famed San Francisco locales: Market Street and Portsmouth Square, Seal Rock, Chinatown, Twin Peaks, The Presidio, Telegraph Hill, Union Square, and Mission Dolores.

The Pullman-built train was a beauty, and lived up to its owners' expectations, attracting both attention and passengers. A former steward recalled: "It was a very luxurious train. Nice silver...fresh flowers on the table every day...in the summertime we were furnished summer tuxedos...a fresh white coat every night."

Unfortunately, COSF was quite different from other streamliners of the golden age in its attraction of tragic events. On August 11, 1939, at 10:02 A.M. the City of San Francisco pulled out of Chicago, snaking past the stockyards in the steamy 95-degree F (35°C) heat, accelerating westward, past the trees and farmland of western Illinois, toward an unexpected fate. The barren remoteness of Utah and Nevada soon supplanted the plains of Nebraska and Wyoming, and in the pitch-black desert night, something went very wrong.

At a point a mile and a half (2.4km) outside of Harney, Nevada, known simply as Bridge 4, the five middle cars careened off the bridge into the almost dry Humboldt River, knocking the bridge girders off their abutments. The diners Presidio and Mission Dolores, and the three sleepers Embarcadero, Twin Peaks, and Chinatown were destroyed, killing eighteen people. The locomotive and first two cars made it across the bridge, while the emergency-brake application left the sleeper Fishermen's Wharf hanging precariously over the edge and the remaining cars on the tracks.

An investigation revealed probable sabotage, and witnesses reported seeing a mysterious "earless man" scampering away from a vantage point immediately following the wreck. Evidence indicated that the outside rail on the curve leading to Bridge 4 had been shifted inward 4½ inches (11.5cm), forcing the train to derail. Southern Pacific offered a $10,000 reward for information leading to the arrest of the responsible party, and twelve thousand people were interviewed over the following twelve years, but no suspects were ever charged.

(An eerie repeat of this wreck occurred fifty-six years later, in October 1995, when Amtrak's Sunset Limited dived off a bridge into a dry river bed after persons unknown disconnected a bolted rail joint and loosened spikes in another case of sabotage. Fortunately, only one person (a dining-car employee) was killed, although there were numerous injuries. The FBI and other investigatory bodies noted the similarities between the two crimes, including the geographic proximity, but once again no arrests were made.)

The COSF continued in regular service, carrying passengers to the World's Fair of 1939 and, with a second train added in 1941, soldiering through the war years at a rate of ten trips per month. Most passenger equipment was well-worn by 1946, so 180 new cars, including fifty sleepers, were ordered for the expected postwar traffic. The Union Pacific also rebuilt a number of older cars.

It took three years for all the equipment to arrive, but the San Francisco, Los Angeles, and Portland streamliners were all running daily in 1947. Coast-to-coast Pullman service was instituted in cooperation with eastern roads, and schedules of other long-distance trains were shortened. General Motors' Train of Tomorrow was purchased following a demonstration tour, and put into service between Seattle and Portland.

Like the owners of other American railroads, the owners of the City of San Francisco struggled with the thorny issue of balancing service and cost, but the streamliner services were kept first-class as the competition with airlines and automobiles intensified in the 1950s. It was this cost-saving approach that led to another near-tragedy on the COSF. The story of the incident that distinguishes the saga of the City of San Francisco from the histories of other great trains began with the train's western partner, Southern Pacific (SP).

SNOWBOUND!

When Theodore Judah surveyed different routes through the Sierras for the Central Pacific in the 1850s, snow accumulations that season happened to be lighter than normal, averaging just 13 feet (4m). To further compound the misinformation, Judah measured the Donner Pass summit, not realizing that snow conditions were much worse just below the 2-mile (3.2km) level section at the pass.

The westbound **City of San Francisco**, with 226 passengers aboard, sits wedged in a drifted cut, its American Locomotive Company (Alco) **PA** diesel units unable to move the train either forward or in reverse. As the disastrous conditions continued to worsen that January morning in 1952, the rescue equipment also became marooned by the fierce storm.

Donner Pass was chosen as the route for the transcontinental railroad, and snowfall was not a problem during the first few years of construction. The winter of 1886–1887 proved the fallacy of Judah's assessments with a vengeance—40 feet (12m) of snow accumulated at the summit, bringing construction to a halt and causing much track and grading to be lost to avalanches. The following winter was even worse.

The CP countered Mother Nature by building protective timber snowsheds along 23 miles (37km) of track by 1869 and 17 additional miles (27km) by 1873. "Headlight" plows on the locomotives gave way to "bucker" plows pushed by as many as twelve locomotives, which rammed repeatedly into drifts to force their way through. In 1887, the rotary snowplow came to the high Sierras, but this massive steam-powered "snowblower" sat idle through two years of light snowfall until the terrible winter of 1889–90, when a massive storm system dumped snow virtually continuously for seventy days. A total of sixty-four feet (19.5m) of snow fell, with drifts up to two hundred feet (61m) deep.

The railroad had discovered that heavy snow was the norm at Donner Pass, and gained enough expertise in snow fighting (with bigger and better rotary plows and spreaders), that the system of snowsheds had been reduced to just 5.6 miles (9km) in length by 1951. The railroad, now called the Southern Pacific, was confident that it would not be shut down again. But the unusually severe winter of 1951–1952 would remind the Southern Pacific of the force of nature.

In January 1952, one of the most severe blizzards of the century struck the Sierra. On January 9, the temperature was 16 degrees F (-8°C), the barometer had dropped 22 points in twenty-four hours, and ten inches (25cm) of snow had fallen on top of the ten feet (3m) of snow already on the ground at Norden. The SP struggled to keep the line open. The railroad employees began to plow the new snow as they geared up for the coming storm, with no inkling that the gale-force winds and heavy snow would continue for more than two weeks.

By the morning of January 12, the storm had reached serious levels, with over thirteen feet (4m) of dense snow on the ground, continuing heavy snow, and a strong west wind. The weather worsened during the day, and the danger of snowslides increased.

Howling winds drifted the snow over the stranded City of San Francisco until the train was all but buried. It was three days later before the passengers could be rescued, and it took another full day to dig out the badly damaged train and clear the track.

◆ ◆ ◆

At 10:18 A.M., Train 101, the westbound City of San Francisco, departed Norden behind three Alco PA diesels with a massive AC-class cab-forward articulated steam locomotive helper in front. Already running several hours late because of the storm, the train was carrying several deadheading train crews (that is, crews making a trip as passengers) for relief of the plow trains at Donner Pass, and three linemen to be dropped off to repair downed communication lines.

At 11:00 A.M., the train hit a huge snowslide that derailed the AC locomotive and trapped the train in the quickly drifting snow. The slide was so severe that it smashed through the cab windows of the helper and filled the cab with snow, requiring rescuers to dig out the trapped crewmen. Another locomotive coupled to the rear of the cars was able to tow them back to Norden, leaving behind a crew of men with shovels.

By Sunday morning, January 13, the Southern Pacific was in trouble. The westbound main line was blocked by buried or derailed locomotives in three locations. Communication was interrupted by downed lines, which were at some points buried in the deep snow and in other parts snapped by the numerous slides. The eastbound track traversed the pass at a slightly higher elevation and had been kept open by the rotary plows, although the new snow was not adhering and slides were a continuing problem.

The westbound Train 101 of January 12 left Norden for the second time at 3:28 A.M. and cleared the pass successfully. At 11:23 A.M. Train 101 of January 13, the next day's City of San Francisco, which had also been held in Norden, was sent west into the raging blizzard with a warning to avoid taking chances that might repeat the previous day's problems.

The second Train 101 cleared the blockade and crossed over to the recently plowed westbound track at Crystal Lake, but a fresh slide then blocked these tracks near Yuba Gap. The engineer successfully blasted through that slide with his pilot-mounted snowplow, but immediately struck another huge six-to-twelve-foot (1.8–3.6m)-deep slide, lost momentum, and stalled. When he tried to reverse, the train refused to budge. It was 12:15 P.M., and the City of San Francisco, with 226 passengers and crew aboard, was stuck fast in a howling storm with uncertain communication.

A passing eastbound rotary crew working on the upper track assessed the situation and plowed to the Crystal Lake crossover, intending to back down to No. 101 and pull it back from the slide with their AC class locomotive. As the rescuers approached the stalled train, the reverse-running plow rode up and off the rails on the snow and ice that accumulated under the rotary hood. Drifting snow soon had the plow firmly gripped. The locomotive, trapped behind the plow, uncoupled from it and backed to No. 101, coupling the tender to the rear of the streamliner. After several attempts at coordinated see-sawing with both locomotives failed to move the train, the AC's steam line was connected to help provide train heat. It was now 4:00 P.M., and the storm continued to pile snow up against the marooned train.

Another rotary crew was sent from the west, plowing through 5-foot (1.5½m) drifts until it reached No. 101, but with no coupler on the plow, moved back west so that four F7 helper units (with pilot plows on each end) could reach the train. Unfortunately, the helpers were waiting at a crossover inside the Emigrant Gap snowshed for the plow to move in the clear, and the plow was waiting for a mistakenly thrown red signal. By the time the problem was rectified, the 90 mph (145kph) gale had deposited three feet (90cm) of new snow on the freshly cleared main.

The F7 set tried to force its way through the snow with only pilot plows and 6,000hp, getting within 3 miles (4.8km) of the streamliner, but came to a twenty-foot (6.1m)-deep slide of indeterminable length at the same location where an earlier slide had been cleared by the rotary. After an attempt to ram through the drift failed, the diesels fought back out and returned to Emigrant Gap.

In another attempt to reach No. 101, the rotary fought drifts that had reached twenty-five feet (7.6m), but when they were within a half mile (800m) of the marooned train, after a long night of considerable effort, a heavy slide buried both tracks behind them, trapping the rescuers with their tender toward the slide. They could do nothing but continue on to the streamliner.

Another train that had a rotary at each end of the cab-forward locomotive was plowing the eastbound track above No. 101, and was on its way to rescue the rescuers when it, too, was struck by a slide and became trapped. It was now 8:00 A.M. on January 14, and gray daylight illuminated the scene. Three cab-forwards, three rotary plows, and the City of San Francisco were stuck fast in a blizzard that showed little sign of letting up, and the Southern Pacific main line was completely shut down.

At noon, another slide completely buried all three plows (overturning one) and the two steam engines. Most of the crew members were inside keeping warm and were able to dig their way out, but one man standing outside was killed. Most took refuge in the streamliner, while others hiked to the Yuba Gap Lodge, where they could get rooms and try to make rescue arrangements by telephone.

The situation on the City of San Francisco had deteriorated from a bit of an adventure to being quite serious. Both the diesels and the cab-forward on the rear end had run out of water and shut down, leaving no heat source after the evening of January 14, other than the diner's cookstove. The passengers were wrapped in anything warm—blankets, towels, and even window curtains. They took turns rotating through the diner for warmth and carefully rationed meals.

Section hands had carried several loads of coal on their backs to the train, but that eventually ran out and the cooks resorted to burning any loose wood on the train. Pullman ladders and even the boards stored under the seats for playing cards went into the stove. Meals were reduced to spaghetti without sauce, a frankfurter, and half a cup of coffee for dinner, and a dab of beans, fried potatoes, and coffee for breakfast.

A doctor and five registered nurses among the passengers ministered to the ailing, including several with heart-attack symptoms, in a temporary infirmary set up in a lounge car.

Rescue attempts on January 15 were hampered by the continuing storm, the closed highways, and another rotary that became disabled when it derailed on the eastbound main. A doctor and medical supplies were delivered to the stricken train by dog sled and Snow Cat. Propane-powered engines were placed under the cars to provide power for air circulation, but they became fouled by the blowing snow that night, and the exhaust fumes seeped into two sleepers. Several people were overcome by the fumes, but the problem was discovered in time for all to recover quickly. The storm had broken during the night, but the clear sky caused temperatures to plummet, and conditions on the train were worsening.

By the early morning of January 16, the highway department was able to clear a single lane on the highway from Emigrant Gap, coming within a few hundred feet (100m) of the stalled streamliner. The SP train crews bivouacked at the Yuba Gap Lodge borrowed a Snow Cat belonging to the telephone company and broke a trail to the train and then from the train to the highway. A fleet of cars and trucks had been assembled to ferry the miserable passengers to Emigrant Gap, where a rescue train waited to carry them west. They walked if they could, and were hauled on toboggans, if necessary. Once they were safely away, the crews carried all of the baggage to Snow Cats, which relayed it to waiting trucks. The last items out of the express car were personally carried by the railroad's agents, as the packages contained several million dollars in new currency bound for the San Francisco mint.

Once on board the warm rescue train, passengers and crew were treated to a big steak dinner "on the Company." The train, with a four-unit F7 locomotive on each end, departed at 8:30 P.M. and arrived in Roseville, California, clear of the storm, at 11:40 P.M. The ordeal for those who were marooned was over, but the Southern Pacific was just beginning the rescue of the City of San Francisco itself.

Emigrant Gap was the staging point for the extrication, which began on the cold, clear, Thursday morning of January 17. Bulldozers cleared snow from near the tracks, creating enough room to maneuver, while section men hand-shoveled the snowsheds to relieve strain on the trusses. A rotary cleared the westbound main, allowing a crew of forty men to spend all night digging out the plow train trapped in front of the No. 101, so that it could be hauled back to the Gap the next morning.

The shovelers got some help when three Caterpillar RD-8 bulldozers arrived early Friday morning, but it was Saturday before the overturned plow (which had also fouled the westbound tracks) and the remaining plow and locomotive on the eastbound tracks were cleared. The wrecker removed the overturned plow and then, with the help of the three "cats," pulled the snowbound diesels away from the train. The bulldozers pulled out a few cars at a time and coupled them to the relief train, which hauled them to Roseville. By 9:00 P.M., the remaining cab-forward and rotary were freed, and they were hauled to Emigrant Gap.

The Southern Pacific main line was finally cleared of obstructions, and those rotaries that were still operating proceeded to clear the remaining trackage all through Sunday. The wind had picked up, and drifting snow continued to be a problem. A few freights struggled through later in the day, but another freight was trapped late that night in the drifting snow, and a Herculean effort was put forth before it was cleared at 6:00 A.M. on Tuesday, January 22.

The sense of accomplishment was short-lived, as Donner Pass was open for only a few hours before yet another blizzard struck, closing the line once more. It wasn't until Saturday, January 26, that trains were able to resume regular operation, and, ironically, the City of San Francisco was the first train over the pass.

THE FINAL YEARS

The great City Trains faced the same difficulties in the postwar years as the other notable name trains, and those patterns have been adequately covered in other sections of this book. The passenger trains could not compete with airlines and cars in speed and convenience and the inevitable budget cutbacks finally affected even the best of the streamliners. Ultimately, just one train continued to travel between California and Chicago, a combine that included cars from the Los Angeles, San Francisco, Portland, and Denver trains, nicknamed "The City of Everywhere," which operated until the advent of Amtrak in 1971. The California Zephyr maintains service to San Francisco via Denver and still traverses the historic Donner Pass.

The California Zephyrs passed one another each day at Grizzly, deep in Glenwood Canyon, located along the Colorado River. The train was operated jointly by the Burlington Route, Denver & Rio Grande Western, and Western Pacific railroads.

THE SUPER CHIEF AND FELLOW TRIBESMEN

The name "Super Chief" had been synonymous with passenger-train excellence since 1936, when it began service on the Atchison, Topeka & Santa Fe's Chicago–Los Angeles route as a heavyweight, once-per-week, extra-fare, luxury train. The Super Chief evolved from the California Limited of 1892, which at that time was the Santa Fe's flagship on that route. The railroad had begun featuring Fred Harvey–operated dining-car service in 1888, and the California Limited carried one dining car between Fort Madison, Iowa, and Kansas City, with stops for meals at Harvey Houses in between. This train was discontinued on May 3, 1896, but reborn the following winter as a seasonal, biweekly, all-Pullman luxury service. The 2,265-mile (3645km) route was covered in seventy-two hours. It proved to be so popular that service became year-round in 1900, and daily in 1905.

The California Limited was the AT&SF's premier train until December 11, 1911, when the extraordinary Santa Fe de-Luxe began the most opulent and elegant railroad passenger service ever offered in the United States. Limited to only sixty passengers and run weekly during the winter season, the six-car consist included a diner, club car (with smoking room, barbershop, and shower) and a ten-section observation-parlor. This was an extremely high proportion of non-revenue space, and the Santa Fe demanded a staggering twenty-five-dollar extra fare for the faster sixty-three-hour schedule. Passengers who paid this first-ever surcharge on the California route were treated to a brass bed (rather than a berth); use of the library in the observation parlor; an orchid corsage for the women passengers; an alligator wallet embossed with the train's name in gold for the gentlemen; and finally, a leisurely and delightful Fred Harvey meal in the thirty-seat dining car. The enjoyment of this meal was considerably enhanced by the vermilion mahogany interior that was kept comfortable with the first railway installation of an "air-cooling and air-washing" device.

Following World War I, another extra-fare, all-Pullman train was inaugurated, with a root name destined to represent the best of the Santa Fe's passenger trains—the Chief. Beginning operation on September 14, 1926, the first Chief maintained the sixty-three-hour schedule of the de-Luxe but operated daily and required a ten-dollar extra fare. Members of the Hollywood film industry warmly embraced the Chief, and the glamorous personalities who traveled on it attracted the media and a load of free publicity for the line (just as they did for the Twentieth Century Limited of the New York Central, which carried the stars on the final leg of their Los Angeles–to–New York journeys).

The Santa Fe maintained other trains and other routes, of course, including the Grand Canyon Limited, which connected Los Angeles and

The Santa Fe's new Super Chief (1939) is anticipated in this artist's rendering of the Budd-built train, coursing along the rails of Raton Pass.

✦ ✦ ✦

Chicago with that tourist mecca. Begun in 1929, this train was part of a short-lived but unique experiment that cut the travel time from New York to Los Angeles from one hundred hours to eighty by combining rail travel with airplane flights. The Santa Fe, the Pennsylvania Railroad, and the Curtiss Aeroplane Company participated as follows: New York to Columbus, Ohio, via PRR, overnight; a Transcontinental Air Transport (TAT) Ford Tri-Motor to Waynoka, Oklahoma, in the daylight; the Grand Canyon Limited to Clovis, New Mexico, overnight; and the final leg by Transcontinental Air.

The Super Chief began as a temporary heavyweight train in 1936—clearly descended from the Santa Fe de-Luxe and the Chief as an "extra-fare, extra-fast, extra-fine" luxury train, but bridging the gap between the heavyweights and the coming streamliners. The new train's Pullmans, diner, and club car were simply worked-over cars from the Chief pool and traded on the superb record of the Chief, but its schedule slashed fifteen hours and fifteen minutes from the Chief's eastbound schedule. The Super Chief broke the magic forty-hour mark at thirty-nine hours and forty-five minutes. The secret was in the motive power.

The wave of streamlining sweeping the railroad world in the mid-1930s produced the Union Pacific's M-10000, the Burlington's Zephyr, the Illinois Central's Green Diamond, and the Gulf, Mobile & Ohio's Rebel—all streamlined, diesel-powered train sets—along with more traditional streamlined steam-powered trains such as the Baltimore & Ohio's Royal Blue and the Milwaukee Road's Hiawathas. The AT&SF was as interested in the new streamliners as the other roads, but carefully ana-

Top: The Alvarado Hotel (shown here in 1905), located conveniently adjacent to the railroad's main line in Albuquerque, New Mexico, was an early example of the collaboration between the Santa Fe and Fred Harvey. Above: The cavernous interior of the dining room at the Alvarado is set for an early dinner. Mary Colter, the Santa Fe's in-house architect, contributed her knowledge of Native American history and art to the interiors of many of the railroad's depots, hotels, and streamlined cars.

Top: The Illinois Central's Green Diamond was just one of the several early custom-built diesel streamliners that taught railroads and locomotive and car manucfacturers valuable lessons, paving the way for the standard designs and mass-production techniques that revolutionized the construction of passenger trains. Above: Following their M-10000, the first streamliner ever built, the Union Pacific ordered three new trains—the M-10001 (pictured here), the M-10002, and the M-10003—with similar styling. These latter versions were custom-built locomotives designed to haul individual coaches, as opposed to the integral train-set configuration of the M-10000 or the Pioneer Zephyr.

◆ ◆ ◆

Pioneering road diesels were ordered for the Super Chief. General Motors' Electro-Motive Corporation (later EMD) supplied the 900hp Winton engines (two per locomotive), and St. Louis Car supplied the bodies. They were intended to run as a pair, numbered 1 and 1A, and provided 3,600hp. Designed by EMC's chief engineer, Richard Dilworth, they were almost identical to demonstrators Nos. 511 and 512, a simple box-cab design that virtually ignored the streamliner mania.

Nicknamed Amos 'n' Andy, the one redeeming visual quality to the new diesels was a spiffy paint scheme—cobalt-blue roof, Saratoga-blue undercarriage, and olive-green body with separating stripes of scarlet and Tuscan red. Sterling McDonald, a Chicago industrial designer who also did the interiors for the DC-3 airplane, came up with the scheme and also designed the illuminated nose sign and observation-car drumhead.

Although No. 1 was returned to EMC after it caught fire, the new diesels performed well during extensive testing, and a preliminary run on the Super Chief in November 1935 proved the viability of the under-forty-hour schedule. On May 12, 1936, the Super Chief was officially born (though this version of the train would only exist for a year or so)—a diesel-powered, ten-dollar extra-fare, heavyweight train that shortened the travel time between Chicago and Los Angeles to one business day (thirty-seven hours, leaving in the late afternoon and arriving in the early morning two days later).

On its maiden voyage, with passengers including celebrities Eddie Cantor and Eleanor Powell, the train departed Dearborn Station,

lyzed the alternatives. It elected to avoid the undersized, permanently coupled train sets, wanting full-sized equipment and the flexibility of a pool of individual cars. The management made the daring decision to go with the new diesel-electric locomotives, which were unproven in road service, in part to cut down on the cost of hauling vast quantities of water for thirsty steam locomotives into the arid desert of the Southwest.

Chicago, at 7:15 P.M. and arrived at La Grand Station, Los Angeles, at 8:59 in the morning of the second day, one minute early. At one point, Amos 'n' Andy reached a remarkable (for the time) 102 mph (164kph). Having proven the viability of the new train and its diesel power, the Santa Fe began preparing for the all-new, lightweight fleet already being wrought from stainless steel at the Edward G. Budd Manufacturing Company in Philadelphia.

Once the Santa Fe committed to the streamlining, it went whole hog. The 1937 Super Chief was aptly named, and far removed from the 1936 stand-in, retaining only the under-forty-hour schedule and the Fred Harvey cuisine. The pioneering box cabs that had been the Santa Fe's first diesel-electric locomotives were replaced by the first units in a long line of stream-lined diesel power built for Santa Fe by General Motors: the rakishly slant-nosed Electro-Motive E1A No. 2 and E1B No. 2A. The new streamlined diesels were semipermanently coupled and considered a single locomotive, and were painted in the soon-to-be classic "warbonnet" scheme of red, yellow, and silver. Eight shiny Budd-built cars in fluted stainless steel included: baggage car 3430; eight-section, one-drawing-room, two-compartment-sleeper Isleta; six-double-bedroom, two-compartment, two-drawing-room sleeper Taos; dormitory-barbershop-buffet lounge Acoma; thirty-six-seat diner Cochiti; a second 6-2-2 sleeper Laguna; and a two-drawing-room, one-double-bedroom, three-compartment lounge-observation Navajo, which carried the purple Super Chief drumhead.

This aesthetic triumph resulted from the efforts of an army of creative people. The Santa Fe, Electro-Motive, and Budd personnel met at Budd's Red Lion plant near Philadelphia, along with designer Sterling McDonald, whose work on the Union Pacific's brown-and-yellow Streamliners and the Santa Fe's heavyweight Super Chief had been well received. He would have primary responsibility for the interiors, whose design was to be based on southwestern Indian art, an aesthetic direction already established in the road's advertising by Roger W. Birdseye. This recognized expert in Indian culture lent his considerable knowledge to the project and provided the names for the cars. The skilled and creative Budd architects Paul Phillipe Cret and John Harbeson, of the University of Pennsylvania School of

Architecture, would translate McDonald's and Birdseye's ideas from sketches into reality. After a week of meetings, the contract was signed for a nine-car, nonarticulated train that would sleep 104 passengers, and house a dining-car crew of twelve.

The final results were unprecedented and not to be surpassed. Elimination of an RPO-mail-baggage car reduced the consist to a mail-baggage car, five sleepers, a dining car, and a full lounge, which included crew quarters and the barbershop. Each of the passenger-carrying cars was to be individually designed, with no two alike. An impressive rare-wood interior was made possible by Harbeson's use of Flexwood veneer, a thin layer of real wood laminated to a sheet of muslin, which was applied over Masonite© hardboard paneling. The woods used included: bubinga, white harewood, macassar, ebony, ribbon primavera, zebra-wood, Brazilian rosewood, ebonized maple, American holly, redwood burl, teak, aspen, and satinwood.

Each of the thirty-two double bedrooms, compartments, and draw-ing rooms used different combinations of wood and fabric. The *Santa Fe Magazine* boasted: "The change from the heavy, dark oppressiveness of the uniformly finished Pullmans of yesterday is delightful." The lounge car, Acoma, was finished mostly in zebrawood, and the diner, Cochiti, sported bubinga walls. The Navajo's observation-lounge section dis-pensed with wood entirely, using striking traditional Navajo designs in the upholstery, with the lower walls painted in copper and the ceiling a turquoise blue. The window panels replicated sand paintings illustrating the "Myth of the Mountains" chant.

The Burlington's Zephyr typified the earliest experiments in utilizing integral power cars and fixed equipment, but the lack of flexi-bility in such a configuration with regard to the addition of cars in order to meet increased passenger traffic sent the railroads in the direction of separate locomotives hauling individual coaches.

Above: The Southwest Indian design motifs are evident in this photo of the lower-level lounge on a Santa Fe full-length dome on the new San Francisco Chief (as identified by the source), but it could as easily be a photograph of the Budd high-level cars built for El Capitan. Below: The swiveling lounge seats in a Pullman Standard–built dome (identifiable by the flat glass roof panels) allowed passengers to enjoy the passing scenery in fully adjustable living room comfort.

Mary Colter, a designer and architect employed by Fred Harvey, was well versed in the distinctly ornamented pottery of the ancient Mimbres Indians. This small southwestern tribe produced bold designs (often depicting animals) consisting of precise lines and geometric and checkered patterns. Coloration was typically red on buff or white, and the designs remained virtually unchanged from A.D. 900 to 1200—successive generations of Mimbreno potters simply reproduced the original art through the centuries. Colter turned to this tradition when designing the china for the Super Chief's diner, selecting thirty-seven authentic motifs for the pattern that was called Mimbreno and would become perhaps the most famous of dining-car crockery designs.

The care and attention to detail that was lavished on the interiors of the Super Chief was also applied to the exteriors. An Electro-Motive illustrator named Leland Knickerbocker conceived an elegant paint scheme that was inspired by the profile of an Indian warrior with his feathers streaming in the wind. The sleek, slant-noses of the silver E1 locomotives were painted red, trimmed with yellow and black stripes, as the figurative war bonnet swept down off the roof, back toward the nose, and then curved down and to the rear, forming a continuous band along the lower edges of both A and B units. The standard Santa Fe circular herald was modified to an oval shape that stretched elegantly across the nose with "wings" that wrapped around to the sides. This dazzling red, yellow, and silver scheme, like the Mimbreno china, would spread across the passenger fleet and lasted until an agreement with Amtrak ended Santa Fe's passenger service on April 16, 1971. The legendary paint scheme faded away (although a blue-and-yellow freight version stayed in service) until Santa Fe revived the warbonnet scheme on hotshot inter-modal freight locomotives in the 1980s.

By the spring of 1937, the Budd Company had completed its work at the Red Lion plant, although EMD was not finished with the locomotives. The rolling stock made a test run to Philadelphia on April 28, and then headed for Chicago as part of the Pennsylvania's Commercial Express, where a series of demonstration runs were scheduled.

Seventy-two passengers—Budd and Santa Fe officials and newspaper and magazine editors and writers—gathered at Dearborn Station on Monday, May 3, for the first of several preview trips. Since the E1s were still under construction, a steam locomotive simmered quietly at the head end of the gleaming stainless steel train. Departing at 9:00 A.M., the train arrived in Santa Fe, New Mexico, at 11:30 A.M. on May 4. After a day of socializing and sightseeing in the Indian country of the train's heritage, the passengers departed on the return trip at 8:15 the following morning.

The spanking new E1s, resplendent in their warbonnet livery, led the second preview run on May 8, which carried a delegation from the Chicago Association of Commerce bound for a meeting with the Los Angeles Chamber of Commerce. The train arrived at Los Angeles' La

Grande Station on May 10 at 8:58 A.M., two minutes early, and was greeted by a crowd of three thousand. The ceremonies were broadcast on the radio, during which the stainless steel consist was described as "a necklace of pearls" by the announcer. Cartoonist John T. McCutcheon used the compliments "superspeed, superservice, and supercomfort." The local press was welcomed aboard that evening for a party.

After two days on exhibit in Los Angeles, the Super Chief was sent to San Diego, where thirteen thousand visitors examined the equipment. The train returned to Los Angeles on Friday, carrying San Diego's leading business leaders and newspapermen, who were previewing the future San Diegan. That train's six cars and a locomotive were already under construction and would enter service within the year.

On Saturday, May 15, the Super Chief departed Los Angeles on its final goodwill run, whisking seventy important Californians to Chicago in the record-breaking time of thirty-six hours and forty-nine minutes—two hours faster than the existing best—at an average running speed of 64 miles per hour (103kph).

Unfortunately for the next day's initiation of the Super Chief's once-weekly schedule, the record-breaking run had burned out a traction motor on one of the E1s. The original box cabs Amos 'n' Andy (repainted aluminum with red stripes) were paired with the plain, aluminum EMD demonstrator No. 512 in replacement service. The passengers quickly overlooked the little glitch when they boarded the train and found the appointments and service on the first all-Pullman diesel-powered streamliner to be beyond compare. The City of Los Angeles departed Chicago the very next day on the Union Pacific streamliner's inaugural run, matching (by agreement with the Santa Fe) the Super Chief's thirty-nine-hour, forty-five-minute schedule and offering comparable service and equipment.

Even before the Super Chief was delivered, the Budd Company's contribution to its development was rewarded with additional orders for equipment to streamline existing trains. Ten diners, six club-lounge-dormitories, six baggage-barbershop-buffet lounges (all for the Chief), and thirty coaches (intended for the Scout but used on additional trains) were delivered in 1937.

The popularity of the name-train streamliner service had exploded, and the Santa Fe alone would add sixteen additional stainless steel train

The lighted drumhead mounted on the rounded rear end of the Santa Fe Super Chief's observation car is inspected by Edward G. Budd (left), president of the Budd Company (which built the car), and S. T. Bledsoe, president of the Santa Fe, prior to the May 4, 1937, test run out of Chicago.

◆ ◆ ◆

sets by 1940: another Super Chief, doubling the service's frequency; a luxury all-coach running mate, the twice-weekly Chicago–Los Angeles El Capitan; a reequipped Chief (six sets); a five-car San Diegan (Los Angeles–San Diego); two consists running as the Chicagoan (eastbound) and the Kansas Cityan (westbound) between those cities; two consists for the Golden Gate (Bakersfield–San Francisco); the Tulsan (Kansas City–Tulsa, Oklahoma); and an additional San Diegan train set. While the Chief was hauled by 4-6-4 Hudson steam locomotives (including the one-of-a-kind streamlined Blue Goose), the remaining trains were assigned to the latest diesels available from GM's Electro-Motive Division—all dressed in red-and-silver warbonnets. Eight additional E1As, numbered 2 through 9, and E1Bs numbered 2A–4A, were delivered between June 1937 and April 1938; E3s 11 and 11A arrived in 1939. Old Amos 'n' Andy, the original box cabs assigned to the heavyweight Super Chief, were rebuilt with somewhat more conventional (but still quite strange) "bulldog" noses and high cabs, painted in the warbonnet scheme, and separated as numbers 1 and 10. They were still somewhat ungainly—certainly no match for the elegant E Units—but they helped ease the power shortage.

This massive build-up also meant that the special features and lavish treatments that made the first Super Chief unique had to give way to more standardized products, although the interiors maintained the southwestern motifs. A conflict had also developed with Pullman, which was not happy about providing its services in sleeping cars supplied by another car builder. After the first Super Chief, Santa Fe's sleepers were built by Pullman-Standard, which supplied fifty-seven stainless steel cars—all with Indian names—for both the Chief and a second Super Chief.

The Chief, the daily, all-Pullman, extra-fare, Chicago–Los Angeles service that began in 1926, easily would have been the flagship train on most railroads. As it was, the Chief had its more sumptuous cousin to compete with. So, on January 31, 1938, the Chief was reequipped with a new lightweight stainless steel train set, although it remained steam-powered and secondary to the Super Chief. In reality, the levels of service and equipment were the same, and the trains were featured as equals in early Santa Fe publicity. The only difference lay in the Chief's slower forty-eight-hour schedule. The Chief carried a consist of: a baggage-barber-shop-buffet lounge, dormitory-club lounge, a thirty-six-seat diner, and

The Santa Fe streamlined a single steam locomotive, No. 3460 (a 4-6-4 Hudson), christening it *Blue Goose*. The problem of obtaining water in the arid Southwest pushed the Atchison, Topeka & Santa Fe to quickly invest in diesel power for its new streamliners.

✦ ✦ ✦

seven Pullmans—including one of the four-drawing-room, one-double-bedroom lounge-observations (Betahtakin, Biltabito, Chaistla, Chuska, Coconino, or Denehotso) on the rear.

The stainless steel/steam-power combination made for a unique train on the Santa Fe; it was further distinguished when the *Blue Goose* was assigned as the power. The last of six 4-6-4 Hudsons delivered by Baldwin in 1937, it was the railroad's only experiment with fully streamlined steam. The shrouding was painted medium blue and light blue, with stainless steel trim on the pilot, and bands of like material along the running boards, and across the tender. The running gear was blue-gray with the driver tires and wheel rims painted aluminum. While the Hudsons

ruled the eastern portion of the route, west of La Junta, Colorado, the less glamorous (but very handsome and efficient) 4-8-4 Northerns worked the hilly terrain on the point of the Chief.

During the early 1940s, the AT&SF continued to purchase stream-lined equipment: seven Electro-Motive E6s (four A units and three Bs), and an A/B set of Alco DL109s; a total of eighty-two assorted stainless steel cars from Pullman-Standard (twenty-nine), Budd (fifty-two), and a single experimental fifty-six-seat Pendulum Chair Car from Pacific Railway Equipment Company. A new five-car all-coach companion to the Super Chief, the twice-weekly El Capitan, was added to the Chicago–Los Angeles route, and its lower-cost luxury was touted as

"A Fascinating Experiment in Practical Democracy" in railroad publicity. In a five-year period, Santa Fe took delivery of the largest fleet of lightweight streamlined equipment in the world, and that fleet would be taxed to the limit by the demands of World War II.

Passenger loadings on both the Chief and the Super Chief jumped from eighty or ninety to 150 during the war years. Passenger-miles for the first half of 1942 increased 88 percent over the previous year—totaling 1,075,941,672 (1,731,190,150km). Dining-car business doubled, with as many as 350 meals being served during ten seatings in a thirty-six-seat diner. The Santa Fe's reputation for service and luxury had to be put aside for the duration of the war, since success was measured more by quantity than by quality.

The war years were hard on the railroads (due to forced service and a shortage of building materials and facilities) and, as the close of hostilities in 1945 freed countless resources and factories from war work, the Santa Fe moved quickly to rebuild both equipment and reputation. Car and locomotive builders were overwhelmed by orders, as recovering railroads launched the last great passenger-train boom in the United States. While new diesels began arriving in 1945—including Alco PAs, Electro-Motive FTs and F3s, and one A-B-A set of Fairbanks-Morse Erie-builts—the first passenger cars of the 156 on order weren't delivered until 1947.

Until then, the railroad concentrated on service improvements, recruiting a staff of onboard nurses from discharged military personnel, and inaugurating the long-planned coast-to-coast sleeper service. On March 6, 1946, the Chief began carrying Pullman cars that were interchanged in Chicago, bound for New York (via Pennsylvania's Broadway Limited and New York Central's Twentieth Century Limited), and Washington (via the Baltimore & Ohio's Capitol Limited). Competing railroads for the market from Chicago to the West Coast also offered through-sleepers from the East, a service that was much appreciated by

LIVESTOCK SPECIALS

◆ ◆ ◆

The high-speed deluxe service that the streamliner brought to passenger trains resulted in better service for more unusual, but not less demanding, passengers—livestock. The booming West Coast wartime economy swelled Union Pacific's livestock shipments between Salt Lake City and Los Angeles from ten thousand cars in 1939 to more than twenty-four thousand cars in 1946, and was very profitable despite animal losses due to the heat on long stretches of the California Division.

Federal regulations regarding the treatment of en-route livestock were very strict—unloading for rest and water every twenty-eight hours, or thirty-six hours with permission of the shipper. Regular-service freight trains were unable to regularly cover the 784-mile (1262km) route in less than fifty-eight hours, so livestock was unloaded at the Las Vegas stockyards. As shipments ballooned, so did the stockyard stench, creating considerable animosity in the booming city.

The speed of the new diesel-powered trains, combined with the increased efficiency of a newly installed Centralized Traffic Control system, meant that dedicated stock trains could cover the route within the thirty-six-hour limit and so eliminated the costs and delays of unloading, not to mention the cost of relocating the stockyard complex. The Union Pacific began the Day Live Stock (DLS),

which actually ran overnight to take advantage of the cooler night air on the desert crossings. Steam power was used initially on the thirty-two-hour, almost nonstop schedule (the train still had to make a watering stop, but the animals could remain in the cars). The train was given priority over all others except for passenger trains.

The Union Pacific reconditioned its rolling stock over the first summer, adding roller bearings and improved brakes and couplers to enable higher speeds. These cars were painted in the UP streamliner colors of Armour Yellow, with bright red lettering. Aluminum roofs and ends deflected the harsh sun of the Southwest, keeping the animals cooler. The new cars, with diesel locomotives, reduced the schedule to thirty hours.

The DLS rivaled the prestigious City of Los Angeles in brilliance and speed, although its schedule was slower than that of the famous streamliner. Nine months of the year, the DLS ran in two sections, with sixty cars in each, and the stock season (August through October) often saw three sections. The schedule was trimmed to twenty-seven hours in 1949, with grass-fed cows from Colorado, hogs from Iowa and Nebraska, cattle from Montana, and sheep from Idaho clipping over the UP rails at a speed close to those of the luxurious consists of the 1905 California Limited.

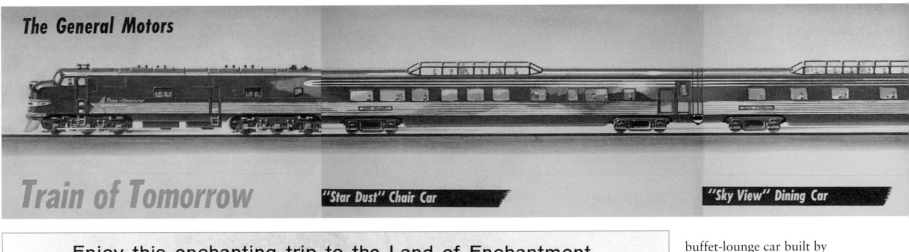

The General Motors

Train of Tomorrow   "Star Dust" Chair Car   "Sky View" Dining Car

Enjoy this enchanting trip to the Land of Enchantment

Chico's

Santa Fe

NEW MEXICO

WEEK-END TOURS

for the 1964 Season

Top: With locomotives built by the Electro-Motive Division of General Motors and cars built by Pullman-Standard, the Train of Tomorrow was constructed to be the most luxurious diesel passenger train of its day; every car featured a dome from which the passengers could survey the passing scenery in comfort. And each car offered its own delights, from the fully reclining, family-sized accommodations of the Star Dust car to the glamorous dining appointments of the Sky View car to the under-the-starlight sleeping "roomettes" of the Dream Cloud car to the cocktail-hour gaiety to be found at the two full bars of the Moon Glow lounge car in the rear. Above: Chico the Indian Boy became one of the best-loved railroad advertising characters in the United States. His image was used extensively to promote the Santa Fe's trains, despite the obvious irony that the advent of the railroad in the United States had played a significant role in the decimation of Native American peoples.

◆ ◆ ◆

the passengers, but the mix of two-tone gray smooth-side cars from the Pullman pool and cars in the colors of the East Coast roads eliminated the visual purity of the matching all-Budd, prewar consists. The fully customized stainless steel "strings of pearls" train sets were a thing of the past.

The 1947 antitrust agreement that separated Pullman's car operation from the Pullman-Standard car-building business freed Santa Fe from the Pullman-mandated restriction on purchasing other manufacturers' sleepers. Santa Fe promptly ordered twenty-seven additional sleepers from the Budd Company and twenty-eight more from American Car & Foundry (ACF). Some of these new cars were assigned to the Super Chief, along with a bedroom-lounge-observation car built by ACF and a dormitory-

buffet-lounge car built by Pullman-Standard.

The Santa Fe launched an advertising campaign to promote its new services. Introducing Chico, the little Indian Boy, the campaign targeted the sixty-five million readers of *Life, Colliers, The Saturday Evening Post*, and other popular magazines and newspapers. As in the prewar era, the public was invited to preview new trains, and elaborate celebratory luncheons were held featuring such noted entertainers as comedian Bob Hope and tenor James Melton. Comfort, luxury, and speed were the train's selling points, with its California destinations adding a bit of glamor.

As the new equipment came on line and the new trains became operational, Santa Fe joined other railroads in a final bid to lure passengers away from automobiles and planes—they ordered the dome car. On the Santa Fe, they were known as Pleasure Domes, and Pullman-Standard delivered the first ones in 1951, as part of the third complete reequipping of the Super Chief in the six years since the end of World War II. The floor plan was a copy of the dome-lounge from General Motors' four-car demonstrator Train of Tomorrow, and included the unique Turquoise Room, the first private dining room on a modern-era train. This space seated twelve for luncheon, cocktail, or dinner parties and could be reserved through the dining-car steward.

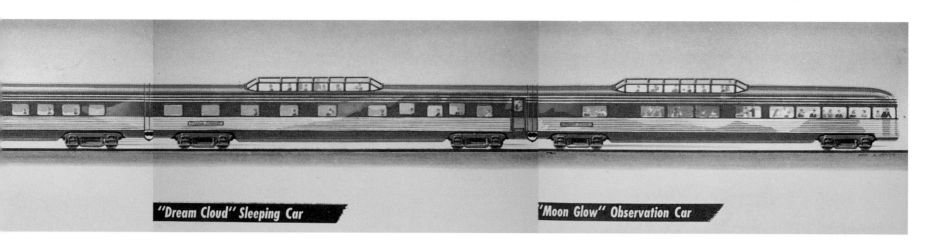

"Dream Cloud" Sleeping Car

'Moon Glow" Observation Car

The theme of the Turquoise Room was reflected in a reproduction of a silver-trimmed turquoise medallion that was displayed in a glass case on the forward wall. Carpeting was turquoise blue, gold-tinted mirrors lined the walls, and gold curtains covered the windows. Beneath the dome, adjacent to the Turquoise Room, was an intimate cocktail lounge, done in tete-de-negro carpet, pinkish-colored mirrors, and cherry-red curtains.

The main lounge was the largest area, with inviting sofas, lounge chairs, and built-in seating that were perfect for socializing or watching the scenery pass by. The beige walls and creamy yellow ceiling, combined with green and terra-cotta upholstery, recalled the warm colors of the southwestern desert, while the drapery pattern was based on Pacific Coast seashells. The upstairs dome section maintained that color scheme, and was outfitted with two pairs of fixed seats front and rear with the center section containing eight swiveling parlor-car seats to maximize the viewing possibilities. Unfortunately, that luxury lowered the capacity to sixteen seats from the twenty-four possible with normal four-across seating. These domes were always coupled to Pullman-built thirty-six-seat diners so that food service could be provided to the Turquoise Rooms.

The renewed train benefited from the favorable publicity generated by a Gloria Swanson film, a romantic comedy called *Three for Bedroom C*, which took place entirely on board the Super Chief. The production company rented six cars and a locomotive from the train's standby consist, dismantled the interiors, and reassembled them in a Hollywood studio. The railroad hoped that the film would entice the public back to the rails, and sponsored Swanson's trip West to the Kansas City premiere. A press entourage accompanied the star on board the Super Chief, adding to the publicity generated.

The Santa Fe was not yet finished with equipment experiments and innovations. In 1952, the railroad invested in a pair of Budd self-propelled RDC-1 railcars for the Los Angeles–San Diego route, but four years later, the cars overturned at high speed at Redondo Junction, with a loss of thirty lives. The repaired RDCs were returned to service on obscure secondary trains and were ultimately sold to the Baltimore & Ohio.

A more auspicious move was the 1954 addition of fourteen of Budd's new Big Domes. These full-length domes featured fifty-seven coach seats and an eighteen-seat lounge on the upper level, while the lower levels accommodated additional lounges of varied capacities, as well as dormitory and service spaces. In the cocktail lounge, seats were arranged around Lucite tables that had sprays of Australian seaweed cast inside. The tables were illuminated from below built-in ashtrays, producing a soft glow with no glare to disturb the passengers riding in the darkened forward-seating area. These cars continued the southwestern Indian motif, with Pueblo beige, Zuni turquoise, and Mesa red on the walls and ceilings, rust-colored fabric on the coach seats, and straw-colored Naugahyde in the lounges. The carpet was custom-woven in a design of charcoal, beige, and turquoise prickly-pear and cactus design.

While they were exciting additions to the fleet, the Big Domes were not an unqualified success, since the large glass area made for difficult cooling, and the full length of the dome restricted forward vision as compared with the standard domes. The new cars did not serve on the Super Chief, but were assigned to the El Capitan, Chicagoan/Kansas Cityan, and the last major passenger train launched in the United States, the San Francisco Chief. Thus, Santa Fe joined Milwaukee Road and Great Northern as the only operators of these cars, although Southern Pacific rebuilt several single-level cars into low-profile, three-quarter-length domes.

The year 1954 was notable for the introduction of a pair of Hi-Level cars—one each built by Budd and St. Louis Car Company for prototype testing on the El Capitan. These revolutionary two-level cars evolved from the Big Domes, placing seating on the top, removed from the noise and vibration of the wheels, with the service areas (such as entry, luggage storage, rest rooms, and air-conditioning equipment) down below. Since the full length was available for seating, capacity increased to sixty-seven passengers, compared with the forty-four to forty-eight in conventional long-distance coaches, and virtually everyone had a dome-seat view. Readily accepted by both crews and passengers, the cars were joined by a fleet of forty-seven more in 1955. The order was divided between coaches, diners, and lounges (known as the Top of the Cap), all with the trademark southwestern decor.

With a loccomotive fleet that dated to the immediate postwar years, the Santa Fe's commitment to innovation extended to new power. A 1966 order for ten General Electric U28CG hood units signaled a drift away from the streamliner image, as these "dual service" locomotives presented a strong "freight train" image. In 1967 and 1968, two new orders brought a different image to the passenger fleet. EMD's 3,600hp FP45s (nine) and GE's 3,000hp U30CGs (six) were very modern-looking "cowl" units that marked a return to the fully enclosed "car body" styling, although traditionalists balked at the angular noses, even with the mitigating warbonnet paint.

Despite the appeal of

The view through the expansive glass of a full-length dome on the Olympian Hiawatha (of the Chicago, Milwaukee, St. Paul & Pacific Railway) was unsurpassed, providing travelers with magnificent views that ranged from the sprawl of the Mississippi River to the prairies and mountains of the Pacific Northwest.

✦ ✦ ✦

these new innovations, the twin demons of the automobile and the airplane continued to sap traffic from the rails, and many eastern railroads, along with the Southern Pacific, began to retrench. Deferred maintenance, reductions of amenities, and train-offs (that is, trains removed from service) were standard procedure as the 1960s began. The mighty Santa Fe remained optimistic, even ordering new equipment and rebuilding older cars. In 1966, AT&SF still operated fourteen million train miles, as compared to 8.4 million on the Union Pacific, 7.8 million for the Burlington, and 6.3 million for the Southern Pacific. Although for Santa Fe, that was a drop of 30 percent from 1957, the SP plummeted 50 percent during the same period.

Santa Fe's optimism may have been unrealistic, but the railroad had already instituted a number of measures that would save money without compromising its high standards of service. The Super Chief's capacity was ninety to one hundred passengers (but it often carried as few as nineteen), and El Capitan was equipped for more than four hundred and

often departed with just half a load. In January 1958, the trains were combined during the light travel times of October–November and January 15–April 30, saving half a million dollars a month. Other trains were trimmed: the eastbound Kansas City Chief was cut east of Kansas City; one of the four Golden Gates was dropped; and observation cars were deemed excessive and were retired, beginning with the fleet built in the 1930s. Despite these retrenchments, 1964 saw delivery of an additional twenty-four Hi-Level cars for El Capitan, virtual duplicates of the 1956 order. This enabled three or four of the earlier high-capacity cars to be transferred to the San Francisco Chief, thereby reducing weight and operating costs on that train, which had grown long (and therefore heavy) over the years.

Using carefully crafted, huge advertising campaigns, employee bonuses for tips on potential customers, bargain fares, and acceptance of credit cards, the Santa Fe was able to increase passenger revenues about 2 percent annually in all but one year of the early sixties. Unfortunately,

MEALS BY FRED HARVEY

◆ ◆ ◆

The often memorable pleasure of dinner in the diner was especially unforgettable on the Santa Fe, where the long tradition of excellence began in the lunchroom at the Topeka, Kansas, depot, when Fred Harvey assumed management in 1876. Frederick Henry Harvey emigrated from Britain in 1850 at the age of fifteen. His first job, washing dishes for two dollars a week in New York, earned him boat passage to New Orleans, where he found work in a number of the best hotels and restaurants. After moving to Saint Louis, where he spent four years working as a tailor and jeweler, he opened his first restaurant. When his partner pilfered the proceeds, Harvey drifted toward the railroad industry, first working on the Missouri River Packet line, then sorting mail on the first Railway Post Office (RPO) at Saint Joseph.

Hôtelier extaordinaire Fred Harvey (1835–1901).

◆ ◆ ◆

Keenly aware of the bright future of railroads, Harvey took a position with the Hannibal & St. Joseph—before moving to the Chicago, Burlington & Quincy—as a freight agent at Leavenworth, Kansas. A man of many interests and much ambition, he also owned a ranch, invested in a hotel, and sold newspaper advertising.

Harvey was appalled by the poor food services available. Although George Pullman's Delmonico, the first true dining car, had been built in 1868, the standard practice for rail travel in the 1870s was to stop the train briefly for meals, available from trackside restaurants. The stops were indeed brief, as the train crew, in cahoots with the restaurant, accepted bribes to blow the departure whistle early, forcing the patrons to rush for the train—leaving their food, as unappetizing as it often was, behind to be served again.

Fred Harvey recognized the need for reasonably priced food that was of good quality and properly served. He first approached the Burlington, but was rebuffed. The railroad officials were very leery of becoming involved in the restaurant business. In 1876, a meeting with Superintendent Charles F. Morse of the AT&SF produced an agreement that evolved into the sprawling empire of railroad-owned, Fred Harvey–operated restaurants, hotels, and dining cars.

The agreement was simple, and the principles lasted for almost a century. Santa Fe would supply the buildings, coal, ice, water, and transportation for supplies, furnishings, and personnel at no cost.

Harvey would keep the profits and Santa Fe would have attractive dining services for passengers, without inheriting the problems of running a restaurant business.

The Topeka depot lunchroom was followed by a hotel in Florence, Kansas, purchased by the railroad and renovated by Fred and his wife, Sarah. The empire grew into a string of lunchrooms at 100-mile (161km) intervals along the Santa Fe's main line to California. Hotels were also built, often at tourist destinations that not only served the railroad's passengers, but generated additional traffic as they became destinations in themselves. The hotels all reflected the Spanish heritage of the Southwest, both in styling and names—Alvarado, El Ortiz, El Navajo, El Tovar, La Fonda, La Posada.

The Harvey Houses were staffed by an army of Harvey girls, young women "of good character, attractive, and intelligent, ages 18–30," according to the newspaper advertisements. They were offered salaries of $17.59 per month, plus tips, and provided an air of respectability at a time when the West was still wild and woolly, and waitresses weren't always ladies of quality. The Harvey girls, who wore prim black-and-white uniforms that minimized their attractions, lived in dormitories under the watchful eyes of stern matrons. The more than five thousand young women whom Fred Harvey brought in helped to civilize the West, since most of them stayed on, often marrying Santa Fe employees. A movie called *The Harvey Girls* (1945) provided Judy Garland, Angela Lansbury, and Cyd Charisse an opportunity to tell the Harvey story, and included the classic song "On the Atchison, Topeka & the Santa Fe."

The Santa Fe began dining-car service in 1888, and Fred Harvey was given the contract to operate the cars. At the time of his death in 1901, at sixty-six years of age, Harvey was operating thirty dining cars, forty-seven restaurants, and fifteen hotels for the Santa Fe, along with the food service on the San Francisco Bay ferry system. The company continued with Fred's sons, Ford and Byron, at the helm, and by 1954 had grown to 124 dining cars staffed by more than two thousand stewards, waiters, chefs, and attendants. But the railroad was losing too much money in the diners, and the Harvey name was losing significance, so the Santa Fe ended the venture in 1969.

Sadly, even a design and performance legend such as the Super Chief couldn't withstand the declining passenger base wrought by the changes in transportation technology in this country. Here, the great train, with its wonderful Big Dome lounge car, is westbound at Raton Pass on its final run in May 1968.

✦ ✦ ✦

1967 was the watershed year. The first eight months showed a 17.3 percent drop in passenger revenues and, when the U.S. Post Office announced the removal of all but two Railway Post Office cars from AT&SF trains (with the loss of $35 million in revenue), the Santa Fe finally threw in the towel. On most railroads, passenger service had survived for years because of this essential postal "subsidy," but with even the U.S. Post Office choosing the speed and flexibility of highway and air, it was no longer practical to operate most passenger trains.

The AT&SF's most highly visible name trains—Super Chief, El Capitan, San Francisco Chief, Texas Chief, and San Diegan—would survive; the rest, including the legendary Chief, would be gone. The remaining trains sustained the high levels of service and maintenance that had been much respected, and in the summer of 1969 (the last year the Super Chief/El Capitan was split into two sections), the Super was an all-Pullman train for the first time since consolidation of the trains in 1958.

This level of commitment caused many people to believe that AT&SF would decline to join Amtrak, but the mounting losses were threatening the survival of the railroad. The National Railroad Passenger Corporation offered a final contract, which Santa Fe agreed to on April 20, 1971, and ten days later, the historic Atchison, Topeka & Santa Fe Railway ended a century of carrying passengers, reverting to a freight-only railroad.

Santa Fe paid fees of $21 million over three years, and Amtrak purchased nearly 450 of Santa Fe's cars (including the six Pleasure Domes and the entire seventy-nine-car Hi-Level fleet), nearly a quarter of the new Amtrak roster. All but one of the Big Domes went to Auto-Train.

New Jersey's Department of Transportation purchased twenty-six coaches for commuter use, and a number of other companies and individuals purchased cars. The railroad allowed Amtrak to use the Super Chief/El Capitan (although El Capitan was dropped from the name in 1973), Texas Chief, and San Diegan names on those surviving trains.

Amtrak maintained an appropriate reverence for the Super Chief that was missing on its other trains, but despite the best of intentions, when it proposed to run the Super in two sections for 1974, with one section having a capacity of three hundred but only one diner, the Santa Fe announced that it was unacceptable to "lower the quality of service to a level hardly recognizable by those accustomed to past Santa Fe standards." The railroad withdrew permission to use the traditional names. The Super Chief became the Southwest Limited, and the Texas Chief was renamed the Lone Star (although that train also disappeared in the service cuts of 1979). As Amtrak improved its own service standards, Santa Fe relented, and the former Super Chief acquired its last title in October 1984—the Southwest Chief.

The former glory of the Santa Fe's vast passenger-train operations lives on now only in the names on a pair of Amtrak trains, the new generation of Superliner cars that evolved from the Hi-Level fleet of the 1950s, and a small fleet of stainless steel equipment retained for company use—a Big Dome, ex–Super Chief diner No. 600, six sleepers, and a club lounge. The Chiefs and all their tribesmen have vanished forever from the American West, and even the indomitable Santa Fe itself was swallowed up by a 1996 merger with Burlington Northern (now called Burlington Northern Santa Fe).

THE CALIFORNIA ZEPHYR

The most revered of the Chicago, Burlington & Quincy's celebrated fleet of stainless steel Zephyrs was easily the Chicago-to–San Francisco California Zephyr. The Burlington had joined with the Denver & Rio Grande Western and the Western Pacific to operate a new steam-powered transcontinental passenger train, the Exposition Flyer, between those cities in 1934. Because the Flyer's 2,532-mile (451km) route was 300 miles (482km) longer than the competition's, the Burlington and its partners had no hope of matching those schedules, but the Flyer could win over passengers with the spectacular scenery of its route, which wound through the Colorado Rockies and the Feather River Canyon in the Sierra.

The success of the Flyer led the railroads to believe that they could introduce a train that would be pro-moted exclusively on the pleasures of scenic travel as an end in itself—a land cruise. After World War II,

The Silver Solarium, a classic boat-tail Budd-built observation car, with its neon tail sign lit, waits for the highball at Chicago's Union Station in April 1970.

✦ ✦ ✦

the management invested $15 million in a new streamliner, the California Zephyr. The generous fifty-five-hour schedule enabled the passengers to enjoy the most scenic portions of the run during daylight hours, despite the sacrifices in travel time required (the Union Pacific and Santa Fe trains pushed hard to remain under forty hours).

Costs and operations of the California Zephyr were divided among the three railroads, according to the mileage run. The Burlington pro-vided three train sets and operated from Chicago to Denver. The Denver & Rio Grande supplied one train and was responsible for the Denver-to-Salt Lake City leg, and the Western Pacific furnished two more trains and finished the run from Salt Lake to Oakland. Passengers completed the journey across the bay to San Francisco either by bus or ferry.

The make-up of the California Zephyr reflected the land-cruise concept. Budd supplied eleven stainless steel cars (with five Vista-Domes) for each train, which carried 245 paying passengers, 138 of these riding

in the coach seats located beneath the raised dome lounges. Sleeping accommodations varied, ranging from sections through roomettes and compartments to a seven-foot-wide (2.1m) double bedroom. The elegant tail-end Vista-Dome buffet-lounge-sleeper-observation car included a drawing-room suite with a private shower.

Another 224 alternate seats were available at no extra cost: 120 in the dome lounges and the remainder spread among the dining car, two buffet-lounges, and the observation lounge. There was plenty of room for passengers to stretch their legs while enjoying the scenery in a dome, a snack or a cocktail in a lounge, or a full meal in the diner.

The usual train staff was augmented by a crew of Zephyrettes, host-esses who pampered the passengers, while a public-address system piped soft music throughout the train. Places for dinner at one of the three sit-tings in the flower-decked diner were reserved in advance. Italian cuisine was the CZ specialty—with antipasto, minestrone, pasta, and perhaps veal scaloppini à la Parmesan with salad and garlic toast, cheese, and a dessert of a Marsala-fortified nut sundae. The meal would be served with a complementary six-ounce (177.5ml) bottle of California wine.

Before slipping into a comfortable berth for the night, the traveler could wind down in a comfortable seat in a darkened dome and marvel at the spectacle of the glowing sky fading to black punctuated by brilliant stars, or perhaps be pleasantly startled as the spears of lightning and crashes of thunder exploded around the glassy perch. Another highlight of a dome seat came as the train moved through the automated car washes in Denver and Portola, California (maintaining clean windows for maximum view was important on the CZ).

The California Zephyr began operation on March 20, 1949, and was advertised as "The Most Beautiful Train in the World." It was successful on all accounts, doing capacity business until the mid-1960s—it was often sold out several months in advance—but traffic slowly eroded until the losses were no longer acceptable. By 1969, this "silver queen" was in deep trouble. Six full train sets were required to maintain the daily schedule, and the train was losing $2 million annually.

The Western Pacific gave up the struggle to survive in March 1970, claiming the losses were too great, even as the government had begun planning the takeover of U.S. passenger trains. When Amtrak assumed passenger service on May 1, 1971, the maverick Denver & Rio Grande (along with several other roads) elected to go its own way by maintaining

its leg of the CZ route between Denver and Salt Lake City, renaming the train the Rio Grande Zephyr and operating it for another decade. Finally recognizing the futility of going it alone, the D&RG relented, shutting down independent operation of its Zephyr on April 24, 1983.

Consolidation of routes under Amtrak had provided an extension of the Zephyr legend, but under another name. The transcontinental route, via Union Pacific to Salt Lake City and Southern Pacific for the final leg, hosted an Amtrak train called San Francisco Zephyr. Once the Rio Grande Zephyr was canceled, Amtrak was free to reroute its train back through Denver, and July 16, 1984, saw the inauguration of the third variation of the Silver Queen (as it had officially come to be known)—the California Zephyr. In the Amtrak years, the fluted Budd cars have been replaced by the new generation Pullman-Standard Super-Liners, but a traveler can still marvel at the stunning scenery from a high-level, glass-enclosed perch for a fifty-hour ride through the historic West.

GREAT NORTHERN EMPIRE BUILDER

The Pacific Northwest was settled quite late in the nineteenth century, and its early economy depended almost entirely upon shipments by sea, with connections to the East Coast via stormy Cape Horn. The completion of the Great Northern Railroad to Seattle provided much faster land transportation to the East and brought hope for a commercial future, but the financial panic of 1893 delayed development.

The situation changed dramatically when the steamer Portland docked in Seattle's Elliott Bay on July 17, 1897, with seventy ordinary men on board whose luggage contained collectively over $1 million in gold. The Klondike gold rush was on, and the region began to boom, with Seattle as the jumping-off point for thousands of men eager to

The twin air pumps were mounted on the nose of the Great Northern's Baldwin-built 4-8-4 Northern No. 2580 to maintain sufficient side clearances. This locomotive was only four years old in this photograph, which shows the Empire Builder stopping at Minot, North Dakota, on September 28, 1933.

Top: The Empire Builder begins its transcontinental journey from Seattle with a 32-mile (52km) jaunt along the beautiful shores of Puget Sound. The matching consist of this April 1973 train is typical of excursion service, whereas in the early years of Amtrak, most trains were characterized by mixed sets of cars from the contributing railroads. Above: A highlight of the trip across the width of the nation would be a high-level ride under the glass of the "Great Dome" Glacier View car.

✦ ✦ ✦

find fortune. Those who chose to forgo the rigors of the climb over Chilcoot Pass could earn their fortunes by supplying or transporting those who were brave (or foolish) enough to try. The city's population doubled over the next four years, riding on the golden wave of boom-town prosperity; Seattle was on its way to becoming a city of importance.

Ultimately, two more rail routes stretched across the country from the Northwest to Chicago, carrying the products of forests, fields, and the sea to eastern markets. Competition for passengers to the Northwest was as fierce as in any market, with the Milwaukee Road's Olympian Hiawatha, the Northern Pacific's North Coast Limited (which split off a Portland section in Pasco, Washington), and the Great Northern's Empire Builder all connecting Chicago with Seattle, although operating on different routes. Each offered deluxe service and the best equipment that their owners could buy, so the routes were popular and ridership was heavy.

It was most appropriate that the Great Northern of James J. Hill, who was known as The Empire Builder during his life, would name its crack train for the man who forced its rails through the West. The Empire Builder came into being in 1929 as a steam-powered heavyweight train. In addition to the business traveler, or the isolated Dakota farmer visiting family, the train attracted vacationers eager to view gorgeous scenery, some of whom were bound for Glacier National Park. The Great Northern also offered a particularly distinctive service—an elegant English-style afternoon tea that became a treasured ritual for many travelers.

The Empire Builder really came into its own in 1947 as a streamliner, the first long-haul train to be completely reequipped during the postwar boom in building passenger trains. The Burlington, which handled the train from Chicago to Minneapolis–Saint Paul, joined with the Great Northern to build five complete Pullman-Standard train sets at a cost of over $7 million. Four years later, the train received another head-to-tail reequipping (for $12 million), and the older cars were given to the Western Star. The twenty-two new dome cars, including six full-length Great Domes, that arrived in 1955 set the CB&Q and GN back another $6 million.

Light meals and drinks were provided to the Empire Builder's coach patrons from this compact coffee shop/snack bar, located under the short domes.

✦ ✦ ✦

The GN streamliner was noted for a number of distinctions: the first duplex roomette service; the first ice-water on tap in the sleepers; and the first wardrobes in the bedrooms. The partners passed on the fluted stainless steel exteriors that had been a signature of the Burlington for many years, opting instead to finish the train in a striking dark-green-with-bright-orange scheme that was trimmed in yellow and silver and still ranks among the most handsome of exterior train designs.

The interiors reflected the culture of the northwest Indian tribes, featuring Winold Reiss murals and reproductions of paintings by western artist Charlie Russell. The 1951 train included the budget-oriented Ranch Car, a coffee shop that offered over-the-counter food service during daylight hours. Soups, sandwiches, pork chops, and pie were provided in an environment reminiscent of a log cabin, complete with rough wood and rustic furniture. The chairs were leather covered and marked with the "G-Bar-N" brand (actually registered with the Montana Livestock Association).

Travelers desiring the formality of the dining car were treated to true first-class service, with custom silver flatware, elegant china, and white linens. The china was particularly handsome, with designs of Glacier Park scenes and flora glazed in natural colors.

An atypical feature of the Empire Builder was the inclusion of two types of dome cars. The traditional short center-dome cars were available for the coach riders, while the impressive full-length Great Dome was placed adjacent to the diner and was available to first-class passengers only. There was room for seventy-four passengers upstairs on upholstered seating angled toward the glazing for improved viewing. The lower-level lounge and bar had seating for thirty-five, with writing tables, magazines, and a dumbwaiter to hoist drinks to the upper level. In later years, as amenities were reduced, the lower lounge was opened to coach passengers also.

Like most of the streamliners of the golden age, the Empire Builder suffered from ever escalating costs at the same time (the 1960s) that passenger loads were declining (although the parallel North Coast Limited actually increased ridership during most of the decade). When the train was still in its prime, in the mid-1950s, it ran as long as fifteen cars but carried only 323 passengers at full load. To provide the expected services required a huge staff: two coach porters; two stewards, five chefs, and six waiters in the diner; a Pullman conductor and six porters for the sleepers; a uniformed passenger-department representative, who handled the public-address system announcements for scenic and operational information; and a conductor, brakeman, and locomotive crew for each operating district.

A staff of that size meant that operating costs, much less capital costs, became ever harder to recoup. Even on the Great Northern, quality began to slide as the railroad worked to reduce losses by trimming service. As service suffered, passengers had even more reasons to take alternate forms of transportation, compounding the difficulties of the three railroads competing for the dwindling traffic.

In one of the largest North American rail mergers, the Chicago Burlington & Quincy, Northern Pacific, Spokane Portland & Seattle, and Great Northern joined in a huge rail network called the Burlington Northern in 1970. While the basis for the merger was the freight business, there was a possibility of combining passenger services also; the 1971 creation of Amtrak transferred passenger-train ownership from the original roads to the new organization, however, and the great trains of the Northwest began to fade away as the new agency trimmed the number of trains.

Over the years, the Empire Builder, North Coast Limited, and Olympian Hiawatha were combined and deleted in various combinations, until now only the Empire Builder remains on the schedule. The Amtrak Superliner high-level cars that evolved from the old Great

Northern and Milwaukee Road full-length domes of the 1950s make the 2,209-mile (3,555km) trip in approximately forty-four hours, and still stop at Glacier National Park. A Portland section continues to split off, but now at Spokane, rather than Pasco.

The leisurely schedule means that most passengers could be classified as pleasure travelers, but the train remains an important link to the rest of the country for residents of such remote places as Rugby, North Dakota; Glasgow, Montana; or Sand Point, Idaho. The Empire Builder's route through some of the most scenic and remote parts of the United States encourages high ridership levels, and the train is one of Amtrak's most popular.

THE MILWAUKEE ROAD'S HIAWATHAS

Competition for passengers was intense on the heavily traveled Chicago Minneapolis–St. Paul route. The Chicago, Burlington & Quincy (Burlington Route), Chicago and Northwestern, and the Chicago, Milwaukee, St. Paul & Pacific (Milwaukee Road) all provided service, and all three railroads quickly jumped into the premier streamlined passenger-train business. While the Burlington's diesel-powered stainless steel Twin Zephyr and the C&NW's streamlined, steam-powered, bright-yellow 400 were notable successes, the Milwaukee Road's legendary Hiawatha, named for the silver-tongued Mohawk orator, captured the imagination of the traveling public.

The Hiawatha debuted on May 29, 1935, powered by Alco-built 4-4-2s, the first constructed in North America since 1914 and the first new steam locomotives designed with streamlining. Assigned class A and numbered 1 through 4, these strikingly handsome Atlantics were dressed in maroon, orange, and gray bathtub shrouds that were trimmed in black and had stainless steel wings on their noses. Heavy patronage required replacement of the original seven-car consists in only sixteen months, but the 4-4-2 speedsters proved to be underpowered on the new nine-car trains.

Passenger loads increased steadily, and net income had grown to $2.63 per mile (1.6km), an enviable profit during the waning years of the depression. In February 1938, the Milwaukee Road announced the second reequipping in just three years, and only a single year after the last. Thirty-five cars built in the railroad's own shops and a new locomotive, the Alco-built F-7 class 4-6-4 Hudson (known as Baltics on the CMStP&P), were to be ready for the inauguration of the 1939 trains, with the schedule increased to a Morning and Evening Hiawatha in each direction. It was this streamlined train, with art deco–styled ribbed passenger cars and a finned "beaver-tail" observation car, that became the very image of the Milwaukee Road.

Above: Otto Kuhler's streamlined Hudsons chewed up the miles between Chicago and Milwaukee at speeds exceeding 100 mph (160kph), with the Hiawatha's passengers trailing comfortably in their luxurious coaches. Below: The Beaver Tail observation car contributed to Kuhler's reputation for "Buck Rogers"–inspired designs, but he maintained that the fins were sun shades.

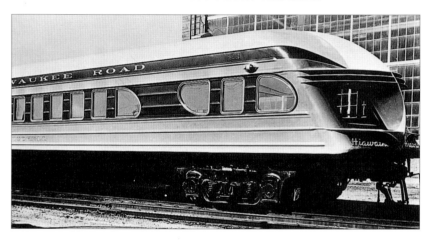

Noted industrial designer Otto Kuhler was given responsibility for the overall appearance of the train, working within the parameters established by the American Locomotive Works and Karl Nystrom, the railroad's chief mechanical officer. Although rival Burlington's Zephyr fleet was diesel-powered from the beginning and the new 1939 C&NW streamlined 400s were to be as well, the Milwaukee Road rejected diesels in favor of new steamers.

These locomotives were truly stunning, with a visual impact equal to Dreyfuss' Hudsons on the New York Central's Twentieth Century Limited or the Southern Pacific's Daylight GS-class 4-8-4s from Lima. Alco delivered six F-7s, numbered 100–105, in late 1938. They weighed 415,000 pounds (188,244kg) each, carried a boiler pressurized at 300 psi, and produced a tractive effort of 50,300 pounds (22,816kg). The 84-inch (2.1m) Boxpok drivers made it possible for the nine-car Hiawathas to run in excess of 100 mph (161kph) where conditions warranted, and the F-7 was capable of quick acceleration and high speeds even with the extra cars needed to accommodate holiday traffic.

While many early attempts at streamlining steam locomotives shrouded the running gear, Kuhler wisely exposed the elegant drivers and polished valve mechanism that represent the visible manifestation of the locomotive's soul. This allowed for easy maintenance, too, which gave it a distinct advantage over streamlined designs that had failed to take this practical issue into account. He also retained the striking paint scheme, although the "sprinting-Indian" emblem was eliminated from the tenders. A series of seven horizontal ribs was applied to the tender instead, in a pattern matching those applied to the passenger cars.

These cars continued Kuhler's theme of "parallelism," the ribs augmented with a maroon window band and letter board, which were applied to the orange sides. The roofs were gray and the smooth-riding stabilized trucks, designed by Nystrom, were a dark rust-brown. The same rust-brown color was applied to a steel box that enclosed the under-car appliances, both improving the car's appearance and protecting the under-car air-conditioning systems, water tanks, and brake equipment from the ravages of weather and loose ballast kicked up by the 100 mph (161kph) speeds. Full-width diaphragms were applied to cars and tender.

The Milwaukee Road took advantage of the rich Indian legend and tradition of the upper Midwest in the design of all the Hiawathas. Cars, names were usually drawn from the Indian culture or local geography for other versions of the Hiawatha, although the 1939 parlor and observation cars were departures from that theme, having been named for people important to the history of the Milwaukee Road. Yet other cars were more traditionally identified, with numbers.

The Railway Post Office (RPO) and baggage-express cars were not considered part of the "official" consist, but appropriately styled cars could often be found carrying high-priority mail and express deliveries. RPOs 2150 and 2151 as well as baggage-express cars 1305 and 1306 were part of the 1938 equipment order and normally served on the Morning Hiawatha, which usually carried more of this material than the Afternoon Hi.

While the demands of World War II put thousands of women to work on the United States' railroads, it would be another generation before they would sit in the cab of a locomotive. Here, Theresa Goll and Betty Clark participate in the dedication of the new Fairbanks-Morse diesels destined for service hauling the Hiawathas.

The 1935 Hiawatha included a combination diner-lounge, but the popularity of the train's food service led to a dedicated diner on the 1937 train. The lounge was combined with an express compartment and called the Tip Top Tap. The 1939 train maintained that arrangement with four cars numbered 153–156. A 29-foot (8.8m) baggage section occupied the front of the 79-foot (24m) car, with the remainder devoted to a taproom, cocktail lounge, and bar. The booth dividers were walnut with Indian-theme bas-reliefs, and the walls were painted coral in contrast to the cream-colored seating. Round portholes admitted light into the taproom and allowed patrons to view the passing scenery, but the rest of the car was windowless. An illuminated sign indicated the upcoming stop for the convenience of the imbibing passengers.

Sixteen reclining-seat coaches, numbered 437–452, were distinguished by the clusters of two and three windows, with the outer corners of each group having rounded corners that were unique to the 1939 Hiawatha. This feature made the cars easy to spot when they were demoted to the passenger-car pool in later years. Each car contained twenty-eight pairs of reclining seats, with nine more in the men's lavatory and four in the women's lavatory (smoking being more of a male-specific habit in the prewar days). The lounge chairs were green, and were made of leather in the men's rooms and mohair in the women's rooms. As was typical in all of the new equipment, there was a generous use of wood veneer and trim. The coach walls were of bleached maple with walnut window frames. The bulkheads and overhead luggage racks were similarly treated. Seats were upholstered in mohair—either green or rust, but not mixed within a coach. Window shades were also green or rust, but opposite the seat colors, and the ceilings were treated with aluminum leaf.

Each of the four dining cars, numbered 109–112, had a dozen four-place tables with individual chairs. The four tables closest to the kitchen were separated from the others by Indian-motif curtains and treated as a separate café, especially during lightly patronized hours. The café ceilings and chairs were green, while the open seating was rust and the ceiling yellow. Unlike the coaches, which had linoleum floors, the diners were carpeted in a predominantly red floral pattern, which contrasted with the cream-colored tables and bleached maple walls.

The Hiawatha's parlor cars were unique. As with other railroads, the Milwaukee Road recognized the growing market in premium-priced luxury service. Assuming 50 percent passenger demand for first-class, the 1939 Hiawatha order included six parlor cars and four parlor-observation cars. Each version included rotating reclining seats, with twenty-eight such seats in the parlor car (and a private drawing room), twenty-four in the parlor-observation car, and seventeen additional lounge chairs in the solarium-observation section.

The exterior of the parlor cars was quite similar to that of the coaches, but the strong design of the parlor-observations provided a striking exclamation point to the end of the Hiawatha. Dubbed "beaver tails" because of the interlocking horizontal and vertical fins (sun visors, according to the Milwaukee mechanical department), these art deco beauties were one of the triumphs of Otto Kuhler's career. A three-unit sofa faced the rear windows, providing a prime view of the scenery receding at 100 mph (161kph).

The Hiawathas were augmented with another equipment order in 1942, but not completely reequipped, and the fleet-footed trains labored through the war years. Postwar reequipping came in 1948 with diesel locomotives and matching passenger cars. The new trains were products of industrial standardization, and the elegance of the earlier art deco individuality was lost as the Kuhler-styled equipment was dispersed among the Milwaukee's passenger fleet.

By the 1960s, much of this equipment was in local service. Even the orange-maroon-gray paint scheme had disappeared under the yellow-gray-red that was adopted following the 1955 shift of the Union Pacific's Overland Route streamliners to the Chicago–Omaha main line of the Milwaukee Road. The taproom cars had been converted to express only, and even the elegant beaver tails had been reduced to mail-storage use.

The reputation of the original Hiawatha became an asset that the Milwaukee Road couldn't ignore, and the name was applied to other trains, such as the Midwest Hiawatha (Chicago–Omaha–Sioux Falls), Chippewa Hiawatha (Chicago–Ontonagon, Michigan), and the Olympian Hiawatha (Chicago–Seattle).

The CMStP&P continued on its unique path through the streamliner era, investing in full-length Super Domes, the Sky Top observation cars designed by Brooks Stevens, and the brawny chrome-bedecked Fairbanks-Morse locomotives styled by Raymond Loewy. Electrification through the Cascade Mountains added another unique element to the long-distance trains, although the system was removed as the Milwaukee Road slowly withered, and finally succumbed to the various problems of North American railroads in the late twentieth century.

Otto Kuhler (1894-1976)

◆ ◆ ◆

While Otto Kuhler gained fame as a stylist of locomotives and trains, he originally came to the attention of the railroad industry through his industrial art. Born in Remscheid, Germany, in the heart of the Ruhr Valley, Kuhler emigrated to the United States in 1923 and settled in Pittsburgh, which provided an industrial setting familiar to him. Kuhler's reputation was established thanks to his well-received watercolors and etchings of industrial subjects.

He moved to New York City and became involved in the 1930s streamlining movement, designing several steam locomotives. His work frequently showcased what was then a futuristic, "Buck Rogers" quality, featuring rocket fins and chrome detailing. In addition to the Milwaukee Road's Hiawatha, Kuhler styling was applied to several Lehigh Valley Pacifics, as well as an entire passenger train, the John Wilkes. Following his work on shrouding the 1935 Royal Blue's locomotive (President Monroe) for the Baltimore & Ohio, he streamlined the Tennessean for the Southern.

Streamlining the straightforward "form follows function" steam locomotive was always controversial to the purist, but the practice was popular during the 1930s nonetheless. At any rate, Kuhler often did his best work when a tight budget required restraint. The 1936 renovation of the New York Ontario & Western's Mountaineer was very reminiscent of traditional British styling—restrained smoothing of lines and shielding of appliances, all under an elegant paint scheme. Limited by NYO&W's $10,000 budget, Kuhler applied a smooth "bib" above the pilot and a skirt along the running boards. The entire train was painted in maroon enamel with multiple orange stripes along the sides.

Otto Kuhler became a consultant to the American Locomotive Works (Alco) and contributed to the styling of numerous locomotives, including the DL-109 diesel of 1940, his final assignment. He retired to New Mexico, where he continued to paint until his death.

The legendary Hiawatha name still remains under Amtrak: fourteen trains operate each day (in 1993) between Chicago and Milwaukee as Hiawatha Service.

CHAPTER SIX

RAILS ALONG THE WEST COAST OF THE UNITED STATES

When the Franciscan fathers traveled north out of Mexico at the end of the eighteenth century, they established a chain of twenty-one missions spaced a day's travel apart. The route connecting them was well traveled and became known as El Camino Real, "the Royal Road." These legendary California missions—San Diego, San Gabriel, San Fernando, Santa Barbara, San Luis Obispo, Soledad, Monterey, San Jose, San Francisco—became centers of commerce and religion, growing into towns and even into cities over the years.

The Mexican War of 1846 transferred control of California to the United States, but it was the discovery of gold at Sutter's Fort two years later that enhanced the importance of the West Coast, and California became a state in 1850. The rough road system used by wagons and stage coaches proved inadequate for the rapidly growing economy, and a railroad was begun along the route blazed by the padres. The San Francisco & San Jose Railroad (SF&SJ) started a north–south route in 1864, after the Central Pacific began to build east from Sacramento in 1863.

THE DAYLIGHTS, LARKS, SHASTA LIMITED

The owners of the SF&SJ incorporated the Southern Pacific Railroad in 1865. Their goal was to build south from San Jose through the San Joaquin Valley to a connection with the Atlantic & Pacific–Santa Fe, which was building west from the Missouri River along a southerly route. The

✦ ✦ ✦

The pride of the Southern Pacific, the Coast Daylight (hauled by No. 4449) cruises effortlessly near San Luis Obispo, California. In the 1950s, there were Daylights on both the coast and valley lines of the SP; there was also the Shasta Daylight. Running between San Francisco and Portland, the Shasta Daylight was diesel-powered from the beginning; today, restored No. 4449 covers this route in occasional excursion service.

Double-headed steam power (Pacific-type No. 2451) leads train 76—the Lark—in this 1940 view. The Lark was an overnight train that ran between San Francisco and Los Angeles.

✦ ✦ ✦

Central Pacific's "Big Four"—Collis P. Huntington, Leland Stanford, Charles Crocker, and Mark Hopkins—acquired the Southern Pacific and pushed the rails to Los Angeles in 1876. The two railroads ultimately merged under the name Southern Pacific.

A second line climbed over the Coast Range at the south end of the Salinas Valley to San Luis Obispo, and from there 113 miles (182km) of track followed the rugged Pacific coast, bridging many deep ravines before reaching Santa Barbara in 1901. Heavy tunneling through the Santa Susana Mountains brought the Coast Line over an improved route to Los Angeles in 1904.

The Coast Line Limited began as a daytime coach train running from Los Angeles to San Francisco (in fourteen hours and forty-five minutes) in 1901, and the Sunset Limited was moved to that line from the San Joaquin Valley route at the same time. A luxury all–parlor car train, the Shoreline Limited, entered Los Angeles–San Francisco service in 1906. A companion overnight sleeping-car train, the Lark (originally known as the Shoreline Lark), was inaugurated in 1910, and was carrying a through-sleeper to Seattle (via the Shasta Limited) by 1915.

The Daylight Limited started out as a Friday–Saturday, summer-season-only train in 1922, hauling coaches and a dining car over the scenic 483-mile (772km) Coast Line route in thirteen hours. It was the fastest train on the Southern Pacific and made no station stops between Los Angeles and San Francisco (although protests from communities along the way eventually convinced the SP to add some station stops). The 1923 season saw Sunday service added, followed a few weeks later by a Thursday train, and on July 12 the Daylight became a daily, year-round train.

The popularity of the daily train entitled it to some unusual equipment, including two observation cars converted in the Sacramento shops with enlarged rear platforms that extended deeply into the car and seated thirty-two passengers. "All-Day Lunch" cars served sandwiches and light refreshments from a counter at one end of a coach beginning in 1924, parlor cars were added in 1928, and new SP-designed, Pullman-built observation cars were delivered in 1930. The observations arrived in a pearl-gray Pyroxilin lacquer paint scheme with dark gray window sash, and the rest of the train traded its dark olive paint in order to match this scheme (which lasted for only a single season). By early 1936, the Daylights had been renumbered to 98 and 99 and the running time cut to eleven hours.

Above left: The heavyweight cars earned their description honestly. Ornate finishes on the interior walls in marble and carved wood added weight to the already heavy riveted steel construction. Above right: The Pullman Company introduced the innovative "roomette" to the passenger rail market around the time of World War II in what amounted to a radical departure from seventy years of tradition. Travelers loved the privacy provided by these roomettes. This one (which the porter has already made up) was assigned to SP's Lark.

The overnight Lark had also attained premier status by the 1920s and had become a favorite of film stars as well as business travelers. The train was assigned the best Pullman cars and in 1929 received the first single-bedroom cars in the West. The following year, two new sunroom Pullmans and elegant new lounge cars painted in a heat-reflecting aluminum were added. The interiors included full club facilities: valet, barber, showers, a soda fountain (this was during Prohibition), and large viewing windows.

As with many other railroads struggling with the financial difficulties of the Great Depression, the Southern Pacific decided to reequip its premier trains in the middle of the decade at a cost of $2 million, hoping to regain passengers lost to a growing intercity bus system. The new trains, to be delivered in 1937, were to be the fastest and most colorful in the West and reflected the penchant for streamlining so common to the era.

Sleek new GS class 4-8-4s with enough power to reach 90 mph (145kph) were ordered from the Lima Locomotive Works at a cost of $136,000 each. They were equipped with a "skyline casing," bullet nose, and running board skirting for smoother lines, and were painted to match the consist. Since the locomotives would run through from San Francisco to Los Angeles, only two were needed for the service, but four more were ordered so that helpers needed for the steep Cuesta Grade and back-up power would always match the new streamliner.

Pullman built the fully air-conditioned, twelve-car train sets, using high-strength Cor-Ten steel for a 29 percent weight savings, and sheathed them with corrugated stainless steel painted in a brilliant red, orange, and black scheme. The consist—a chair-baggage car, a single full-chair car, three two-car articulated chair-car units, a tavern–coffee shop car, diner, parlor car, and parlor-observation—was 978 feet (298m) long, and carried 465 passengers and a crew of forty-five.

Credit for the paint scheme and logo goes to the Southern Pacific's Charles Eggelston, who spent months trying countless combinations before SP president Angus McDonald chose the red-orange-black scheme, which seemed to him to reflect California. The chair-baggage No. 300 was painted to test the scheme before final approval. The logo he chose was a sun-like ball with

Top: The famed Daylight, which was often referred to in its day as "the most beautiful train in the world," was powered by handsome Alco-built GS-class 4-8-4s. Above: During World War II, the red-and-orange paint was replaced by black; this engine has also been fitted with a "blackout" headlight visor, which obscured the headlight beam from potential enemy aircraft.

✦ ✦ ✦

attached wing and the word "Daylight" written in script.

There was no scrimping on the car's interiors: seating, heating, lighting, kitchen, and dining equipment all received careful scrutiny, and close attention was paid to passenger comfort. The seating was an adaptation of the Heywood-Wakefield reclining contour seating that had been designed for airplanes, and a moving neon lighting system spotted in a Chicago nightspot was adapted for the tavern car's bar.

Changes had also been made to the right-of-way, with nearly 80 miles (129km) of new 112- and 131-pound (per yard) rail installed, numerous curves realigned, and a great deal of fine tuning done so as to enable the Daylight's schedule to be cut to nine hours and forty-five minutes and the Lark's schedule to twelve hours flat.

Special yellow round speed boards were erected under the standard oval boards in locations where the new streamliners were allowed higher speeds.

The new locomotives arrived in Los Angeles in late January 1937, and the first new train left the Pullman plant on February 22. Several test runs were made in early March, and railroad workers stood and watched in amazement as the brilliant train passed, the engineer saluting back with the deep-throated air horn. After two 158-mile (253km) runs over the Santa Susanas, a test run to San Francisco was made to attempt the 9½-hour schedule, but the train arrived an hour-and-a-half late despite the fact that there were no reported problems. The crews were uneasy with the new locomotives and were not yet used to the higher speeds. The second test was flawless (and on time), and the train was pronounced ready for service.

On March 21, 1937, the trains were taken to their respective terminals and readied for the first revenue run. NBC broadcast the 7:00 A.M. ceremonies live to the nation on the radio, and boarding passengers received a souvenir booklet that described the equipment and contained a full-color center spread. At 8:15 A.M., the trains were christened, the locomotives began to stretch out their fully loaded consists (No. 4411 in Los Angeles and No. 4413 in San Francisco), and the maiden voyages began, the bright colors of red and orange in sharp contrast to the passing green hills.

The Daylight ran at capacity for the month of March, carrying 20,226 passengers. April saw that number dwindle to 18,674; in May the number was up to 23,999; and 25,931 passengers rode in June. The grand total of 88,830 was a world record for passengers carried on a single-section long-distance train over a period of four months. This success far exceeded the delighted Southern Pacific's expectations, justifying the expense and effort expended on "the most beautiful train in the world."

The capacity loads continued, putting a strain on the tavern-coffee shop cars, as passengers seemed determined to linger there for much of the trip. Pullman received an immediate order for two full coffee shops and two full tavern cars; the combination cars were transferred to other trains.

On August 4, Miss Patricia Robeson became the one hundred thousandth passenger on the Daylight and received a handsome rawhide bag. Celebrations were held at the close of the first year of operation—the Daylight had carried 253,573 passengers, who collectively had paid over $1.5 million in fares.

Shortly thereafter, fourteen new GS-3 locomotives, faster and more efficient as a result of small design changes, arrived to help with the loads. The Southern Pacific had been running second sections with conventional equipment, much to the consternation of passengers expecting much more. Wanting to maximize passenger capacity but fearful of overloading (and slowing) the locomotives, the SP nonetheless switched from a twelve-car train to a fourteen-car train to keep its customers satisfied. Several cars were transferred from subsidiary Texas & New Orleans' underutilized Sunbeam, which featured similar cars with the same paint scheme and was sometimes called the Texas Daylight. Two more fourteen-car trains were ordered from Pullman, and two additional chair cars were pulled from pool service for repainting, bringing the existing consists up to fifteen cars each.

But continued heavy loading still required second and even third sections, setting new passenger-hauling records in 1938 and 1939. In twenty-one months of service, the trains had carried 470,840 passengers, for an average of 370 per run. During the World's Fair in July 1939, patronage peaked with a total of forty-six thousand people from all of the sections. The Southern Pacific officials were getting desperate, frantically trying to provide adequate service while pushing Pullman for the new equipment.

On January 1, 1940, the Brotherhood of Railway Clerks won the theme prize in the Rose Bowl Parade with a 66-foot (20m) Daylight locomotive built entirely of flowers, and the next day the float's brand-new steam-powered brethren were at their respective terminals. After two days of operations as second sections, the new Pullman trains replaced the older equipment (on January 5), enabling the well-used cars to be shopped for refit-

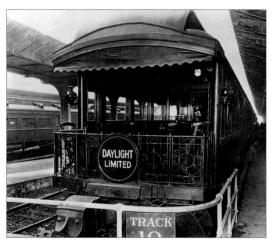

The Southern Pacific was not satisfied with the classic open-rear platform, so the railroad built two observation cars with deep exterior recesses with more passenger capacity and better protection for the adventurers who wished to ride outside. One of these observation-lounge cars is shown here bringing up the rear of the Daylight Limited at the San Francisco depot circa 1923.

ting. On March 30, the former trains returned as numbers 96 and 97, known as the Noon Daylight, and second sections were retired.

Later that year, fifty-one additional cars were ordered, twenty-two to reequip numbers 98 and 99 and the rest for the Lark, Noon, and San Joaquin Daylights, along with twenty new Golden State locomotives that were designated GS-4. These cars would match the 1939 order except for new propane kitchens, ice-activated air-conditioning, and improved truck design. The reequipped Lark was painted in a new two-tone gray color scheme. Total cost was $7 million, and another $8 million was allocated to new freight equipment.

Anticipating U.S. involvement in the war, the Southern Pacific prepared for the expected traffic loads. The railroad ordered ten more GS-4s along with a number of 4-8-8-2 freight locomotives, and began to upgrade the heavyweight fleet. When the new cars began arriving in June 1941, the era of complete trains delivered as a cohesive package (including radio and press promotion) was past, and the new cars trickled in via the Union Pacific on the City of San Francisco. The Daylight cars operated for a while on that train, filling in for the equipment on the City of San Francisco that had been damaged when snowbound the previous winter (see Chapter Five).

With the Pearl Harbor attack on December 7, the SP responded to government edicts pertaining to nonessential services by mothballing thirty-one passenger trains, including the Noon Daylight. The straight parlor and tavern cars were deemed nonessential and therefore pulled from the morning Daylight, the motive-power pool was reduced to the minimum, and six chair cars were added, bringing the consist to twenty cars. The Daylight operated at this record length for the duration of the war.

In April 1946, the tavern and parlor service returned to the peacetime train, and the Southern Pacific announced a $2 billion recovery program, which included refurbishing the Daylight's motive power and equipment. By 1947, the ten-year-old Daylight had settled down to eighteen cars; the last two parlor-observations were transferred to a new train, the Shasta Daylight; the first main-line freight diesel had come to the SP; and a new diesel-powered passenger train, the Golden State, had been introduced. Time was running out for steam on the Southern Pacific.

By the end of 1952, passenger traffic was shifting to the airlines, which were scheduling ever-increasing numbers of flights between San Francisco and Los Angeles, and the SP could see the bleak future. The last equipment purchase for the Daylight was in 1953, an order to Pullman for six chair cars. The railroad also looked into many dome-car designs before commissioning its own.

Existing cars were rebuilt with low three-quarter-length domes that cleared all overhead obstructions on the route, the unique domes projecting only 21 inches (53.5cm) above the roof line.

On January 7, 1955, after eighteen years of service, the last GS-powered powered Daylights left their stations, and steam was a thing of the past on the elegant streamliner. Several of the deep-throated air horns were removed and installed on the new Alco diesels, preserving the warning sound that local residents had grown used to.

The SP was suffering from the same passenger losses faced by other railroads, and the Daylight often dipped to eleven cars during 1956–1957, the shortest trains since it became a streamliner. But on March 21, 1957, the Daylight celebrated its twentieth birthday, having hauled more than eight million passengers, and those riding that day were treated to cake by "the friendly SP."

The losses suffered by the railroad reached a staggering $60 million by 1958, and the SP considered alternatives to reduce costs. The expensive multicolor paint schemes on the passenger cars and diesels were high on the list of things to go. Diesels began emerging from the shops in the infamous "bloody nose" scheme—dark gray with a red nose that wrapped around the sides in a winged configuration. Passenger-car color schemes featured red letter boards and bare stainless steel. A rebuilding program was launched to eliminate the need for new purchases.

The great trains of the Coast Line were withering away. The Daylight was down to nine cars in 1959, the triple-unit diner was replaced by a single-unit car, and the Lark was reduced to seven Pullmans. After 1960, even the diner was replaced, by an Automatic Buffet (vending machines), for the lightly traveled winter months.

By 1966, passenger traffic on the Coast Line had declined from 4.5 million in 1952 to fewer than one million (excluding commuter runs), but the deficit had been trimmed to $16 million. The Lark was down to six passenger cars and two head-end cars, averaging ninety-five passengers per night. The SP was denied permission to discontinue the dying train following a bitter dispute with the California Public Utilities Commission (P.U.C.), but the cancellation of the mail contract in 1967 ended the argument. Despite accusations that the SP had intentionally driven away passengers by telling customers that the train was sold out for three weeks—and shipping luggage by truck, which got it there three days late—the Lark was gone on April 7, 1968. Mail would be shipped by piggyback freight or flown. Passengers had their choice of eighty flights per day each way, or could drive on Interstate 5.

As passenger traffic waned and equipment aged, even a great train such as Southern Pacific's Lark lost most of its glamor. The streamliner image once personified by EMD Fs and Alco PAs had already been supplanted by the straightforward look of an SDP45 (with an old B Unit) as the Lark passed through Chatsworth, California, for the final time in 1968.

◆ ◆ ◆

The last run was a real production, with booklets distributed that bid farewell to the Lark and a sixteen-car train ran in each direction. Rail fans sang "Auld Lang Syne" and partied into the night as the Coast Line was reduced to a single train each day—called the Coast Daylight—which faced even further cutbacks.

Sunset Limited cars began to run through to San Francisco from New Orleans to save on maintenance costs, but the Sunset frequently arrived late in Los Angeles, delaying the connecting Daylight as well. The diner was eliminated in 1968, replaced with Coffee Shop–Automat cars, and the ten-hour trip dragged on in the well-worn coaches. The classic Alcos and EMD E Unit diesels were nearing the end also, so the SP invested in ten SDP-45s from EMD to power the remaining trains. By January 1969, the Daylight was down to six cars.

The problems on the Southern Pacific were little different from those on most other Class 1 railroads, although some of the other railroads tried harder to solve those problems. When Amtrak announced the plans for operating long-distance passenger trains, there were sixteen routes radiating from Chicago in the pared-down system, and the Coast Line had been discontinued. SP management was delighted because it felt that the passenger trains interfered with the money-making freights (which generated a much larger income at a fraction of the operating cost) traveling on the same trackage. But a public outcry caused a quick reversal, and the Amtrak era began in 1971 with a Seattle-to–Los Angeles Coast Starlight plying the rails that had once been traveled by the most beautiful trains in the world.

CHAPTER SEVEN

PASSENGER TRAINS OF CANADA

Canada's railway history grew past the industrial line stage when a 14-mile (25km) line connecting Laprairie, Quebec, and Saint-Jean-sur-Richelieu, was opened in 1836. These short, local service railroads predominated until the 1852 incorporation of the Grand Trunk, which grouped a number of smaller lines into a coherent system and allowed for additional construction. The Grand Trunk was primarily an east-west system concentrated along Canada's southeastern corner in Ontario and Quebec, connecting to the United States at Detroit on the west and at the Saint Lawrence River on the eastern seaboard. Since shipping was interrupted by ice deposits in the winter months, a line penetrated the United States into Maine, reaching the year-round harbor at Portland.

Growth of the industry was concentrated along this corridor for many years, expanding into the Maritime provinces while bypassing the vast western plains. This pattern was understandable since most of the Canadian population, industrial developments, and agricultural sites were (and still are) located within this area.

TRANS CANADA LIMITED, IMPERIAL LIMITED (DOMINION), SOO PACIFIC, MOUNTAINEER, CONTINENTAL LIMITED, CONFEDERATION, CANADIAN

The completion of the U.S. transcontinental railroad in 1869 challenged the Canadian government, raising concerns that the southern portions of the western Canadian territories might drift toward alliance with the United States through economic ties developed from transportation patterns. The isolated residents of British Columbia stubbornly demanded a rail connection to the east as a condition for joining the new Dominion of Canada, and the eastern-dominated government finally agreed in 1871.

◆ ◆ ◆

The Canadian Pacific No. 374 is garlanded both to celebrate the coronation of Queen Victoria and to commemorate its arrival; it was the first passenger train to have crossed the Canadian continent, on July 4, 1886.

Some of the heaviest construction occurred on the North Superior Shore, as the Canadian Pacific crews struggled to carve suitable pathways through terrain that alternated between hard granite and deep bogs. Pictured here is the west portal of Jackfish Tunnel.

The construction of a Canadian transcontinental railroad was scheduled to begin within two years and to be completed in ten. The funds to be used were a $25-million contribution made by the government combined with woefully inadequate privately raised financing. The struggle to push westward from the shores of the Kaministiqua River in the future location of Fort William, Ontario (through the hard granite and bottomless swamps of the North Superior Shore), and eastward from Port Moody, British Columbia (across the forbidding wilderness of the Canadian Rockies), progressed very slowly—

The Canadian Pacific 4-6-4 earned the class name Royal Hudson after it hauled the train of the royal family in a 1939 visit to Canada. No. 2860, pictured here, still operates in excursion service out of Vancouver.

far more slowly, in fact, than anyone had imagined. By 1885, the private backers of the nearly completed Canadian Pacific Limited (now known as CP Rail) were facing personal bankruptcy and futilely lobbying the government for more funding when fate intervened in the person of the infamous rebel Louis Riel.

Riel was a Métis (half-French, half-Indian) agitator who had led a failed rebellion in 1870, after the Hudson's Bay Company had transferred title of their western lands to the Canadian government. Having made a peace of sorts with the government, he then sat in Parliament,

Top: Canadian Pacific's Jubilee class 4-4-4s reflected the British styling influence. One of these locomotives reached a speed of 112 mph (180kph) in 1936, the fastest speed ever achieved under steam in Canada. Above left: The spectacular scenery of CP's route through the Rockies inspired the railroad to experiment with domes and observation-lounges early on. These heavyweight solarium cars "carried the markers" (that is, brought up the rear and sported lights) for the Trans-Canada Limited and the Soo Lines Mountaineer and contained showers and other appointments that were designed to accommodate female travelers. Above right: CP's influence spread to Europe: this Austrian "Canadian Pacific Pullman" was named America.

The Rocky Mountaineer

◆ ◆ ◆

The most spectacular rail travel in North America at this writing cannot be experienced behind the red, white, blue, and silver power of Amtrak, nor the blue and yellow of VIA. As has happened in Europe, private industry has moved into the rail travel business in Canada, tapping the market for luxurious rail cruising. The Rocky Mountaineer currently makes six round-trips every four weeks between May and October, operating from Vancouver through the spectacular Canadian Rockies to either Calgary or Jasper, in the province of Alberta.

Service began in 1990 under the Great Canadian Railtour Co., which purchased at auction a failed VIA operation, The Rocky Mountains By Daylight. The train uses two leased ex–Santa Fe B36-7 diesels from General Electric, seventeen renovated coaches from the tail end of the Canadian National's streamlined era, and a specially constructed dome car of a brand-new design. Rader Railcar built the dome, which has an open rear observation platform, kitchen, and dining area below the dome.

The train winds through the canyons of the Thompson and Fraser rivers to Kamloops, British Columbia, where the train is split into Calgary and Jasper sections. Passengers spend the night in hotels in Kamloops, and can leave the Jasper section in Banff if they wish. Superb food is featured in the diner, and first-class passengers can use the dome or enjoy the passing view from the open rear platform.

Designed to be enjoyed as a splendid (albeit expensive) vacation, the Rocky Mountaineer has tripled ridership since the first year and seems to be proving that passengers will still pay for superb pleasure travel that hearkens back to many fine train journeys from the golden age of the passenger train.

Like Amtrak, the Canadian National experimented with the Turbotrain, which was a return to the fixed-train-set origins of the streamliner. The original imported French units were built by ANF Frangeco; the later U.S.-built units were from Rohr Industries and United Aircraft. The experiment yielded mixed results. VIA inherited this UA unit, which went into corridor service between Montreal and Toronto.

◆ ◆ ◆

Craigellachie, 28 miles (45km) west of Revelstoke, British Columbia, and 2,529 miles (4,046km) from Montreal. The first regularly scheduled transcontinental train, the Pacific Express, was delayed until the following summer, when the legendary service that attracted passengers from around the world finally began.

Traffic congestion on the CP soon encouraged the construction of additional routes to the Pacific, so the Canadian Northern and Grand Trunk (through subsidiary line Grand Trunk Pacific) were also building west by the turn of the twentieth century, and both roads traveled through Yellowhead Pass, a much easier (although longer) route through the Rockies than CP's more southerly Kicking Horse Pass route. The Canadian Northern and Grand Trunk had reached Vancouver by 1915, but poor economic conditions caused the Canadian Northern to fail almost immediately, forcing formation of the government-owned Canadian National Railways. The Grand Trunk, Grand Trunk Pacific, and Intercolonial were absorbed by the Canadian National by 1923, creating the second true transcontinental system.

As Canada moved into the golden age of passenger trains, two mighty rail systems crossed the country, competing for passengers with the best service and equipment each could offer. As the Great Depression loomed on the horizon, the CP alone offered five crack transcontinental trains daily: the all-sleeper Montreal; Toronto–Vancouver Trans Canada Limited; the Montreal–Vancouver Imperial Limited (later succeeded by the Dominion); and the Soo Pacific and all-sleeper Mountaineer, both of which went from Chicago to Vancouver. These trains carried passengers comfortably across vast expanses of sparsely settled land. CN offered similar service on its own, more northerly route with the Continental Limited (its flagship train), the Confederation, and a few other trains.

The Canadian Pacific anticipated the dome-car craze of the 1950s sixty years earlier with a pair of coaches that were modified by the addition of rooftop cupolas to provide better views of the spectacular scenery of the Canadian Rockies. Both CP and CN provided open-air observation cars as well.

Following the difficulties of the Depression and the debilitating heavy loads that trains everywhere in North America had to carry during World War II, the Canadian railroads took separate paths in their rebuilding efforts. Canadian Pacific had more confidence in the future of passenger service and took an aggressive approach to equipment replacement, while the government-controlled Canadian National was slower to respond. CP

but soon after left in disgust. He organized a second uprising in spring 1885, forming a provisional government to represent the rights of the Métis people. The CP reacted to news of the uprising aggressively, offering its services to the Canadian government, which promptly dispatched troops from Ottawa. With boats and sleds carrying the army over uncompleted sections of the railway, the massive force was swiftly moved across northern Ontario and arrived in Winnipeg in only four days. The rebellion was subdued before developing much momentum and a grateful government released additional funds to the railway builders.

A simple stone cairn marks the spot where the final spike in the vast span of tracks was driven the following November, at a place christened

contracted with Budd for 173 new stainless steel passenger cars, including dome cars, to reequip the Dominion and to put together an entirely new train—the Canadian.

The new Dominion and the Canadian offered paired service daily from Montreal and Toronto in the east to Vancouver in the west. The Canadian covered the route in half a day less than the Dominion, which was assigned the bulk of the mail, along with secondary passenger traffic (both of which resulted in additional station stops). The Canadian became the premier train and a railroading legend, while the Dominion slowly languished, being reduced in service during the nonvacation seasons, and finally dying in 1965.

The new equipment created a sensation across Canada, at least partly because of a twenty-six-hour reduction in the westbound schedule (although conditions limited the eastbound cut to only 10½ hours). An extensive media campaign and a barnstorming trip across Canada and

the northern United States created much public interest in the new train. The April 1955 issue of *Vogue* magazine was entirely devoted to CP's Canadians, and the drama of the new train's route, and what the well-dressed traveler would want to wear for the journey.

From its inauguration on April 24, 1955, the spectacular scenery and first-class service made the Canadian the first choice of transcontinental pleasure travelers on both sides of the border, with many U.S. passengers forsaking the Empire Builder, Olympian Hiawatha, and North Coast Limited for the pleasures of the Canadian Pacific route (although it was common to take a U.S. train in the opposite direction). The Canadian boasted the longest dome-car journey in the world, 2,776 miles (4467km), and provided two of the glass-enclosed perches for passengers to admire the passing prairies, lakes, and mountains.

Near the front of the train was a dome car with first-floor economy meal service at one end, a bar-lounge and kitchen beneath the dome, and a

"The Newfie Bullet," Newfoundland Railway's Caribou

✦ ✦ ✦

One of the more charming vehicles of the golden age of passenger trains, the Newfie Bullet ambled across the Canadian island province of Newfoundland between the ferry landing at Port aux Basques and the capital and commercial center, St. John's.

The Newfoundland Railway was begun in 1884 as an 82-mile (131km)-long, 3-foot-6-inch (1.1m)-gauge line from St. John's to Harbour Grace. Originally conceived by Stanford Fleming (of the Canadian Pacific) and built by a U.S. syndicate, the railway line's last spike was driven by a young midshipman from HMS *Bacchante*, which was visiting the harbor at the time. This young sailor became His Majesty King George V. Unfortunately, the railway failed financially and reverted to its British financial backers.

In 1890, Robert Gillespie Reid, a Scot who began as a stonemason and became a multimillionaire bridge builder in the United States, contracted to complete an additional 262 miles (419km) of track to Notre Dame Bay and operate the railway. The work was to be completed in five years at a cost of $15,500 per mile, with a forfeiture bond of $250,000 to the colony of Newfoundland (not a province until 1949) if not finished on time. Two years later, despite extreme difficulties and being well behind schedule, Reid extracted a contract revision to extend the route 300 more miles (480km), terminating at Port aux Basques. The advent of World War I ended Reid's involvement with the project, however, and the colonial government took over operation.

The railroad—as well as the colony—suffered terribly during the Great Depression, but fortunately Newfoundland was the North American point closest to Europe; as a result, the U.S. and Canadian governments revitalized the economy with major base-building programs. The boom times saw construction of a major air base to handle high volumes of troop traffic, and freight for the Atlantic crossing doubled overnight.

When Newfoundland joined the Dominion of Canada as the tenth province in 1949, the Newfoundland Railway was absorbed by the Canadian National Railway (the final acquisition of the government-controlled system). At the time of the takeover, the railway rostered four-

teen steam locomotives and three diesels. There were no rail car ferries, requiring all cars to be unloaded to boats and reloaded onto the narrow-gauge cars until 1967, when the ferry *Port aux Basques* entered service. The CN also invested in fifty-three new diesel locomotives and fourteen hundred pieces of rolling stock between 1952 and 1960. The MV *William Carson*, the world's largest ice-breaking auto ferry, joined the fleet, carrying five hundred passengers and 120 cars from Sydney, Nova Scotia, to Port aux Basques in six hours.

Passenger service was typically limited to four mixed trains daily and Nos. 101–103, the Caribou, was the "crack train." Nicknamed The Newfie Bullet, the train operated from Port aux Basques to St. John's daily during the summer and three times per week during the other seasons. Speed was limited to 50 mph (80kph), but normally ran at 35–45 mph (56.5–72.5kph) and often slower and was scheduled to take as long as twenty-six hours to complete the 600-mile (960km) trip.

A typical train of 1966 had two diesel locomotives (GMD 1200hp specials) and ten to fourteen cars, including one or two boxcars, a steam generator car (seasonal), express car, diner (serving as a lounge), three or four coaches, a sleeper for the dining-car crew, and two or three sleepers for passengers. Stops might be made to add or drop freight cars along the way, as well as for intermediate stations.

The coaches and diners resembled CN's mainland modernized heavyweight equipment, but were shorter, narrower, and had lower ceilings. The same reclining seats were spaced closer, there was no air conditioning, and the lack of tight-lock couplers meant slack action was considerable. Curiously, the elegant tableware in the diner was emblazoned NR, even under CN management.

There were still four mixed trains on the schedule in 1974, but CN began operating bus service across the island, dubbing it Expedo Express. The Caribou did not survive the coming of VIA, but the new passenger train operator retained and expanded the bus service. The Newfoundland Railway remained a CN operation and was the last narrow-gauge railway hauling freight in North America until it was abandoned in the early 1990s.

twenty-six-seat lounge at the other end. A varying number of coaches, sleepers, and a diner followed (depending on the season), and finishing off the train was a dome-observation-lounge-sleeper that included three double bedrooms, a three-bedroom suite with bath, and a comfortable observation lounge nestled in the rounded glass-enclosed rear end. All of the

cars were equipped with a three-channel sound system—two devoted to different taped music programs and the third for train announcements.

Canadian National reacted a little slower to the developing trend in passenger-train service, but eventually placed the largest order ever by a North American railroad—389 cars valued at over $60 million—in 1953.

These new cars were destined for the ordinary traveler, thus were of high quality but not fancy. Therefore, CP's Canadian was considered the premier cross-country train over the CN Super Continental, although both began service on the same day.

Though the appeal of the new equipment was insufficient to stem the traffic decline of the late 1950s, CN was not yet ready to surrender to the airplane and highway. Improved marketing, timetables, and fare structures were just the beginning. Rebuilt equipment was joined by purchases from retrenching U.S. railroads. The Reading's Crusader equipment was brought north and became the Montreal-to-Champlain Quebec, and the Milwaukee Road's ex-Hiawatha Super Domes and Skytop Lounge observation cars joined the CN fleet. The domes were refurbished as club lounges, with a mixture of easy chairs, sofas, and tables with coach seating below, and renamed Scenerama cars for service on the scenic Winnipeg-to-Vancouver portions of the Super Continental and Panorama.

While this period was the apex of the streamlined era for the Canadian National, traffic continued to erode for both lines and the government was forced to step in once again. VIA Rail Canada was incorporated on January 12, 1976, for the purpose of taking over passenger-train operation, and issued its first joint CP/CN timetable under the VIA name in October. Separate trains would leave Montreal and Toronto, merge in Sudbury, Ontario, and operate as a single train to Winnipeg, where they would again split onto their individual routes to Vancouver. It was a heartbreaking emasculation of two great trains, and ultimately just the Canadian survived. The Super Continental was gone from the timetable.

VIA purchased the CN and CP passenger-car fleets in 1978 and, on April 1, 1979, assumed full financial responsibility for the passenger services formerly operated by Canadian National and Canadian Pacific. In 1988, VIA began a rebuilding program to modernize its rolling stock. In the case of the Canadian, this meant a restoration of 1950s opulence (although with modern air-conditioning equipment).

✦ ✦ ✦

Harsh winters caused the retirement of Ontario Northland's TEE power cars, but the coaches continued in service behind conventional diesel locomotives. Keeping the streamliner alive in the 1990s, the Northlander is shown here leaving Toronto behind an EMD FP7.

The rationalization and trimming of services was as devastating as the Amtrak experience had been in the United States. As of January 15, 1990, VIA continues to operate the Canadian, but it follows much of the CN route. Day coaches are carried at the front of the train for short-haul passengers; reclining-seat Daynighter cars in the middle section are provided for economy travelers; and sleeping cars, including private compartments, section berths, and drawing room suites, are included. A coffee shop-cafeteria lounge car is located near the day coaches, a diner is placed near the middle, and the traditional domed observation-lounge car brings up the rear.

The historical image of a long stainless steel snake coiling through the Canadian Rockies is gone, supplanted by CP stainless mixed with the blue-and-yellow colors of VIA, but a dome seat through the grandeur of Yellowhead Pass remains an experience to savor.

THE NORTHLANDER

A new passenger service was initiated in 1977, when the Ontario Northland (ON) instituted six-days-per-week service on an 11½ hour schedule between Toronto, North Bay, and Timmins, using second-hand Trans-Europe Express (TEE) train sets purchased from the Swiss and

Dutch rail systems. The sleek fixed four-unit train sets left Toronto at 12:50 P.M., traveling over the Canadian National Railway's tracks to North Bay, then on the ON into the north country through Temagami, Englehart, Matheson, and Porquis, arriving in Timmins at 11:35 P.M.

The TEE trains were conceived to eliminate much of the difficulty encountered with train travel on the Continent with the multiple border crossings required on many trips (see Chapter Eight). While the service was standardized as much as possible, there was great variety in the

tional problems due to the lack of flexibility. Cars could not be added to accommodate heavier loads, and turning entire trains at terminals was time consuming. The Swiss and Dutch TEE sets sold to the Ontario Northland had operator cabs at each end, eliminating the turning problems.

There were five of these trains built, beginning in 1955—three were owned by the Dutch Railways and two by the Swiss Federal Railways—for service between Amsterdam and Zurich. The locomotives were built by Werkspoor in Holland; the coaches and pilot cars by Schweizerische Industrie-Gesellschaft in Neuhausen, Switzerland; and the electrical equipment was provided by Brown-Boveri et Cie AG. The locomotives each contained three diesel-generator sets: two (at 2,000hp total motive power) drove the traction motors and the third provided 380/220 volt electricity for the coaches. The power unit rode on three-axle trucks with two traction motors each.

The trains entered European service in June 1957 and were capable of achieving speeds of up to 101 mph (168kph) in testing, but were limited to 69 mph (110kph) in regular operation. The five train sets carried 114 passengers (with thirty-five places in the diner) between Zurich, Amsterdam, Brussels, and Paris on a four-day cycle, knocking four hours off the fourteen-hour Zurich–Amsterdam run.

When the Ontario Northland needed quick delivery of new equipment to upgrade their service to the province's northern region, they looked into the idea of purchasing the recently retired Dutch-Swiss TEE units and ultimately acquired four of them. After a rebuilding and repainting in Holland, the units had bells and lettering added at the ON shops in North Bay.

The new Northlanders were stylish and comfortable, and warmly accepted by the passengers, but the rough track and snowy winters of Northern Ontario (which could reach -30°C) were hard on equipment designed for less severe conditions. The locomotives were temperamental and frequent breakdowns played havoc with schedules. For a time, buses followed each train, ready to rescue the passengers when a breakdown occurred. Finally, the locomotives were replaced with dependable FP7 units that had been modified to provide electrical power for the trains, and the Northlanders performed dependably until the coaches were retired 1992.

Now looking very different from its beginning, the Northlander continues to serve Ontario's North Country using less exotic coaches from Toronto's GO Transit system. While not as luxurious as the TEE train sets, the new equipment offers higher capacity at an acceptable level of comfort and dependability.

◆ ◆ ◆

A pair of angular F40PH diesels lead the Canadian along the shores of Lake Louise, Alberta. The EMD locomotives began to replace the traditional but aging E and F Units on North American streamliners beginning in 1976.

equipment, which was built by the individual rail systems to various designs.

The fixed-train-set concept, which was also the original approach taken by the builders of the early American streamliners, created opera-

CHAPTER EIGHT

TRAVELS ACROSS EUROPE

Great Britain could well be called the "fertile crescent" of railway development. From the trailblazing work of Richard Trevithick, who built the first locomotive to run on rails, at Penydarren, Wales, to the inspired engineering of George Stephenson and Isambard Kingdom Brunel, who pioneered innovative construction and operating techniques on fully functioning railways, much of the early mechanical progress resulted from the genius of the tiny island country.

The engineers and navvies who built the railways of the British Isles saw their achievements replicated throughout the Empire, and exported in the form of equipment and ideas to much of the rest of the world as well. But as time passed, because the industrial societies of Britain and much of Europe were well established before the advent of railroad technology, their railways evolved quite differently than in North America, Australia, and the rest of the newly developing world.

European railways connected existing industries and cities to nearby markets. In the populous and contiguous nations of the European continent, cities and towns were—and are—relatively close together, so that short stretches of railways met most commercial needs; as a result, little thought was given to integrated national systems in the early days. A less dense but still well-traveled network carried passengers and freight between Europe and the countries of the eastern Mediterranean: Turkey, the former Palestine, and Egypt. In contrast, the governments of such emerging nations as the United States and Canada quickly saw the need for long-distance, often coast-to-coast, railroads that would open up vast, uninhabited areas to settlers and future industrial growth, and so provided public funding and land grants to encourage these risky endeavors.

These different approaches to railway development were embodied in locomotive and rolling stock design, with the biggest, heaviest, and most powerful locos being built for use in Canada, the United States, Australia, Africa, and Russia. British and European railways tended to operate many more trains on frequent schedules, enabling the use of shorter trains and smaller locomotives. Although important or international trains featured elaborate dining facilities and sleeping cars, there was less need for the long-distance "Great Trains" seen in the new countries.

◆ ◆ ◆

Sir William Stanier's handsome streamlined Pacific was designed for the new Coronation Scot streamliner. This particular locomotive, Coronation, was involved in a disputed speed record during its trials when the London, Midland & Scottish Railway reported a speed of 114 mph (181kph) on the run.

On one hand, the proximity of Old World cities means that today the downtown-to-downtown transit times of modern trains match those of the airlines, so that the European railway systems have remained more viable as passenger carriers than the railroads of North America. On the other hand, the number of legendary trains on the continent is as limited as the number of workaday trains is great. This chapter discusses several of the principal trains of the golden age of European rail travel.

TRAINS OF THE BRITISH EMPIRE

Passenger trains in Europe tended to run over short routes because of the close proximity of the region's towns, cities, and countries. Such as it was, this state of affairs was a macrocosm of the situation in the United Kingdom, the small size of which necessarily limited the opportunities for such long-distance rail journeys as those across the United States. Nonetheless, passenger service has always been a vital part of train service in Britain, and the most significant lines were those that connected London with Scotland and Ireland. The most famous of these long-

ROYAL
BORDER BRIDGE

Tom Purvis

"THE CORONATION"
CROSSING THE ROYAL BORDER BRIDGE BERWICK-upon-TWEED
IT'S QUICKER BY RAIL
FULL INFORMATION FROM ANY L·N·E·R OFFICE OR AGENCY

The routes from London to Scotland were the most heavily contested in Britain. The London North Eastern Railway's Coronation was hauled by one of Nigel Gresley's streamlined class A4 Pacifics on its six-hour run from London to Edinburgh. This dramatic poster shows the Coronation on the stone arch viaduct at the border.

distance trains were the Flying Scotsman, the Royal Scot, the Coronation, the Coronation Scot, and the Irish Mail.

The 412-mile (642km) route from Euston Station, London, to Glasgow, Scotland, is one of the most historic in Britain. Known as the West Coast Main Line, it incorporates sections of two legendary pioneer lines built by revered engineers: Robert Stephenson's London & Birmingham and the Grand Junction of Joseph Locke. Also incorporated were the fast-running main lines of Locke's Lancaster & Carlisle, through the Lakeland Mountains, and the Caledonian, from Carlisle to Glasgow. A parallel line through the Trent Valley bypassed the industrial congestion around Manchester and there was also a connection north and east to Edinburgh, Dundee, and Aberdeen, via the North British Railway. The southern portion of the route carried the famed Irish Mail out of London.

This busy main line was operated jointly by the London and North Western and the Caledonian Railway until the passage of the Railway Act of 1921, which created a single system known as "the Grouping." On January 1, 1923, the two lines were amalgamated into the London, Midland & Scottish (LMS) Railway. Matters continued like this until the 1948 nationalization of the railways again separated the line into the London, Midland, and Scottish regions of British Rail.

In the 1880s, there were two additional independent routes that offered lavish service between London and Scotland, but by the time of the 1923 amalgamation of the independent lines into "The Big Four," the only rival routes were those on the east and west coasts. The easterly route—the London North Eastern Railway (LNER)—connected London's King's Cross Station with Edinburgh.

While there were many important trains on the Scottish routes, perhaps the most famous were the luxurious LMS Royal Scot—a continuation (undertaken in 1927) of a schedule that had been in operation since June 1, 1862—and the equally plush Flying Scotsman of the LNER. From the early days onward, both trains left their terminals at 10:00 A.M., underlining the competetive spirit between the railways. From 1888 on, timetables were occasionally abandoned (the trains left London on time, but would leave subsequent stations as soon as they were ready rather than wait for the appointed departure time) and the trains raced to Edinburgh, and later to Aberdeen, with the LNER signalmen at Kinnaber Junction, the interlocking to joint trackage, holding up rival trains to allow their own to pass through first. The fastest east coast trains occasionally covered the 541 miles (866km) in as little as 8 hours 38 minutes—an average speed of over 62 mph (100kph)—before the turn of the twentieth century.

By the 1930s, the most modern locomotive designs and the latest passenger equipment were being assigned to the Scottish trains. When the new three-cylindered 4-6-0s built by the LMS were brought in to haul the train, both train and locomotive were christened Royal Scot; the 6100, the first of fifty copies of the Royal Scot class locomotive, was shipped to

North America for a goodwill tour in 1933. Hauling a brand new train of coaches, sleepers, club car, and observation car and temporarily fitted with a headlight and bell, in keeping with North American practice, the Royal Scot was exhibited at the 1939 New York World's Fair before traveling thousands of miles across the railroads of the United States, and then on the Canadian Pacific tracks across Canada.

In 1937, the LMS inaugurated a new express. Celebrating the coronations of Edward VIII (who abdicated his crown after only eleven months as monarch in order to marry a divorcee, Mrs. Wallis Simpson from the United States) in January 1936 and George VI (Edward's brother, the Duke of York) in December 1936, Sir William Stanier

The LMS competed with the LNER's Coronation for the London-to-Scotland traffic with its own high-speed streamlined steam train, the Coronation Scot.

A STRANGER IN A STRANGE LAND

◆ ◆ ◆

A brash American, while on a journey through Britain, had just joined two Englishmen in a first-class compartment when he removed a large cigar from his breast pocket. One of the occupants harrumphed, "Perhaps you are not aware that this is a nonsmoking compartment."

"Oh!! Is it?" replied the American, lighting the stogie.

The Englishman growled, "Perhaps you are unaware of the stiff fine involved for smoking in a nonsmoking carriage?"

"Oh, really?" was the casual reply, as he continued his smoke.

Now quite angry, the Englishman shouted, "Now see here! I'm going to have the guard throw you out of this compartment for your impertinence!"

"Oh, are you?" replied the smoker.

The train soon slowed to a halt at a country station, and the American quickly stepped off the train and summoned the guard. "Sir, there is a man in this compartment who is traveling first-class on a third-class ticket."

"May I see your ticket, please?" requested the guard. The Englishman's ticket was indeed for third-class. The guard removed him and his luggage, and he was left sputtering on the platform as the train pulled out.

Presently, the second Englishman inquired, "Pardon me, but how did you know that our neighbor was traveling on a third-class ticket?"

"Because," replied the American pleasantly, "his ticket was the same color as mine!"

produced the fully streamlined Princess-Coronation class Pacific (4-6-2) steam locomotive for the Coronation Scot, a 2:00 P.M. train to Glasgow. The LNER followed with its own streamlined Coronation, which reduced the London-to-Edinburgh schedule to six hours—at 393 miles (629km), it was the world's longest nonstop rail journey.

Following World War II, nationalization brought many changes to the Scottish routes. British Rail began electrifying the former LM&S line, and diesel power replaced steam elsewhere. The Royal Scot and Flying Scotsman continue their daily journeys to the North Country, now with fully modern equipment. With a 5,000hp electric locomotive on a twelve-coach train, the time to Glasgow has been reduced to five hours at an average speed of 80 mph (139kph) for the 401-mile (642km) trip.

British Rail has applied the new high-speed technology to the line, with "advanced passenger train" (APT) sets further reducing the time

The King's Time

♦ ♦ ♦

The Irish Mail carried on a charming tradition for almost ninety years. Every evening, "The King's Time" was set on a watch at the General Post Office in St. Martin's-le-Grand and carried by courier to Dublin via train and steamship, thereby maintaining the "proper" setting of the clocks throughout Ireland. This practice continued until the BBC began broadcasting Greenwich Mean Time 12:00 noon at ten seconds to the hour.

A Claughran-class 4-6-0 built by the London & North Western Railway leads the Irish Mail past the great stone lions that guard the Britannia Tubular Bridge in 1929. Built by Robert Stephenson in 1850, the bridge carried the London, Midland & Scottish railway across the Menai Straits to Holyhead.

1850—the rail journey had to be interrupted at the Menai Strait. At that point in the journey, passengers, baggage, and mail were detrained at Bangor, trundled by carriage across the existing suspension bridge, and then put aboard another train for the final run to the ferry at Llanfair. The 100-mile (160km) crossing of the Irish Sea brought the travelers to Kingstown, now Dun Laoghaire, for the final short railway leg to Dublin. All of the same delays applied when traveling in the other direction as well.

The schedule was established by the Post Office, and the contract of 1860 required an average rail speed of 42 mph (68kph), with several intermediate stops between Euston Station, London, and Holyhead. Elapsed time was 11½ hours, between London and Dublin. The principal service was at night, with a Euston departure at 8:45 P.M., but a secondary day train was also scheduled for 8:30 A.M. Both trains included a Traveling Post Office (TPO) car, and the day train

to four hours, using tilting coaches to make the 100-mph (160kph) average speeds comfortable for passengers on the winding route.

Communication between London and Dublin has historically been vital to both commerce and government. When the time arrived, in the 1840s, to finalize a rail connection between the capitals, a great controversy arose between the backers of two primary proposals. Each was championed by a legendary railway engineer—Robert Stephenson argued for his projected Chester & Holyhead Railway, while his friend and rival Isambard Kingdom Brunel favored extending the broad gauge from Worcester through the heart of Wales to Porthdinlleyn, on the Lleyn Peninsula.

Stephenson's route was ultimately selected and was completed in time for the August 1, 1848, inauguration of the Irish Mail, the world's first named train (although the name would not be carried on the letterboards of the train until 1927). For the first two years of service—that is, until Stephenson completed his brilliant Brittania tubular bridge in

included a restaurant car, while the night train carried sleepers. Unfortunately, the Dublin-bound nighttime Irish Mail's arrival at Holyhead was at 2:00 A.M., a most unpleasant hour for passengers to transfer to a steamer at the blustery end of Admiralty Pier.

The available technology made this tight schedule difficult to meet, and much effort was devoted to reducing the time required by intermediate mail and servicing stops. The world's first track pans (water-filled troughs set between the rails) were installed near Aber, east of Bangor, enabling the fireman to lower a scoop and refill the tender at speed. Mail standards were installed, allowing the suspended mail pouches to be snatched by a hook on the passing post-office car for immediate processing.

The success of the Irish Mail encouraged the development of additional trains to meet the growing demand. Its successor, the London & North Western Railway (L&NW), increased passenger express service with two more Dublin trains, using its own steamers, which departed from Holyhead's inner harbor at more convenient hours. Ireland's political unrest following

Passengers clamber aboard the post–World War II Orient Express at the Athens depot in 1951. Note the wooden clerestory roofed middle coach with truss rods; this quite possibly could be an old Pullman-built car.

✦ ✦ ✦

World War I reduced traffic considerably, causing the L&NW to eliminate these trains, but maintain the inner harbor connection for the Irish Mail.

With "the Grouping" of 1923, the London & North Western became part of the London, Midland & Scottish Railway, and by the hundredth anniversary of the Irish Mail, the train was operated by the nationalized British Rail. While mail pickup on the move was discontinued in 1971, British Rail was still operating 144 Traveling Post Office cars in 1990. The service carried twenty-five million letters per day on forty-two daily trains—including the venerable Irish Mail.

THE ORIENT EXPRESS

Georges Nagelmackers was the guiding force behind European sleeping-car services, and his Compagnie Internationale des Wagons-Lits et des Grands Express Européens (the Wagons-Lits Company) performed much like the Pullman Company did in North America. Wagon-Lits built Europe's first eight-wheel bogie (truck) sleeper in 1880 (previous cars had been supported by four or six fixed-wheel-sets), and its first proper restaurant-kitchen car in 1881. The company was then ready to introduce Europe's first true international passenger express.

The popular Paris–Vienna route was chosen for an all-first-class train in 1882, and its immediate success encouraged eight railways to cooperate with a similar train all the way to the Near East the following year. Originally, because of Russia's efforts to protect its shipping interests by blocking a continuous rail line to Turkey, passengers had to transfer to a ferry for the Danube crossing south of Bucharest, Romania, board another train for crossing to Varna, Bulgaria, and then board an Austrian Lloyd Liner for the final leg to Constantinople. But soon trans-European rail travel would become a standard of excellence throughout the world.

A legend was born in 1883—the Orient Express, the European deluxe train operating across the continent to Constantinople (rail was finally completed to the Turkish border in 1884) and equipped entirely with Wagons-Lits equipment. Also operated entirely by Wagons-Lits, the train epitomized the elegance and romance of rail travel, attracting the adventurous in addition to the wealthy. Indeed, it was common for passengers to dine in full formal attire and to be entertained with live music.

Service to Constantinople had a less-than-auspicious beginning, since the new equipment had not yet been delivered when the first train departed Paris on June 5, 1883, with only two sleepers, a diner, and mail-baggage cars. The twice-weekly service left Paris at 7:30 P.M. Tuesday and Friday, arriving eighty-four hours later in Constantinople at 7:00 A.M. the following Saturday or Tuesday.

It was not until October 4 that Nagelmackers invited a group of forty dignitaries and journalists to experience the opulence of the Orient Express, with its newly delivered bogie cars. Because of the expected

The reincarnated Orient Express maintained the high level of service and style that had come to be expected aboard that great train. Upholstered seating, table lamps, linens, and silver made a meal in the diner compare with that in a fine restaurant.

GEORGES NAGELMACKERS
(1845–1905)

✦ ✦ ✦

The son of a wealthy Belgian banker, Nagelmackers was shipped off to the United States in 1868 by his parents (who hoped to remove the young man from the possible consequences of a boudoir indiscretion), where he was exposed to the elegant service and luxurious equipment of the Pullman Palace Car. The lack of such amenities in primitive European bunk cars meant that long-distance rail travel was a journey to endure, rather than the comfortable, even pampered, experience typical on Pullman sleeping cars and diners.

Nagelmackers was convinced that the concept would succeed in Europe, despite the lack of cooperation that prevented easy interchange of passenger cars between self-reliant railroads, much less countries. He returned to Belgium and resumed his career as a mining engineer, all the while planning his sleeping-car venture. Nagelmackers was unable to secure financing (he was dismissed as a dreamer for even suggesting that railway cars should have lavatories), so in autumn 1872 he used his own money to build a few tiny four-wheeled coaches that were convertible into Pullman-like sleepers. In spring 1873 he began operating them between Ostend and Cologne. The underfinanced business was facing bankruptcy, despite modest success, when Nagelmackers met Colonel William d'Alton Mann, of the U.S. Army Engineers.

Mann wanted to enter the sleeping-car business, but had failed in an attempt to crack the British market and was rightfully wary of competing with George Pullman in the United States. He and Nagelmackers joined forces in 1873 to build Mann Boudoir Sleeping Cars in continental Europe.

The company prospered, thanks to the credibility fostered by an early contract with the French Railway System and the use of a Mann car by

Georges Nagelmackers brought comfortable sleeping cars and luxury to passenger trains across the European continent.

✦ ✦ ✦

the Prince of Wales (later King Edward VII) for a highly publicized journey through Europe and Russia. This trip opened the door to successful international operations, particularly the lucrative Paris-to-Vienna route, and the railroads began to appreciate the value of expanded sleeping-car services. By the end of 1874, the company operated forty cars, and Nagelmackers soon gained the confidence of investors and enough capital to buy out Mann's interest in 1876.

Nagelmackers then formed the Compagnie Internationale des Wagons-Lits et des Grands Express Européens, commonly known as the Wagons-Lits Company, to take over first-class service in the Pullman manner. Realizing the important relationship between travel and food, Nagelmackers included elegant restaurant cars that served exquisite meals. In 1883, the legendary and deluxe Orient Express was begun, and the train was equipped entirely with Wagons-Lits equipment. By the turn of the century, five hundred Wagons-Lits sleepers and diners were rolling over 90,000 miles (144,837km) of track per year.

In the 1880s, George Pullman had begun expansion into Europe, competing with Wagons-Lits for the luxury market, but he almost immediately offered a merger with Nagelmackers, which was dismissed. Pullman successfully operated special trains in partnership with travel agent Thomas Cook, and the rivalry continued in earnest for many years, although Wagons-Lits ultimately joined the arrangement.

After the deaths of Georges Nagelmackers and George Pullman, the companies merged as the International Sleeping Car Company and dominated travel on the continent for another forty years.

rigors of the journey and the potential for ambush by the less "civilized" citizens of the east side of the Carpathian Mountains, no females were invited. (In fact, Bulgarian bandits attacked the train at least once in the twentieth century.)

The guests on that historic journey were enormously impressed by the elegance of the equipment. The three sleeping cars included partitions carved and inlaid with teak, walnut, and mahogany; silk bed sheets; and

gold-plated plumbing in the bathrooms, which had marble sinks. An elegant car that included a men's smoking compartment, a library, and a "ladies lounge" (for such a time when women would travel on the Express) followed the sleepers, but the dining car was the crown jewel. Carved wood provided a sumptuous backdrop to oil paintings and crystal chandeliers; fine china, sterling silver, and crystal adorned linen-covered tables. Nagelmackers understood the important relationship

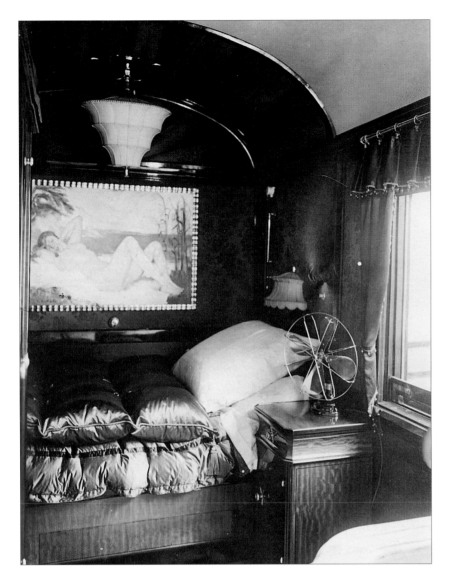

between food and travel, and provided a separate car to carry the vast quantities of food, wine, champagne, and brandy necessary for such a journey.

The first magnificent dinner the dignitaries enjoyed on the virgin trip lasted until midnight. The next day the travelers were disappointed to learn that the diner had developed an over-heated bearing during the night and been left at Augsburg, Germany. While Nagelmackers had provided for such an event, the backup diner waiting in Munich was an older six-wheeled car that ran so roughly that the passengers complained that they couldn't pour or drink the wine without spilling. But the sleepers, with their smoothly rolling bogies, prompted a journalist to report, "It runs so sweetly that you can even shave in comfort at fifty miles an hour [81kph]."

The train stopped at a small station between Budapest and Temesvar, Timisoara (in Romania), so that a gypsy band could board. For a few dozen miles, the diner was transformed into a cabaret as the strolling musicians entertained the guests. Waltzes and czardas segued into Turkish tunes in honor of the First Secretary of the Ottoman Empire, who was one of the guests. A medley of French songs culminated with a spirited Marseillaise, the chorus only slightly interrupted when the burly, bearded chef burst through the kitchen door in full voice. After two and

✦ ✦ ✦

Left: No expense was spared during construction of the Istanbul Orient Express. Rich woods, plush upholstery, and sumptuous paintings were used liberally in the interiors. Below: The Orient Express cruises through the French countryside in this 1910 view.

a half hours, the gypsies disembarked and the atmosphere aboard the train returned to its more placid state.

Fortunately for subsequent passengers, the ambience and tone of this first Orient Express journey were largely retained in regular service.

With the completion of the missing trackage links, a pure rail journey all the way to Constantinople became possible, and the train operated steadily until service was withdrawn in 1914, at the outbreak of World War I. In 1919, the magnificent train was returned to service for a year, but was assigned to the exclusive use of the Triple Entente's military brass on a Paris–Vienna–Warsaw route.

The revisions to the European map that emerged from the war were cause for a revised Orient Express, as well. Postwar politicians were anxious to reinstate international railway service between western Europe and the Balkans, but wished to bypass the lines through Germany and the former Austro-Hungarian Empire. The 1906 opening of the twelve-mile (19.5km)-long Simplon Tunnel (between Brig, Switzerland, and Iselle, Italy) had provided an alternate route through the Alps that was later double-tracked when a parallel bore opened in 1922. With the

counsel and agreement of the Wagons-Lits Company, the Simplon-Orient Express was born in April 1919.

This new train was the beginning of a network of Wagons-Lits routes connecting northern and western Europe with the Balkans and the Near East. A first section of the Simplon-Orient Express carried cross-channel boat passengers from the port of Calais to Paris, where the main portion of the train, the sleepers to Istanbul (formerly Constantinople), Athens, and Bucharest were added. The train left Paris with five sleeping cars, the restaurant car, and a brake van or caboose (later replaced with a Wagons-Lits fourgon, which included a small shower). After an exquisitely scenic climb over the Alps and through the long, dark passage of the Simplon Tunnel, the train stopped at Milan and Trieste, where the restaurant-car crew was changed. The two Bucharest sleepers were dropped off at Vinkovci, northwest of Belgrade, and the remainder of the train proceeded to the Yugoslav capital.

As the Wagons-Lits network grew, Belgrade became the rendezvous for a number of the exotic trans-European deluxe trains. By the 1930s, the Arlberg-Orient, the Ostend-Vienna, the resurrected Orient-Express,

The 1906 completion of the Simplon Tunnel opened the European rail routes to Italy and beyond. At Brig, an electrically powered Swiss Federal Railway train emerges from the parallel second bore, completed in 1921.

Cecil Rhodes' Cape-to-Cairo Railway

◆ ◆ ◆

The importance of railroads to emerging nations was quickly recognized, and Britain's technology was exported around the world, particularly where the Empire would benefit. The dreams of empire-builders featured railways taming the wild landscapes of Canada, New Zealand, Australia, and South Africa.

Cecil Rhodes (1853–1902), son of an English clergyman, had earned a vast fortune with his African diamond mines when he decided that he was the man to bring civilization to the Dark Continent by building a Cape-to-Cairo railway. With his own funds—supplemented with additional money bullied from the government—he set out to link his mines at Kimberly with the seaport of Cape Town, always keeping in sight the imperial vision of steel rails running the length of the continent. He once remarked, "The railway is my right hand, and the telegraph my voice."

The line was built to a gauge of 3 feet 6 inches (1.1m) and had reached Kimberly when gold was discovered in the Transvaal. That required an extension to Johannesburg in 1892, despite opposition by the Boer settlers, who favored a line built by their own government. Trackwork was complete to Bulawayo, Rhodesia (now Zimbabwe), in 1897 and had reached the town of Bukama, Congo (now Zaire), before Rhodes' death. At that time, trains could travel 2,600 miles (4,160km) from Cape Town, but were still 3,500 miles (5,600km) from Cairo.

The loss of Cecil Rhodes' financial backing and influence thwarted further progress, as did World War I and the political turmoil that followed. Although it is still impossible to undertake a Cape-to-Cairo railway journey, with the help of a few ferries, 100 miles (160km) or so of road, a thousand or so miles (roughly 1,600km) of boat travel, and a great deal of winding about, one can make the trip overland.

Despite his failure to bind the length of Africa in British steel, Rhodes made an enduring contribution to the golden age of rail travel with the Cape Town–to–Pretoria portion of the route. Today, the South African Railways' Blue Train, "the most luxurious train in the world," carries 108 passengers in what amounts to a rolling five-star hotel along that section of track.

The history of the Blue Train began at the conclusion of the Boer War. In 1903, a new service connected the Union Castle mail steamers from England with the interior cities of the Transvaal. Since the passengers were accustomed to the luxurious appointments of the steamers and the best continental train service, the rolling stock was designed to equal the best railway cars in Europe. The train was operated jointly by the Cape Government Railway and the Central South African Railway, and ran two days a week in each direction. Departing Cape Town at 10:45 A.M., it arrived in Pretoria, the administrative capital 999 miles (1,608km) away, at 4:30 in the afternoon of the following day.

When the Union of South Africa was formed in 1910, the independent railways of the Cape and of Natal were merged with the CSAR to form the South African Railways. In commemoration of the amalgamation, the Pretoria express was named the Union Limited. Although this train exclusively offered extra-fare first-class passage, another train ran on the five days the Union Limited did not. These "all class" trains made many intermediate stops and took thirty-nine hours, more than nine hours longer than the Union Limited, to reach Pretoria.

The Union Limited's popularity—despite the higher fare—made necessary the addition of more coaches and larger locomotives. The CSAR 4-6-2 Pacifics were replaced by giant 4-8-2s in the 1930s. Fortunately, the high quality of the trackwork and relatively slow maximum speeds of 55 mph (88.5kph) allowed the use of wider and taller locomotives than most narrow-gauge lines could accommodate.

New equipment and a new blue-and-cream paint scheme were accompanied by a new name in 1939—the Blue Train. The new coaches had clerestory roofs and were outfitted like deluxe cabins on a ship. The compartments had writing tables, custom note paper, and blue leather upholstered seating. The dining car was appropriately luxurious and on the rear end was an observation car. The traveling staff was carefully trained to accommodate any passenger needs.

Large coal reserves in South Africa meant that steam-powered engines lasted longer there than in many other parts of the world. By the early 1960s, however, only the central portion of the route was under steam. Electrification of the Pretoria–Kimberly and Cape Town–Beaufort West portions, and the adoption of diesel-electric power on the remainder cleaned up the train's image (by eliminating the smoke).

The Blue Train's thirtieth anniversary was celebrated spectacularly with a return of steam. In April 1969, a special anniversary train was run with carefully polished and primped steam locomotives hauling the train in both directions. A trophy was awarded to the most festively appointed of the six locos assigned to the run, and large, enthusiastic crowds turned out to watch the train pass. The equipment on the Blue Train was replaced again, in September 1972.

A ride on the Blue Train remains a cherished goal of serious travelers, and the train continues its special service with fully air-conditioned and sound-proofed coaches riding on air-cushioned trucks. All accommodations are private rooms, three of which include private toilets. Passengers dress formally for dinner. Speeds of 40 mph to 50 mph (65–85kph) have reduced the Cape Town-to-Pretoria journey to twenty-six hours on one of the few remaining of the opulent land cruisers that once served the major cities of the industrial world.

TRANS-SIBERIAN EXPRESS

◆ ◆ ◆

In many ways the Trans-Siberian Express (more properly called the Russia) is as legendary as the Orient Express, but for reasons other than luxury. The Trans-Siberian Railway is the longest single line in the world, spanning 5,777 miles (9,297km) and nine time zones between Vladivostok and Moscow. The government-sponsored line was deemed critical to national security and as a means of encouraging settlement in the remote wilderness of Siberia.

Construction began in 1892, working simultaneously from both ends, and by 1898, the single-track line was half finished. Gauge was set at 5 feet (1.5m) and clearances were very generous: 11 feet 2 inches (3.4m) in width and 17 feet 2 inches (5.2m) in height (the gauge was slightly narrowed to 4 feet 11 inches [1.5m] in 1972). Passenger service began in 1899 with the Siberia Express, which ran between Moscow and Tomsk, and the Wagons-Lits company operated the sleeper cars before the Revolution.

As could be expected, construction was very difficult. In some places along the route, the permafrost can be as deep as 1,000 feet (305m) and never thaws to less than 3-to-5 feet (91cm–1.5m) deep. Snow falls for nine months of the year and the temperature can reach as low as -74 degrees Fahrenheit (-58°C). Crossing Lake Baikal originally required ferry service until the completion of the Chinese Eastern Railway around the southern end of the lake (taking the line through China) in 1904; in 1938 China's unstable political situation caused the Soviet government to begin construction on the Baikal-Amur Northern Mainline. This new alignment shortened the route by about 300 miles (484km).

Power on the Russia was orginally provided by steam locomotives imported from Britain, but the son of U.S. locomotive builder Ross Winans established a domestic locomotive works at St. Petersburg in 1840 to make the locos. Understandably, the massive railway needed locomotives that provided massive power. The most common steamers were the 13,000 E class 0-10-0s, and in 1934 a gigantic 33-foot (10m)-wheelbase 4-14-4 was built (unfortunately, the behemoth turned out to have a nasty habit of straightening the tracks around curves). A large number of 2-10-0 and 2-10-2 freight locomotives was also used, but passenger service was dominated by the 4,000 S-class Prairies (2-6-2s) on shorter trains and 2-8-4s and 4-8-4s on the longer, heavier trains.

The first dependable diesels arrived from the United States during World War II, and domestic production evolved from those designs. A heavy investment in electrification had been completed on the entire route, allowing the thyristor-controlled 6520kW-class VL80R to operate in the 25kV, 50Hz mountainous section. Earlier electrification was undertaken at 3000 volts DC.

The Trans-Siberian Express, like many other Russian trains, offers two classes of travel: "Hard" (leather- or plastic-covered seating) and "Soft" (fully upholstered seating). Similar differences are the rule in sleeper cars as well: Hard-class provides convertible bunks in four-berth compartments or open coaches, while Soft-class has larger compartments with four large couchettes. This train also includes European-style conventional sleeping cars with two- and four-berth compartments.

The Russian peasants had a saying: "Russia is not a country, it's a world." The extent of that world is apparent on the Trans-Siberian Express as it makes its weeklong journey across the vastness of "Mother Russia."

The Trans-Siberian Express provides a vital link across the vast expanse of Russia, a link as important as the American and Canadian transcontinental railways of the nineteenth century. The train, photographed here in June 1973, represents one of the world's last great train rides, covering nine time zones along its route from the Pacific shore to Moscow.

Above: The Trans-Siberian Express leaves Moscow bound for Vladivostok on July 21, 1941, carrying a vital military load. The rail lifeline was critical to the Soviet war effort. Below: For passengers traveling first class, the Trans-Siberian Express provided appropriately luxurious service. This dining car is well provided with linens, silver, and comfortable seating.

and the Simplon-Orient connected there. On several days of the week, the Simplon-Orient would pick up additional sleepers from either Berlin, Ostend, Amsterdam, Vienna, or Prague. Continuing east, the Simplon-Orient paused at Nis, Yugoslavia (where the Athens sleepers were dropped off), to be eventually delivered to the port of Piraeus for the convenience of passengers transferring to cruise ships. The remaining cars continued through Sofia to Istanbul, completing an 1,899-mile (3,056km) journey from Paris.

Luxury rail travel from Europe did not end at Istanbul. In 1926, when Ankara became Turkey's new capital, Wagons-Lits contracted to extend its service and began operating the Taurus Express to the Middle East in 1930. Simplon-Express passengers were ferried across the Bosphorus to another all-sleeper-and–restaurant car train that carried one section to the border with Iraq (the standard-gauge line to Baghdad was not completed until 1940) and another to Tripoli. A private bus carried passengers from Tripoli south to Haifa, where another Wagons-Lits train proceeded to the bank of the Suez Canal. There was no rail bridge at that time; therefore, another ferry ride to Kantara, Egypt, was necessary before boarding an Egyptian Pullman train for the final leg into Cairo. Total travel time from London was seven days.

While this long travel time might seem masochistic to modern travelers, the only real alternative was via steamship, which took just as long. The trans-European luxury trains, therefore, carried the high-ranking diplomats, businessmen, and nobility of the day as well as premium-rate international mail packages. Both King Ferdinand of Bulgaria and his son, Boris, were avid steam-locomotive buffs, and the newspapers frequently carried photos of Boris at the throttle of a Bulgarian loco—sometimes the Simplon-Orient.

Germany's streamlined Fliegende Hamburger ("Flying Hamburger"), an early streamlined train set, waits in the Frankfurt station, which at the time was still under construction. The two-car unit, powered by Maybach diesel engines, was built in 1933.

A TEE train marches up the grades through the Austrian Alps. An extensive system of electrification allows efficient and speedy passenger service throughout the European continent.

◆ ◆ ◆

As was the case on most luxury trains around the world, the postwar traffic on the Orient Express did not return in sufficient force to justify maintaining the level of service that travelers had come to expect. Service was reduced to ordinary coaches until 1962, when the trains terminated

at Belgrade as the Direct-Orient. In 1977, the historic Orient Express finally ceased running altogether.

For most luxury passenger trains, that would have been the end, but the grand traveling hotel that had been known as the Orient Express was the stuff of legends. Detective Hercule Poirot rode the train in Agatha Christie's *Murder on the Orient Express*, and many other novels and films used the opulent setting as a background to a story. Thus, the train was revived in the 1980s, operating as the Nostalgic Orient Express and using some restored equipment from the 1920s. With service from Zurich, Switzerland, to Istanbul, the luxurious train once again attracted travelers who believed that the journey was as important as the destination. These modern excursionists have proven that there are other generations wishing to experience fine travel, continuing the century-old tradition of the Orient Express.

THE TRANS-EUROPEAN EXPRESS (TEE)

The 1950s saw the growth in commercial ties between the mainland European countries. The formation of the European Coal and Steel Community in 1952 heralded the strengthening of these bonds, years before the 1958 creation of the European Economic Community (EEC), more commonly known as the European Common Market. This economic growth was sure to generate a tremendous increase in international business travel that would be snapped up by the emerging commercial airlines, unless Europe's railways cooperated on a new kind of rail service that passed across borders as easily as an airplane.

F.Q. den Hollander, president of the Netherlands Railways, foresaw the urgent need for a fleet of first-class trains that would connect western Europe's main business centers. In order to be successful, the railways would need to meet a schedule that would permit round-trip travel in one day, allowing sufficient time for business transactions in the middle of the day. The intercity trains operating at the time were slowed by having to provide second-class cars, cars for baggage, and mail cars, along with the first-class accommodations. The need for intermediate stops and the transfer of coaches between trains also added to the delays, as did the changing of crews and customs inspections at the borders.

The Reichsbahn had provided speedy intercity service in prewar Germany, using two- and three-unit diesel-powered self-propelled cars that offered only first-class service on a network connecting the country's primary business and industrial centers with Berlin. These luxuriously appointed 100 mph (161kph) train sets were the first in Europe. The pioneer unit, known as the Fliegende Hamburger ("Flying Hamburger"), ran from Berlin to Hamburg at an average speed of 77.5 mph (124.5kph). By

1939, when the war brought an end to the service, the Fliegende Kölner was the fastest, covering the 158 miles (254km) from Berlin to Hanover at an average speed of 83 mph (134kph). The full network of trains made possible a comfortable single day linking of the major German cities of Munich, Nuremberg, Stuttgart, Frankfurt, Cologne, and Bremen with Berlin, and provided a model for the postwar Trans-European Express service.

Den Hollander urged an international approach to the new network, using a universal luxurious train set operating at a standard level of speed on each route and managed by an international commission that was divorced administratively and financially from the participating railroads. Seven national rail systems agreed in 1954 on the fundamentals of the TEE—France, West Germany, Luxembourg, the Netherlands, Switzerland, and Italy—but balked at several key issues, particularly those involving sovereignty. The points they did agree on included a supplementary fare, exclusively first-class service that would not interfere with the loadings on the standard international trains, and an initial network of ten international routes connecting seventy-three centers of business and industry.

Specifications for the trains required a top speed of 87 mph (140kph), food service, and no more than three-across seating. Customs and immigration matters were to be dealt with on the moving train, thus eliminating border delays. The standards of seating, lighting, and air-conditioning were explicit, as was the uniform red-and-cream color scheme.

Lost in the complicated politics was the concept of a unified independent management, and with that loss, the idea of uniform train sets faded as well. TEE management was assigned to a loose association of the seven railways, with each one, in turn, serving a four-year term as manager of a small TEE Commission that would attend to administrative details. No real political power or financial independence was allowed, and each national system retained the revenue for fares originating in its countries. As long as the broad specifications were followed, railways were free to provide equipment to any design they chose. Some basics could not be agreed upon: whether to provide open seating or compartments, and whether to provide separate dining cars or serve meals at the seats. A proposal that the base fare include main meals was opposed because Wagons-Lits (the caterer for most of the routes), the DSG in Germany, and the Swiss vendor all thought that integration of prices was an excessive administrative burden.

Also dropped was a proposal for TEE service personnel to assist with baggage and accompany passengers to their seats (much like redcaps in the United States), as was a corps of TEE conductors who would collect both tickets and passports to simplify border crossings. The seven railways did cooperate on an integrated ticketing system that allowed for simple booking on any TEE network train.

This German train (shown at rest in a classic steel and glass train shed) represents the typical TEE system equipment.

✦ ✦ ✦

Many of the partners were still enthusiastic for integral streamlined train sets, similar to the early streamliners developed in the thirties in both Germany and the United States. The train sets could be double-ended (a control cab at each end), eliminating the need to reverse locomotives end for end at the terminals and therefore avoiding potential delays. Their smooth, wind-cheating shape implied modernism, although at the speeds the trains would run, the benefits of the aerodynamic design were limited to appearance.

Diesel-electric-power cars were anticipated, because of the lack of compact multivoltage equipment that would allow electrically powered trains to operate across western Europe's four different systems of electrical current: 1,500 volts DC in the Netherlands and parts of prewar France; 3,000 volts DC in Belgium and Italy; 15,000 volts AC in Germany, Austria, and Switzerland; and 25,000 volts AC in most of France's postwar electrification.

Unfortunately, the meager benefits of these fixed train sets were easily offset by their inflexibility. A power unit that needed servicing broke up a train set; when conventional locomotives were ultimately used, the predicted terminal delays were found to be greatly exaggerated. There was an extra cost for the diesel generators on each unit that was operat-

The Spanish Talgo equipment is able to adjust to the gauge differences between Spain and the rest of Europe.

✦ ✦ ✦

THE SPANISH TALGO TRAIN

◆ ◆ ◆

The Spanish national system, Red Nacional de los Ferrocarriles Españoles (commonly referred to as Renfe), operates a TEE train using its own patented "Talgo" equipment, which consists of lightweight, short (43-foot [131m]-long), low-slung coaches that ride on a pair of independently suspended single-wheeled half axles at one end and are supported by the adjacent coach and its pair of wheels at the other. The Spanish trains operate on a gauge of 5 feet 6 inches (1.7m), rather than the standard 4 feet 8½ inches (1.4m) of the rest of the TEE system, so Renfe devised an ingenious accommodation to the break-of-gauge dilemma. The Catalan Talgo, running between Barcelona and Geneva, slows to 6 mph (9.7kph) at the border station of Port-Bou as it runs through a section of track that is equipped to adjust the train's wheel gauge on the move.

While the Talgo equipment is comfortable and includes a small bar and Wagons-Lits–operated kitchen, the suspension design is somewhat of a return to the early European coaches and not as smooth-riding as bogie (truck)-mounted cars. Since they are not interchangeable with standard equipment, the Talgos also suffer somewhat from the operational flexibility problems suffered by the early TEE multiple-unit sets. In the United States, Amtrak has experimented with a Talgo train set, along with a number of other European designs, in high-speed service.

ing on already electrified trackage, and the power units were not available for other assignments when not in use for passenger service. Finally, the designs of multiple units had never reached a level that matched the smooth-riding qualities of locomotive-hauled coaches.

France began the assault on equipment standardization with a decision to adapt the RGP multiple-unit diesel, first designed for domestic intercity service in 1954. The units badly blurred the visual distinction between ordinary trains and the Trans-Europe Express—not what was originally intended. The Italians built ungainly two-car train sets that were quite long and lacked air-conditioning. The Swiss Federal and Netherlands Railways jointly provided Dutch-built train sets with a six-axle power car (essentially a diesel locomotive). The first units constructed especially for the TEE by the German Federal system were the final integrated multiple-unit train sets that they had built for long-distance service and were the best of the early TEE equipment. Smooth-riding and equipped with disc brakes, they offered a choice between compartment and open seating, and included a bar as well as a separate restaurant.

The international system began operations on June 7, 1957, but a key element was missing. There was no connection from the industrial centers of northern Italy to Paris and Zurich. The imposing grades and curvature on the climb through the Alps on the Gotthard and Simplon routes required diesel power plants capable of excessive output to maintain reasonable speed. But the Swiss were convinced that multicurrent electric traction was possible and built four five-coach electric TEE train sets in 1961 for service between the cities of Milan, Zurich, and Basel.

These new Swiss trains were still double-ended multiple units, but they raised the service expectations of the TEE significantly because they were powerful and could operate across all four of western Europe's power systems. The twelve-wheel power car on each set was essentially a 3,400hp locomotive, although the electrical equipment was sufficiently compact to leave room for a kitchen-pantry, baggage room, and quarters for both train and customs staff. The 257-ton (231t) train managed a steady 55 mph (88.5kph) up the long 1-in-40 grade climb to the 3,786-foot (1154m) summit at Gotthard Tunnel. Even with the 55 mph speed limit enforced by the constant, sharp curvature, the original schedule was trimmed by twenty-three minutes southbound and thirty-seven minutes northbound between Zurich and Milan.

The high power and flexibility of the Swiss design allowed the new train set to be assigned to the Paris–Milan Cisalpin, which followed the crack Paris–Dijon Mistral, the pride of France, by a slim four to five minutes. The two trains covered this 195-mile (314km) racetrack at average speeds of over 80 mph (129kph), and the Cisalpin covered the 511 miles (822km) from Paris to Milan (including the Alps and five intermediate stops) at a respectable 63.5 mph (103kph).

SIG, the Swiss vehicle manufacturer, had created a number of unique features: enclosed vestibules, which improved both sound insulation and climate control; comfortable semireclining armchair seating; and double-glazed windows with internal venetian blinds that operated electrically at the touch of a button. The cars featured open seating and included separate lavatories for both sexes. The feel of the diner was quite light and airy, with a red-and-yellow color scheme and lightweight freestanding chairs, which occasionally sent passengers sprawling when the engineer squeezed the highest possible speed from the train while rounding a curve.

The popularity of the Cisalpin caused the Swiss to add an additional coach to each train set in 1965, and to then build an additional train set for peak-period use. The extra equipment (being semipermanently coupled) usually was coupled to an already scheduled train that was unable to accommodate the seat requests, thereby doubling the normal train length.

By the early 1970s, the operational inflexibility of the multiple-unit fixed train sets was becoming too heavy a burden. If the Cisalpin was fully booked, the railroad faced two unpleasant alternatives. Additional passengers could be turned away, or the second train set could be called out, adding 297 extra tons (267.5t) of weight and 3,400hp to the train for what might be only a small additional passenger load. TEE passengers also preferred meal service at their seats, which pleased the railway managers, who could eliminate the extra seating and weight of a dedicated dining car.

These factors suggested that another reequipping would be valuable. A new Cisalpin began service in the summer of 1974, with electric locomotives hauling TEE coaches. The route was also extended through Milan to Venice, for the summer tourist season. While new and powerful four-voltage French-built CC40100s, capable of 150 mph (241kph), had gone into service on the Paris–Brussels–Amsterdam TEE route, they were deemed unsuitable for the mountainous portion of the Cisalpin's run. The three railways elected to abandon the concept of through-operation without power change, and decided to provide their own power on home rails. The few minutes necessary for the two changes were insignificant in light of the total schedule between terminals, but it was one more step away from den Hollander's original concept.

Above: The French TGV (*très grande vitesse*, or "very high speed") trains consist of eight articulated coaches with a power unit at each end. Twelve electric motors drive the trains at regular speeds above 125 mph (200kph) on a private right-of-way between Paris and Lyons. First class–only trains carry 287 passengers, while the mixed-class trains carry 111 first-class and 275 second-class passengers. The success of these trains has inspired expansion of the high-speed system. An advanced model of the TGV, the Eurotrain, now plies the underwater tunnel between England and France, the Chunnel, at even greater speeds. The Eurotrain is the longest passenger train currently in service in the world.

♦ ♦ ♦

That direction continued across Europe. The French and German systems were equipping their flagship domestic trains to the same level of opulence as the TEE equipment, and the Germans even began assigning identical equipment, painted in the TEE red and cream, to their domestic intercity trains. The Spanish national system (Renfe) had joined the TEE network in 1969, using its own patented Talgo lightweight equipment, and since it operated on 5-foot-6-inch (1.7m) gauge, rather than 4-foot-8½ inch (1.4m) gauge, the concept of an easily identified standard luxurious train set was beyond salvation.

Nevertheless, the TEE system did succeed in linking the business centers of Europe with a network of fast, comfortable, extra-fare trains that could compete with the airlines. By 1972, the network was almost entirely electrically powered, with only seven of thirty-five trains hauled by diesel-electric locomotives. In 1989, the Trans-Europe Express carried five hundred thousand passengers on thirty-five trains, operating more than twenty-seven routes and serving 125 stations in nine countries (Austria and Spain having joined the original seven).

CHAPTER NINE

PASSENGER TRAIN WRECKS

As with any other form of transportation, accidents and fatalities sometimes occur on trains. When the excitement of the citizenry and the potential
for profits encourage rapid growth in new technology that gets ahead of safety
improvements, injury and death are often the consequence. The first fatality
caused by a train was recorded on December 5, 1821, when David Brook, a carpenter walking
along the tracks of the Middleton Railway in England in a blinding sleet storm, was run over by a
train of coal wagons.

The first passenger known to have been killed was William Huskinson, member of Parliament
(for Liverpool). At the opening ceremony of the Liverpool and Manchester Railway on September
15, 1830, he was struck by Robert Stephenson's *Rocket*, fracturing a thigh. Huskinson was taken
by the locomotive Northumbrian to Eccles (near Manchester), where he died. Engineer George
Stephenson set a world speed record on that mercy mission, running at 36 miles per hour (58kph).

The Camden & Amboy Railroad recorded the first serious accident in the United States on
November 9, 1833, near Hightown, New Jersey. When a broken axle caused a carriage to overturn,
twelve of the twenty-four passengers were injured (including Cornelius "Commodore" Vanderbilt),
and one subsequently died. Vanderbilt was hurled from his carriage and down a thirty-foot (9.1m)
embankment, breaking several ribs and puncturing a lung. Because of these near-fatal injuries on his
first train ride, the Commodore refused to invest any of his immense fortune in railroads until thirty
years later. He ultimately became one of the greatest of the rail barons, controlling the vast New
York Central System. Incidentally, one of the uninjured passengers was former President of the
United States John Quincy Adams.

Australia's first fatal railway accident occurred on June 25, 1859, on a special train celebrating
the completion of the Geelong & Melbourne Railway line. As the train approached the Ocean
Child Hotel, Henry Walter, the railway's locomotive superintendent, was fatally injured when he
was knocked off the engine as it passed under a bridge. The country's first fatal wreck occurred

◆ ◆ ◆

It is a fundamental law of railroad physics that two trains cannot occupy the same track at the same time. This July
10, 1909, wreck at Bayshore, Long Island, well illustrates how wooden freight cars splintered in even a minor wreck.
A similar collision involving a passenger car would have been even more disastrous.

Left: Before photography was widely used, newspapers and magazines depended on artists to produce visual images of notable events. These wooden passenger cars of the Camden & Amboy are badly damaged in this mid-nineteenth-century crash, but there is no evidence of fire, which would have greatly increased the carnage. The train struck the surrey of one Dr. Hannigan, who was deaf and could not hear the warning whistle. Below: The fiery wreck of May 8, 1842, at Meudon, France, near Versailles, was notable for the heavy loss of life caused by the locked compartment doors. The practice of locking the passengers in was immediately thereafter prohibited as a result of the shocking carnage caused by this accident.

STAGED TRAIN WRECKS

One of the more curious forms of entertainment in the 1890s was the staged "cornfield meet." Huge crowds of people would pay a dollar a head to watch the thrilling spectacle of two locomotives crashing head-on at high speed. One of the earliest staged wrecks was at the 1896 Iowa State Fair, which drew eighty-nine thousand spectators.

The same emotion that draws people to disasters—fires, floods, tornadoes, riots, and so on—was tapped by promoters such as "Head-On Joe" Connolly, who destroyed 146 locomotives (mostly worn-out 4-4-0s) in seventy-three wrecks staged over thirty-six years. Sometimes, he attached old wooden coaches loaded with kerosene and flaming charcoal burners so that the splintered wreckage would explode into flames.

Such spectacles were not without risk, however. The Great Train Wreck, staged on September 15, 1896, by William G. Crush, General Passenger Agent of the Missouri-Kansas-Texas Railway (the MKT, or "Katy") drew thirty thousand spectators to a valley in Texas. The audience lined both hillsides, and when the two empty trains collided, the resulting boiler explosions hurled debris into the crowd, leaving a considerable number dead or injured.

when a train derailed at Haslem's Creek, near Lidcome, on July 10, 1868. Excessive speed on a curve caused the derailment, which killed two and injured thirteen.

As train speeds rose and passenger loads increased, so did the death and carnage. On May 8, 1842, an axle broke on one of the two locomotives hauling a fifteen-coach Versailles-to-Paris express, bringing the train to an almost instant halt. Several coaches piled on top of the locomotive, and the wreckage caught fire. Locked compartment doors prevented escape, and forty-eight passengers burned to death, which prompted the end of the practice of locking train doors in France.

The United States remained free of major rail disasters until the pivotal year of 1853, when 234 people were killed in 138 wrecks. In the first twenty years of U.S. railroading, an approximate total of only fifty fatalities had occurred, with no more than half a dozen deaths attributed to any one incident. There were many likely reasons for this relatively long period of innocence: trains ran slowly, about 15 mph (24kph), because of poor track quality; traffic was light, since there weren't many trains in operation; and trains rarely operated after dark, and if a night passenger train was run, a pilot locomotive preceded it to verify the safety of the right-of-way. In 1835, there were only 1,098 miles (1,767km) of track in the country, and still only 9,000 miles (14,484km) by 1853.

There were hazards in these early years, of course. The Best Friend of Charleston, the first commercial locomotive built in the United States, exploded on June 17, 1831, killing the fireman (a slave), who had become annoyed by the constant hissing of steam coming from the safety valve and had tied it closed. The South Carolina Railroad subsequently made a practice of including a barrier car piled high with cotton bales behind the locomotive to protect the passengers from the flying debris of any future explosions.

One of the worst problems during the early days of railroading was the deadly snake-head. Some early rail was made of a strap-iron running surface attached to wooden beams. These iron attachments would wear down and loosen until the strip would suddenly break loose under the force of a moving train, the loose end curling upward until it pierced the floor of the cars, doing dreadful damage to the passengers as it "snaked" through the train.

The first U.S. wreck of the fateful year of 1853 occurred on January 6, when a Boston & Main train was derailed by a broken axle at Andover, Massachusetts, and tumbled down an embankment. President-elect Franklin Pierce was injured, and his twelve-year-old son killed, which generated considerable publicity for the wreck. On March 4, a Pennsylvania Railroad mail train plowed into the rear end of a stopped emigrant train at Mount Union, Pennsylvania, setting a new record of seven deaths.

Then came the first of two disasters that shocked the nation. An express and an emigrant train collided at a crossing near Chicago, killing twenty-one of the people aboard. Just eleven days later, a train ran

The 1873 disaster at Meadowbrook, Rhode Island, was typical of many early train wrecks. The derailed wooden cars splintered and caught fire, either from coals spilled from overturned heating stoves or from the locomotive fire box. These fires often caused more casualties than the wreck itself.

through an open draw bridge at Norwalk, Connecticut, plunging into the river and drowning forty-six unlucky passengers.

The number of calamities grew at an alarming rate throughout the second half of the century. Engines derailed, boilers exploded, bridges collapsed, trains collided, and fires from overturned heating stoves set fire to splintered wooden coaches. In 1890, 6,335 people died and 35,362 were injured on U.S. railroads, only forty years after the fatality-free year of 1850.

Train wrecks can be easily divided into categories, according to type of failure: right-of-way failures, including bridge collapses, washouts, and broken rails; equipment failures, including boiler explosions, broken axles, and brake problems; operations failures, including engineers missing signals, switching mistakes, misunderstood train orders, and excessive speed; and obstructions on the track, including other trains, road vehicles, animals, or debris.

Top: On August 14, 1865, a Housatonic Railroad locomotive struck the rear of a stopped passenger train, telescoping into the interior of the last car and starting a fire. It seems most unlikely that any of the passengers of the "Ladies Car" would have survived the telescoping to be evacuated through the windows, as is depicted here. Above: Railroad crossings at grade were especially dangerous locations before improvements in signaling and communication made possible the coordination of trains on the intersecting lines. One of the earliest of the railroad-crossing disasters was this 1853 collision between an express and an emigrant train near Chicago; twenty-one people were killed.

RIGHT-OF-WAY FAILURES

Quick and cheap construction methods, particularly in the United States, led to many bridge and track failures and subsequent carnage. Rapid expansion over great distances, with little on-line traffic to help pay the bills, soon outstripped available capital, so it was inevitable that grading and track-laying would be done as quickly as possible.

This hasty construction procedure began in the United States when the government rewarded the new railroads with grants for land that lay alongside the completed track. The financial health of a railroad could be critically dependent upon the ability to resell this trackside property to farmers and industrialists who would ultimately ship their products on the line, so it was common for railroads to quickly lay the track down and then return later for upgrades, once the cash began to flow.

Shortcuts meant that fills would continue to settle, cuts might be left with steep sides that occasionally slid, temporary wooden trestles and bridges might span low spots or streams, and the track was often left unballasted. Most routes would inevitably remain single-tracked with occasional passing sidings, and inchoate methods of keeping trains separated were not yet even close to being fail-safe.

In contrast, engineers working on the British rails often covered relatively short routes, and were more inclined to build for permanence. Substantial masonry or iron bridges along with well-established double-track main lines made for a safer right-of-way. Even so, Charles Dickens was injured on June 9, 1865, when his South Eastern Railway train derailed at Staplehurst, Kent, after it ran onto a viaduct where track repairs were under way, killing ten workers. Dickens never fully recovered and died precisely five years later, on June 9, 1870.

As the nineteenth century went on, growing rail systems, greater speed, and heavier traffic continued to overwhelm any safety improvements that had been devised. Steel rail, air brakes, signaling systems, steam heat, the telegraph, and better couplers all improved safety, but as Lucius Beebe said, "The Grim Reaper has not altogether been outdistanced by progress." The carnage continued: the crash of an excursion train at Camp Hill, Pennsylvania, burned sixty-six children to death in 1856; a coal stove broke in a derailed car that plunged off a bridge at Angola, New York, burning another forty-two travelers in 1867; and the Lakeshore Express plunged through a high bridge near Ashtabula, Ohio, in 1876, carrying eighty passengers to a fiery death.

It wasn't necessary for a bridge to collapse to cause death. Australia's notorious Inkerman Bridge over the Burdekin River was built as a low, sloping trestle with 135 spans in its half-mile (800m) length. The builders set deck level at only 10 feet (3m) above normal water level, to allow for flood debris to flow safely over the bridge during high water. The water level of the Burdekin rose and fell rapidly, particularly during the rainy

While many of the illustrations that newspapers ran were billed as "drawn on the spot," others were based purely on conjecture. This Otto Stark engraving attempts to re-create the terror of the passengers at the moment of impact on the interior of a doomed car during an 1888 collision near Steamburg, New York.

✦ ✦ ✦

season, and trains were often held up, waiting for the water to fall. Twice, trains became trapped on the bridge when floating sticks protruding through the ties snagged the brake gear and dumped the air (that is, suddenly released the air pressure in the brakes). This was difficult to correct, as the cars overhung the trestle deck.

In a March 9, 1945, incident, it took fifteen minutes for engineers to find an open valve under the tender and move the locomotive off the bridge to reach the problem area, during which time the water unexpectedly rose several feet. This trapped the guard and six passengers, who climbed onto the roofs of the cars as the cars began to heel. While train personnel released cattle from a stock car, the train was swept off the bridge. The guard and four of the passengers survived by holding onto the tails of swimming cattle until they could reach trees floating in the water and be rescued. The bridge was replaced with a much higher series of steel trusses in 1957.

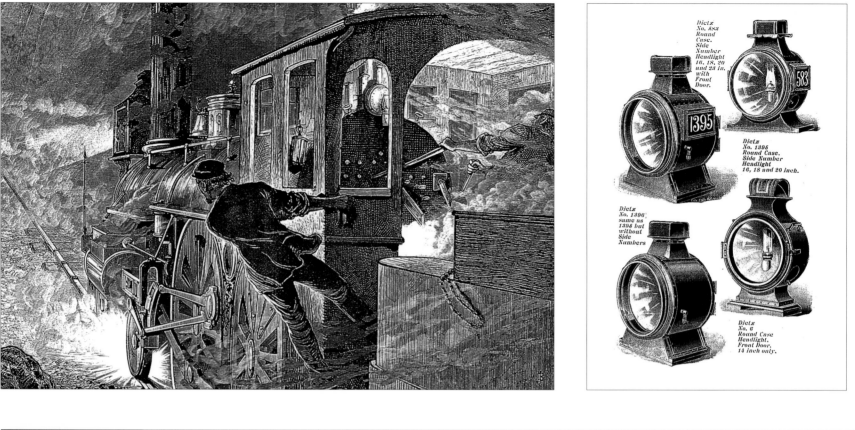

Top left: Before the invention of automatic block signaling, which warned a following train that another train was close ahead, the brakeman of a train was responsible for its protection when the train was stopped on the track. Lit "fusees" (flares) stuck in a tie and hand-carried lanterns were good visible warnings, but when visibility was poor, another important device was the torpedo, a small explosive cap that could be fastened to a rail with flexible lead straps. When a locomotive wheel rolled over the torpedo, a loud explosion warned the crew of danger ahead. Upon hearing such an explosion, the brakeman on the following train would immediately apply the brakes. Top right: Headlights were not deemed important in Britain, but North American railroads quickly recognized them as critical to safety. These illustrations from the Dietz catalog show several available styles of kerosene-burning lights. Beginning in 1881, onboard steam-powered generators were installed; this paved the way for a conversion to safer, electric lamps. Above: Chicago & Eastern Illinois No. 1, a mail train, was involved in a wintry locomotive-to-locomotive collision near Thornton, Illinois, on February 9, 1885.

CASEY JONES
(1864–1900)

✦ ✦ ✦

Perhaps the most celebrated locomotive engineer, John Luther "Casey" Jones hired on as an apprentice telegrapher with the Mobile & Ohio at the age of fifteen, dreaming of becoming an engineer. He became a fireman at the age of eighteen, then moved to the Illinois Central (IC), passing his engineer's examination in 1890.

Next to his wife, Illinois Central 2-8-0 No. 638 became the most important thing in his life. This locomotive was assigned to Casey in 1893, after having been exhibited at the Columbian Exhibition, and he installed on it his famous six-chime whistle, whose whippoorwill call was instantly recognized along his run, from Jackson, Tennessee, to Water Valley, Mississippi.

Casey gave up his beloved locomotive in 1899, when he was offered a regular passenger run on the IC's premier train—the Chicago-to-New Orleans Cannonball, which he would handle from Memphis to Canton, Mississippi. Engineers took the time schedule very seriously, and it was a matter of extreme personal pride to keep a train running on time.

On April 29, 1900, Casey and his regular fireman, Simm Webb, brought the northbound Cannonball into Memphis on time and learned that the southbound train had been delayed. The engineer scheduled to take the train south from Memphis was ill, so Casey and Simm filled in, leaving the Poplar Street Depot at 12:50 A.M., an hour and a half late on a dark foggy night.

They made up a full hour (where the scheduled running time was two hours and forty-five minutes) on the first 100 miles (161km) of straight, level track to Granada, Mississippi, and were almost on time at Durant, 55 miles (88.5km) farther on. There they picked up orders to meet the northbound Cannonball at Goodman (where there was a passing siding) and then to "saw-by" two side-tracked freights farther south at Vaughn. Casey sped into the foggy night at 70 mph (113kph), with his whistle singing, determined to make Canton on time.

The meet at Goodman went as expected, but the situation at Vaughn was rapidly deteriorating. A saw-by is a complicated maneuver during which the combined length of the meeting northbound and southbound freights exceeded the length of the available siding, blocking the main line so that a third train cannot pass. An engineer would normally simply pull past the north end of the siding until his rear end cleared the switch, enabling the trains on the siding to pull north onto the main line behind him until the south switch was clear. It was this back-and-forth sawing motion that inspired the name of the maneuver.

At Vaughn that night, the situation was complicated by another northbound passenger train, No. 26, which was to take the third track at Vaughn, a short siding. While sawing north to allow No. 26 into the siding, an air hose burst on the southbound freight, leaving a caboose and three cars fouling the main line in the path of the speeding Cannonball.

The stalled freight's brakeman ran frantically up the track, setting a warning torpedo on a rail and continuing about a half mile (800m) farther down the track, until he saw Casey's headlight through the gloom. The train sped past, ignoring the waving lantern, and Casey didn't hit the brakes until the explosion of the torpedo, but by then the glowing red markers of the caboose were in sight. Casey shouted, "Jump, Simm! Jump and save yourself!"

Simm jumped out of the cab, but Casey Jones rode No. 382 into the standing freight train—and into legend. The reasons behind Casey's reckless approach to Vaughn are unknown. He was aware of the saw-by meet, and he ignored the lantern warning. Even so, he managed to reduce speed considerably, and was the only fatality. A friend of Casey's named Wallace Saunders (an engine wiper in the Canton shops) contributed to the legend when he began to rhythmically chant, "Casey Jones, Casey Jones." The chant spread, and was heard by a professional songwriter, who polished the lyrics and added music, giving us the most famous railroad ballad in American folklore.

Casey Jones and fireman J.W. (Bull) McKinnie pose on Illinois Central 2-8-0 No. 638, Casey's "personal" engine from 1893 to 1899. The locomotive was famed for its carefully polished brass and six-chime "whippoorwill" whistle. It was in No. 382 that Casey became a legend, however, by driving the locomotive into the rear of a stalled freight train.

THE WASHINGTON UNION STATION RUNAWAY

◆ ◆ ◆

One of the most spectacular U.S. train wrecks happened on January 15, 1953. Pennsylvania Railroad's sixteen-car Federal Express was southbound from Boston, crowded with visitors heading for the presidential inauguration of Dwight D. Eisenhower, when sticking brakes caused a stop in Kingston Swamp, Rhode Island. A stuck angle cock on the third car was found to be the culprit, the brakes were checked, and the train proceeded after a fifty-six-minute delay.

At New Haven, Connecticut, the crews changed, but no mention was made of the brake incident, and the train headed south for New York, Philadelphia, and Baltimore, with no further problems. At Baltimore, Harry Brower took over as engineer on GG1 electric No. 4876 and barreled through the rural Maryland countryside at 80 mph (129kph), until

his first brake application, just two miles (3.2km) out of Washington's Union Station—the Federal didn't slow down at all.

Brower set the emergency brake, which should have locked all the brakes on the train and brought it to an immediate sliding stop—but it didn't work. The Federal Express was running out of control on the downgrade leading to the dead-end track at the terminal. The engineer could only blow his horn repeatedly, warning that he was coming.

The operator at a tower a mile (1.6km) out from the station heard the blasts, realized what they meant, and called the station with the warning, "There's a runaway coming on track sixteen—get the hell out of there!" There was barely enough time to clear the elegant, vaulted concourse of passengers, porters, and vendors before the the train hit.

Above: Fortunately, when the Federal Express plowed through the station master's office, that particular official had left the room to set up the departure boards, which at the time were manually operated. Opposite: Workmen assess the task of clearing the wreckage of Pennsylvania Railroad GG1 No. 4876 after it crashed through the concourse of Washington Union Station. Because the 230-ton (207t) GG1 was too heavy to lift, it was left in the basement until it could be cut up into manageable pieces, and a temporary wooden floor was installed over the site so that the crowds attending the Eisenhower inauguration could be accommodated. The damage caused exceeded $1 million. It was back in service ten months later.

◆ ◆ ◆

With a thunderous roar and a terrible screech, the huge GG1 crashed through the wall, plowed across the concourse, smashed through the station master's office, and demolished the main newsstand. Just as it was about to penetrate the main waiting room, the floor gave way, and, like a dying animal, the locomotive and two coaches fell into the basement baggage room. The station clock was stopped at 8:00 A.M., setting the precise time of the wreck.

Amazingly, although the injuries totaled eighty-seven, there were no deaths, but property damage exceeded $1 million. The cause of the wreck was found to be the same closed angle cock that was first discovered in Rhode Island.

Because the insurer, Lloyd's of London, required it, GG1 No. 4876 was hauled (in pieces) from the basement and sent to Altoona for repairs and returned to service on the Pennsy. It finished out its days hauling commuters for the New Jersey Department of Transportation. Washington's Union Station was repaired and continues to serve rail passengers and, following its restoration and partial conversion to a commercial mall, shoppers and tourists.

EQUIPMENT FAILURES

From the earliest days, equipment failure was often cited as the cause of accidents. As railroad technology matured (and became more complex), failures became even more likely. Safety improvements were constantly being made in the equipment: better metallurgy and design helped to solve the problem of broken axles, wheels, and rails; the air brake improved braking power and limited runaways; and steel car construction minimized telescoping. But the growing complexity of the equipment, combined with lax maintenance, often led to failures of other kinds.

The most serious Australian train wreck occurred on Easter Monday, April 20, 1908, when a doubleheaded Victorian Railway Easter train from Bendigo plowed into the rear end of a stopped Ballarat train at the Sunshine depot, 8½ miles (13.5km) from Melbourne. The moving train smashed through the guard's van and three coaches of the stopped train, telescoping several of the other cars. There were no injuries on the Bendigo train, but there were forty-four deaths and 431 injuries on the stopped train. Many who survived the actual impact suffocated or burned in the resulting fire.

The guard on the Ballarat train survived a close call. He had just whistled off his train when he heard the roar of the approaching locomotives and dived onto the platform as the car splintered behind him.

The engineers on the Bendigo train admitted that they had seen both the caution and stop signals as they approached the station. They had had plenty of time to stop, and their air-brake gauges indicated adequate pressure, but the train refused to comply. One engineer blamed the Westinghouse brake system, which had been subject to malfunction, releasing the brakes at the moment of heaviest application.

An investigation by experts yielded various criticisms of the coaches' brakes, ranging from "certainly feeble" to "poorly braked." Some had no functioning brakes at all. Then a series of thirteen brake tests using the Bendigo train failed to find a braking problem, and the engineers were tried for manslaughter. Charges were ultimately dropped and no cause was officially determined, but the accident illustrates the difficulties encountered with the early air-brake technology.

OPERATIONS FAILURES

In addition to equipment failure, occupancy of the same section of track by more than one train caused many accidents. It could be a head-on collision ("cornfield meet") caused by faulty or misread train orders that allowed a train to leave a passing siding too early, a missed signal that

Trains made up of a series of wooden cars were often subject to "telescoping," a horrifying calamity in which one car slid over the floor and between the walls of another, like the tubes in a telescope. On August 10, 1887, a Niagara Falls–bound Toledo, Peoria & Western train crashed through a trestle and telescoped at Chatsworth, Illinois. The death toll was eighty-two.

set track switches that hurtled two trains together. Human error and a failure to obey the rules were at the root of many disasters.

Canada's first major train wreck occurred near Chatham, Ontario, when a Great Western track-ballast train collided with a passenger train in 1854, killing forty-seven. Britain's worst disaster was May 22, 1915, at Quintinshill, near Gretna Green. A signaling failure allowed a military train to plow into a standing train, telescoping it from the original length of 639 feet (195m) to 201 feet (61.5m). A speeding express train arrived from the opposite direction just fifty-three seconds later and crashed into the wreckage. The wreck and resulting fire killed 227 people.

So many railway disasters were deemed the result of human error that a New York newspaper editorialized that "A vast majority of railroad disasters are directly owing to the stupidity and neglect of the employees, and the apathy and avarice of the railroad officers."

Until the invention of the telegraph, the primary method of separating trains was the railroad timetable, which set departure times and contained rules to cover late trains and other abnormal situations. It was essential to rigidly adhere to the scheduled times, since once a train left a station, there was no way to contact it until it arrived at the next station. The system worked reasonably well, but breakdowns and fog caused many a delay, and there were far too many cases when the opposite-running train failed to arrive at its destination on time. The rules frequently allowed for the standing train to depart at cautionary speed after a fixed amount of time had passed, moving to the next available passing spot. All too often, the slowly moving train would meet the fast-moving opposite-running train (which was running late and trying to make the station before the standing train was allowed to leave) on a curve or other place with restricted visibility.

THE CHATSWORTH WRECK

◆ ◆ ◆

The wreck at Chatsworth became a part of midwestern folk lore. T.P. Westendorf composed a song called "The Bridge Was Burned at Chatsworth." A typically vivid verse went as follows.

The mighty crash of timbers
A sound of hissing steam
The groans and cries of anguish
A woman's stifled scream.
The dead and dying mingled,
With broken beams and bars
An awful human carnage
A dreadful wreck of cars.

Disaster inevitably resulted.

In some cases, a staff or token signifying the right of the train to be on the track (with only one available for each section of track) was given at the entry to a particular section to a train's crew, which would carry the emblem to the end of that section of track. If a crew was in possession of the staff, it could be confident that no other train would be on that section, unless of course there was a violation of the rules. This was an imperfect system at best, because one train could not immediately follow another in the same direction, since the staff in question would be at the other end of the section.

The invention of the telegraph made it possible to communicate between stations. The telegrapher could report passing trains to the dispatcher, who could issue orders changing the meeting place of trains.

Above left: Although several other signaling methods had been tried, it was the semaphore, a visual telegraph, that became the first standardized railway signal system. Introduced in England by Charles Hutton Gregory in 1841, the semaphore's three positions could signal "proceed," "caution," or "stop," both by blade position and by colored lights. The addition of a second blade provided information on the status of the upcoming two sections of track. The development of electricity and powerful batteries allowed the railroads to convert to multicolored signal lights that were automatically activated when a train occupied a track section. **Above right:** Heavy fog contributed to a missed signal and this collision in London in 1937. The location of the wreck, in the middle of a bridge, added to the difficulty of the rescue efforts.

This flexibility greatly improved the organization of train movements but still depended on human intervention, which left plenty of room for error. The dispatcher's information had to be correct, the message had to be understood and properly passed on by the telegraphers, and the train crews had to understand the order and carry it out properly. Many an engineer was found dead in a wreck with the dispatcher's orders—often disregarded or misunderstood—in his pocket.

Electrically operated track circuits opened up the possibility of both automatic train detection and electrically interlocked signals, which would reduce the need for manually operated signal towers. George Westinghouse formed the Union Switch & Signal Company, one of several similar manufacturers, to develop the more reliable automated signaling systems that are still in use today.

Even then, wrecks caused by human error have not been eliminated. On January 4, 1987, a Conrail crew ferrying a string of locomotives fell asleep and rolled past several signals, partway off a siding and through a closed track switch at Chase, Maryland. The crewmembers eventually awoke, but were unable to back into the siding, because the train straddled the switch. They were then struck by the northbound Amtrak Colonial moving at over 100 mph (161kph). Sixteen crew members and passengers on the Amtrak train were killed in the collision. The Conrail engineer was found to be under the influence of drugs. This tragedy set the stage for new transportation safety regulations requiring mandatory drug testing.

Sabotage on the railroads was rare, but this 1939 wreck of the City of San Francisco was attributed to a mysterious "one-eared man" who was suspected of shifting a rail, thereby sending the City of San Francisco careening off a bridge into the Humboldt River on August 14, 1939. The sleeper Chinatown sprawls on its side atop the wreckage of the bridge and four other demolished cars; twenty passengers died and 114 were injured.

✦ ✦ ✦

OBSTRUCTIONS ON THE TRACK

From the early days of the wide-open right-of-way, buffalo, cows, and other large beasts created problems for railroads, especially in the United States, Canada, and Australia. Light locomotives, such as the *John Bull* of the Camden & Amboy Railroad, the first Stephenson Planet-type locomotive imported to the United States (1831), could easily be derailed. To address the derailment problem, a two-wheeled truck (bogie) and pilot were fitted to the front of the *John Bull* by Isaac Dripps, the line's master mechanic. This was the first example of the locomotive pilot, or "cowcatcher." As the railroads pushed west, the pilot evolved into a very elegant, long, pointed, wooden device that pushed obstructions to the side, preventing them from slipping under the wheels and causing a derailment. *John Bull* is preserved at the Smithsonian Institution in Washington, D.C.

Other important safety devices were developed early on. The first headlight is attributed to the South Carolina Railroad in 1831, when a crew pushed a flat car loaded with flaming pine knots in front of the locomotive. Candles and whale oil were burned in reflector lamps through the 1840s and 1850s, until gas and kerosene lamps were introduced in 1859. Electric headlights first appeared in 1881, with the oscillating (Mars-type) headlight debuting in 1936 and the sealed beam lamp in 1946.

The first steam whistle was invented by Adrian Stephens (1795–1876) of Wales in 1832. Its use as a warning device on locomotives started in 1835 in England, spread to North America in 1836, and to France in 1837. Bells were fitted on American locomotives in great numbers in 1835, when the state of Massachusetts passed legislation requiring them.

As the number of carriage roads grew, grade crossings became ever more likely locations for dangerous accidents. At first, the heavy locomotives simply shattered the lighter-weight wagons and carriages, but by the 1920s, motor vehicles had grown too large for pilots to easily sweep them away, and crossing accidents came to be the greatest hazard for train crews. Despite the inventions of various warning devices and even gates to block the roads, motor vehicles and trains continue to collide, with inevitably devastating results for the vehicles and sometimes for the trains as well.

Large trucks are particularly dangerous. When laden with heavy loads such as concrete, stone, logs, or heavy machinery, a truck can easily derail a speeding passenger train. When loaded with flammables such as gasoline, the resulting explosion and fireball can be instantly fatal to crews in the front of diesel locomotives, not to mention the passengers. In one such accident, a Santa Fe passenger train hit a tank truck loaded with over 6,000 gallons (22,712l) of crude oil at Rosedale, California, on March 1, 1960. The resulting explosion ignited the derailed train, killing fourteen people.

A makeshift bus loaded with migrant farm workers crossed in front of a fast-moving Southern Pacific train on September 17, 1963. The violent collision, at Chualar, California, killed thirty-two of the workers and severely injured the rest.

Rural grade crossings, often protected by only a pair of crossbucks (the standard North American X-shaped warning sign), continue to be the sites of disastrous accidents. A farm family of seven on their way to work were killed on June 8, 1990, when they were struck by Amtrak's Pioneer at 6:25 A.M. outside Nyassa, Oregon, near the Idaho state line. The train was moving at 79 mph (127kph) when it struck the pickup almost head-on. The truck was embedded in the locomotive's nose and carried forward for almost a mile (1.6km) before the train could stop.

SAFETY REGULATIONS

The public outrage that invariably followed the early carnage continued to increase as the growing technology became more potentially lethal to greater numbers of people, and this outrage was fueled by crusading newspapers that often included horrific illustrations in their accident coverage. But safety regulations were often delayed or tabled when state legislators were lobbied by the influential—and wealthy—railroad barons.

After eighty-two people were killed when an excursion train crashed through a 15-foot (4.6m) wooden trestle that had caught fire at Chatsworth, Illinois, the public outcry forced the U.S. government to take action. A study of the history of rail accidents led to a 1901 requirement that railroads were to report all collisions and derailments to the Interstate Commerce Commission (ICC). In 1910, the requirement was extended to all accidents involving injury or property damage, and the ICC was given the authority to investigate any serious accident.

Over the years, railroad safety improved significantly. Steel cars with tight-lock knuckle couplers and reinforced vestibules eliminated the problem of telescoping cars, which had been so devastating to passengers. Steam heat replaced coal stoves, reducing fire hazard. Steel bridges replaced rickety wooden ones, and rolling mills produced heavier and more consistent rail. The train was well on the way to becoming the safest form of travel.

The presence of roving livestock on the unfenced right-of-way led North American railroaders to install pilots, or "cow-catchers," on locomotives. The Camden & Amboy's *John Bull* was the first recipient of this early style of scoopsike platform, which extended out in front of the locomotive.

GEORGE WESTINGHOUSE
(1846–1914)

◆ ◆ ◆

One of the most prolific inventors ever, George Westinghouse first applied his fertile mind to the pressing problems of railroad safety. His problem-solving technique was straightforward—"observe, critique, invent"—and he was awarded 361 personal patents over a forty-eight-year career, a rate of one patent every one and a half months.

As train speeds and lengths increased, the railroads faced a serious problem with braking. Various designs of steam brakes had been applied to locomotives, but stopping a train required brakemen to scramble across the roofs, turning individual brake wheels that mechanically applied the brakes on each car. The method was too slow and too dangerous to be practical. Trains often ran away on grades before sufficient braking power could be applied; there was no way to stop quickly; and many a brakeman slipped, falling to his death. Attempts to string chains between cars to connect all the brakes together failed.

The knowledge that a compressed air-powered drill had been used to build the 7-mile (11.5km) Mont Cenis Tunnel in the European Alps inspired Westinghouse to apply the same technology to railroad braking systems. In 1869, the twenty-two-year-old persuaded the Pennsylvania Railroad to try out his automatic air brake on a special three-car train. The railroad insisted that Westinghouse pay for the entire cost of installation as well as accept full responsibility for any damage to the railroad's equipment. Although his financial condition was desperate, Westinghouse agreed.

In the first test run, a trainload of officials accelerated out of the Pittsburgh depot and immediately passed through Grant's Hill Tunnel at 30 mph (48.5kph). At the exit of the tunnel, they encountered a teamster and his horses, who had ignored the warning signals and crossed in front of the onrushing train. The engineer gave the brake handle a twist and, with a rush of expelled air, the train braked to a halt just short of the rearing horse. The somewhat bruised and battered—but alive—officials and guests declared the test a success.

On July 9, 1869, Westinghouse founded the Westinghouse Air Brake Company (later known as WABCO), beginning with 150 employees. The new air-brake device underwent a number of modifications and improvements, including the 1872 triple valve, which enabled automatic braking if

George Westinghouse's revolutionary automatic air brake first went into regular service in 1869.

◆ ◆ ◆

a broken coupling or derailment separated the air hose connections between cars, which would release (or "dump") the air pressure. The number of runaway car accidents was thus greatly reduced. The 1887 quick action brake enabled simultaneous operation of all brakes in a fifty-car freight train. Westinghouse air brakes were soon used throughout the world.

Once the braking problem was solved, Westinghouse turned his attention to handling the problem of multiple trains on the same track by exploring electrically operated signals and switches. With his acquisition of the Union Electric Signal Company of Boston, he gained access to the closed-track circuit patents of Dr. William Robinson, along with several other safety and signaling appliances. He then purchased the Interlocking Switch and Signal Company of Harrisburg, Pennsylvania, which held the patents for the Saxeby & Farmer and Youcey & Buchanan interlocking machines, and consolidated the firms as the Union Switch & Signal Company in 1881. The company quickly became a leader in railroad signaling and safety devices.

Other significant Westinghouse inventions included the railroad friction draft gear, an electric street railway, high-powered gas engines, an automatic telephone system, and automotive air springs. In his studies of electricity, he defied convention and developed the alternating current (AC) system for power and light that we use today.

Despite numerous awards and honors bestowed upon him from around the world, Westinghouse remained a modest man. He was rarely photographed and did not allow his biography to be printed until he was in his fifties. He died from a heart ailment on March 12, 1914, just a few weeks after receiving his 346th patent. Fifteen more would be awarded following his death. The industrial empire that carries his name continued for many years as the Westinghouse Electric & Machine Co., championing research and innovation and reaching into fields as disparate as household appliances, diesel and electric locomotives, electrical transformers, and nuclear power. The Westinghouse Electric Corporation still exists today as a multinational conglomerate operating in similarly diverse fields of research and development.

Although the technology has developed to enable trains to travel at well over 100 mph (161kph), they have been restricted to newly constructed, grade-crossing-free, and completely private rail lines—allowing slow freights and crossing vehicles into the mix is simply too dangerous. Amtrak, for instance, does allow some freight traffic on its high-speed Northeast Corridor, but normally passenger-train speed is restricted by the engineering of grades and curvature that has been optimized for freight trains.

Human nature being what it is, there are always drivers who will race a train to a crossing, engineers who will fudge the speed limit, railroad employees who will try to work under the influence of alcohol or drugs, and managements that ignore the danger of fielding exhausted crews. As long as these situations persist, then the best engineering in the world will fail, and there will always be fatalities and injuries associated with rail travel.

Top: The wreck of Amtrak's Colonial in January 1987 was caused by a group of Conrail locomotives that ran a signal and came to a stop right in the path of another Amtrak train traveling at more than 100 mph (161kph). It was estimated that fewer than three seconds elapsed from the time the Colonial's engineer saw the obstruction until the impact. Sixteen passengers and crew perished in the fiery collision, while another 100 were injured. Here, rescuers and passengers struggle through the wreckage shortly after the collision. Above: Collisions at grade crossings with trucks carrying flammable liquids have accounted for the heaviest carnage in modern railroading. This 1960 collision between a Santa Fe passenger train and an oil truck at Bakersfield, California, killed seventeen, including the engine crew and truck driver.

1847 Liverpool Railway

CHAPTER TEN

DEPOTS, STATIONS, AND TERMINALS

The early railroad operators paid little attention to waiting-room accommodations for their patrons. Following the lead of their predecessors, the stagecoach lines and canal companies (which rarely provided special buildings for either freight or passengers), railroads typically departed from hotels or inns located along the tracks. If fares were not collected directly by the conductor on the train, tickets could be purchased at the departure points or other businesses in the towns served. Some pioneer railroads provided simple ticket booths, and even the earliest Baltimore & Ohio structure (Mount Clare in Baltimore) began as a ticket office, with no passenger shelter at all.

Old advertising provides ample evidence of the early days: "Starts every morning from the corner of Broadway and Race Street—Pioneer Fast Line to Pittsburgh, through in 3½ days" (1837); "A through train for the accommodation of western passengers will leave the vicinity of Broad and Callowhill Street. A McHaffey Supt. Columbia & Philadelphia Rail Road" (1837); "Departure from State Street, Albany. Mohawk & Hudson" (1834).

By 1831, Mount Clare had become a full-fledged "station," and the B&O followed with another substantial structure at Frederick, Maryland, thus establishing the first two true depots in the United States. Mount Clare, along with the adjacent roundhouse, has been restored as the excellent Baltimore & Ohio Railroad Museum.

The first depot in the world is credited to the Liverpool & Manchester Railway, whose Liverpool Road (Manchester, England) station opened September 15, 1830. The oldest station, however, is at Cuautla, Mexico. Railroad use began in 1860, and the station was converted from a convent built in 1657.

Whether a small-town depot or a big-city "union terminal," the structures varied greatly in design while maintaining the same basic functions: sales office for tickets; baggage collection and disposition; express office (for packages); provision for less-than–car load (LCL) freight; telegraph

✦ ✦ ✦

The grand train shed at Liverpool, England, circa 1870–1880, was typical of large urban stations around the world. The long-span roof made of iron or steel (which was relatively new at the time, Bessemer having perfected his refinement process in 1875) is punctured with numerous skylights and vents to maximize interior light and allow smoke to escape.

Above left: It seems that the Feather River Inn had enough traffic to justify a rudimentary depot for its well-dressed patrons. The log cabin-style was appropriate to the California mountain vacation area. Above right: In contrast to the Liverpool trainshed, the Northwestern Pacific's Ben Lomond Depot reflected the modest needs of a rural area in northern California. The number of waiting carriages indicates that this town, located north of San Francisco, was well on its way to becoming a populous suburb.

✦ ✦ ✦

office; and provision for issuing train orders. Small-town depots would include all these functions in one building. In a larger city, they might be split into separate facilities.

In more famous locations with lots of traffic, substantial masonry structures were erected, frequently designed by architects. Such luminaries as Frank Furness, Stanford White, Daniel Burnham, and Henry Hobson Richardson built numerous handsome stations, as did architects employed directly by the railroads.

COUNTRY DEPOTS

As railroads established themselves as a connection to the outside world, the depot often became an important focus for community activity—a social center and source of news and gossip. Train departures and arrivals were big events in small towns as mail, packages, friends, and family came and went. No arrival or departure went unnoticed. Political candidates made speeches from the rear platforms of private cars, husbands went to war, crates of baby chicks arrived in the baggage car, watches were set by the depot clock, and telegrams were sent and received. Activity was continuous, even between trains.

Many railroads standardized the designs for rural stations, making provision for several different building lengths to meet local needs. They were usually of a simple wood-frame construction, with a bay window

for the telegraph operator so that he could observe trains approaching from both directions. Next to the bay stood a manually operated signal board to inform the crews of approaching trains that written orders were waiting. In some remote locations, living quarters for the station agent and his family were included. In snowy New England, even small-town depots often included a small roofed area over the tracks to protect the loading area.

If the station was small enough, the station agent would be responsible for all duties: selling tickets, collecting and dispensing baggage and express packages, sweeping the floor and platform, and stoking the stove. He could also be the telegraph operator, handling train orders as well as telegrams. If conditions warranted, there might be a baggage man who would also be responsible for freight if it was a combination depot. Mail needed to be handled, often being snatched by a hook from a mail crane on the fly as the local mail sack was literally kicked off the train by the mail-car personnel. The unofficial railroaders would hang around the platform, idling away the summer hours watching trains come and go.

SMALL- AND MEDIUM-SIZE CITY STATIONS

As communities grew in size, often partly because of favorable rail connections, the railroad station became less important as a center of gossip and news but, as the entrance to the city, more important as a civic structure. The architecture of the station became more appropriate to its role in the community. Stone and brick, covered platforms, and prominent clock towers were frequently used to underscore the station as solid, substantial, and important. Railroads sometimes included offices in the structure, especially at division points where crews changed and shops were located.

Railroad-owned hotels could be a part of, or located adjacent to, the station. The Baltimore & Ohio favored such structures, and two promi-

nent examples were at Cumberland, Maryland, and Grafton, West Virginia. The Chesapeake & Ohio built the legendary Greenbrier resort alongside its tracks in the Allegheny Mountains, creating a destination for wealthy vacationers. The Santa Fe laid tracks leading to the Grand Canyon and built a hotel there, the El Tovar. The Canadian Pacific Railway operated a number of hotels across Canada, among the most prominent of which was the Banff Springs Hotel at Banff National Park in the Canadian Rockies.

The agent in a small depot had to wear multiple hats: ticket seller, telegrapher, baggage and freight handler, and even floor sweeper. Most of the tools necessary for the job are visible in this photo: racks of tickets and tags, calendar and timetable on the wall, rubber stamps, punches, book of freight rates, telegraph key. There is also a varmint hide on the wall, a testament to the agent's marksmanship.

SUBURBAN STATIONS

Suburban stations sprang up as city residents succumbed to the urge to move to the country, and rural residents found work in the city. Suburban depots varied greatly in architectural style and quality of materials, often reflecting the affluence of those residents who used the train daily. Older, once rural, depots were often replaced with new structures better suited to the morning and evening rushes. Long, covered platforms allowed for quick, protected boarding through multiple doors as the train eased to a brief stop.

URBAN DEPOTS

Major cities often had several large depots, if each local railroad generated enough traffic to justify them. Sometimes the facilities of several railroads were combined into one major structure, a "union station." This simplified ticket sales as well as the transfer of passengers and baggage between trains of different railroads. These larger structures also might have either railroad or rental offices on the upper floors, with large train sheds covering many tracks. Civic pride demanded that these important structures properly reflect the stature of their home town.

The world's largest station is Grand Central Terminal in New York City, which integrates subways, commuter railways, and long-distance passenger carriers in a single elegant structure. The current depot is the third, constructed between 1903 and 1913, and there are forty-four platforms on two underground levels, with forty-six tracks on the upper level and twenty-six on the lower level. Daily use grew to 180,000 passengers on 550 trains daily, including commuters. A record was set on July 3, 1947, when 252,288 people passed through the 48-acre (19.5ha) complex in one twenty-four-hour period.

Construction of this massive facility required the excavation of a million cubic yards (914,400cu.m) of soil. Two million more cubic yards (1,828,800cu.m) of granite were blasted and removed from an excavation that was 40 feet (12m) deep, 770 feet (235m) wide, and a half mile (800m) long, in the heart of midtown Manhattan. The terminal was built

◆ ◆ ◆

The handsome brick-and-stone depot at Durand, Michigan, reflected an importance that exceeded the size of the town. The grand terminal is a testament to the fact that Durand was the site of the crossing of the north-south Ann Arbor and the east-west Grand Trunk (Canadian National), as well as the junction of a GT secondary line. The picture is likely posed, as railroads tried to schedule trains so as not to clog the system like this. There are several 4-4-0s and 4-6-0s on the tracks, as well as open-platform wooden coaches, which dates this picture roughly to the early 1900s.

Above left: The frame depot at West Cornwall, Connecticut, included living quarters for the agent on the second floor. Above right: The handsome depot at Canaan, Connecticut, was built at a junction and crossing of the New York, New Haven & Hartford with the former Central New England, which was later absorbed by the NY, NH & H. This important junction required a substantial depot to serve passengers heading north to the Berkshire Mountains or west to Poughkeepsie, New York, from Hartford. In 1908, sixteen New Haven trains stopped here, and the Central New England scheduled twenty. The upper floors were likely used for railroad offices.

❖ ❖ ❖

on the same site as the earlier two depots, and temporary facilities enabled full operations to continue during construction.

Trains arrive and leave in a long tunnel under Park Avenue, requiring the use of electric locomotives in the underground portions. Two exterior levels are provided for vehicular traffic, with an elevated road surrounding the building at the 'second floor.'

The main concourse of Grand Central Station was called "one of the finest interior spaces ever erected" by several newspapers of the day. A vaulted ceiling soaring high over the vast concourse was painted a pale sky blue, with electric lights and gold leaf describing the heavenly constellations. Through the great south window could be seen a constantly changing parade of people passing along the glass-enclosed walkways. In the center of both the upper and lower levels stand large information booths to handle the needs of tens of thousands of commuters and long-distance travelers.

Pennsylvania Terminal (Penn Station), also in New York, was begun in 1903 to a design by the noted architects McKim, Mead & White. Started simultaneously were access tunnels under the Hudson and East Rivers, a massive two-track fill across the Hackensack Meadows, and a coach yard in Long Island City. The magnificent waiting room of Penn Station was patterned after the Roman Baths of Caracalla and was one of the largest in the world. It was 277 feet (84.5m) long, 107 feet (32.5m)

wide, and 150 feet (45.5m) high. The train concourse served thirty-two underground platforms and was inspired by the Basilica of Constantine, with great latticed steel columns rising to a vaulted roof of iron and glass.

As the railroad's public showcase, no expense was spared when it came to finishes and details. Shortly after it was built, historian Nathaniel Burt declared it to be "A Trojan Horse right here on Manhattan Island, a massive insult to the Vanderbilts [whose interests included Grand Central Terminal]." In 1945, 190 million passengers passed through the magical spaces, but this great depot fell victim to soaring land values in the 1960s. To the despair of historians and architects, the great halls and concourses were demolished, leaving only the underground portions to serve as the Pennsylvania Railroad's link to Manhattan. The destruction of Penn Station did have one positive outcome, however: it mobilized people to protect other historic sites around the city from demolition.

Other major stations include: Washington, D.C.'s Union Station, with thirty-two platforms; Saint-Lazare, Paris, with twenty-seven; and Clapham Junction, Britain's largest station in area as well as its busiest junction (twenty-two hundred trains passed through every twenty-four hours in the 1980s). At the height of rail travel, these large urban depots were a veritable beehive of activity. Chicago's Union Station boasted that

Left: The crush of commuters during the morning and evening rush hours required suburban stations to have long platforms for quick loading into multiple cars, as well as extensive roofed areas in case bad weather prevailed. These realities of twentieth-century life are well illustrated by this depot in Scarsdale, New York.

Below: The weathered frame depot at Saugus, California, is representative of the Southern Pacific's standard small-town depot design. The first floor bay window housed the operator, who had a clear view down the tracks. The forked device on the pole in front of the operator's bay allowed the train crew to safely pick up train orders (written operating instructions from the dispatcher) without stopping. The operator wrote out the orders and tied the slip of paper to a long string that looped over the forked arm. A signal (order board) alerted the engineer if he had orders, and whether or not he had to stop (some critical instructions had to be signed for). If the train didn't have to stop, the fireman would lean out the window and poke his arm through the loop, snagging the string and retrieving the orders on the fly. Another set could then be strung for conductor (who was in the caboose), although some devices had twin arms to handle both sets. Without such a device, the operator had to stand next to the tracks and "hoop up" the orders on a hand-held pole. Radios have all but eliminated the need for written orders.

twenty-four information clerks answered thirty-six hundred questions, porters handled one hundred thousand sacks of mail, and patrons of the depot's restaurants consumed seven hundred pies every twenty-four hours.

The great train sheds of these large urban terminals were engineering marvels when they were built. Huge iron and steel trusses frequently spanned distances exceeding two hundred feet (61m). The stations typically included as much glass as possible, both on the sides and in the roof itself, using large areas of skylights or glazed clerestories to bring natural light into the cavernous interiors. Ample ventilation was needed at the peaks to enable smoke and steam to escape. Even so, it was a challenge to keep the glass clean for the thousands of people, both commuters and long-distance travelers, who passed through daily.

RESTORATION AND REUSE

The term "train station" brings to mind many different images, depending on one's personal experiences. A small-town depot is very different from a large, cosmopolitan rail center, and commuting to a large depot is different from the childhood experience of going down to the local station to meet visiting relatives. But most people of the late-twentieth-century

Top and above: Occasionally, major tourist destinations were important enough that tracks might be laid to the location for the convenience of passengers and to the profit of the railroad. The Grand Canyon was one of these attractions, and the Santa Fe built a 64-mile (102km) line from Williams to the south rim. The Southwest-style El Tovar Hotel was built by the Santa Fe to accommodate tourists. The hotel was operated by the Fred Harvey organization, which was also responsible for the Santa Fe's dining cars.

Opposite bottom: Early November light streams into the great waiting room of Pennsylvania Station in New York City in this early view. This monumental space, which measured 277 feet (84.5m) long, 107 feet (32.5m) wide, and 150 feet (45.5m) high, represented only one portion of the terminal area. Left: The exposed steelwork of Penn Station's concourse and platforms contrasts with the classical finishes of the waiting room above, but those lacy columns and arched girders are appropriate reminders of the engineering advances pioneered by the Pennsylvania Railroad. Below: In 1945, 109 million passengers passed along Pennsylvania Station's twenty-one tracks and 5 miles (8km) of platforms. The railroad embraced steel passenger-car construction to mitigate the perils of the miles upon miles of tunnels necessary to reach the terminal and maneuver within it.

✦ ✦ ✦

industrialized world could probably describe the depot, station, or terminal that was the gateway to their town. Such reverence for a civic structure is rare; perhaps only the venerable town hall or county courthouse holds a similar position in most communities.

This emotional bond that people feel for train stations has led to the preservation of many fine old depots around the world, when thousands of other more plebeian structures have met the wrecking ball. The current levels of passenger service in most U.S. and Canadian cities rarely require the vast train sheds and monumental structures that were found necessary in the first half of the twentieth century, so financially viable alternative uses for these structures are often found, sometimes combined with railroad uses. Even so, Amtrak has restored many smaller depots as such, particularly in its Northeast corridor.

Left: Grand Central Terminal, which was nicknamed the "Gateway to a Continent," was considered the most beautiful edifice in New York City at the time of its construction. Spread over 48 acres (19.5ha) in the heart of Manhattan, the structure covers forty-eight below-grade platform tracks, as well as numerous others needed for servicing the terminal. Above: Grand Central Station is pictured here during an abnormally quiet moment in the wartime traffic. During World War II, the great windows were covered over with patriotic murals in response to blackout requirements, but the elegance of "the most beautiful room in the world" is still obvious and the twenty-five hundred gold-leaf stars still glowed on the cerulean blue ceiling alongside the sixty stars that were illuminated with electric bulbs.

A Collection of Interesting Depot Facts

◆ ◆ ◆

The world's highest railway station is on the meter-gauge line from Rio Mulato to Potosi at Condor, Bolivia, where the altitude is 15,705 feet (4,787m).

The world's highest standard-gauge railway station is on the Peru Central at Galera, at an altitude of 15,673 feet (4,777m).

The world's lowest railway station (which closed in 1949) was at Samakh, Israel, at the south end of the Sea of Galilee, where the elevation was 613 feet (187m) below sea level.

The train shed roof with the longest span was built for the second Broad Street Station, Philadelphia, at 300 feet (91m). It was completed in 1892 by the Philadelphia & Reading RR, under engineer William Henry Brown.

The largest station roof in Great Britain is Saint Pancras, London, with a span of 240 feet (73m) and a height of 100 feet (31m) above the tracks. It was completed in 1868 by the Midland Railway, William Henry Barlow, engineer.

The largest station roof in South America can be found at Retiro Terminal, Buenos Aires. The 820-foot-long (250m) roof spreads 328 feet (100m), using two spans. It was fabricated in England by the Hamilton Iron Works of Liverpool and shipped to the former Argentine Central Railway, and was completed in 1915.

The busiest depot in the world is at Châteleot, Paris, where 144 trains pass through the junctions at each end in the peak hour.

The station without a railroad—Dartmouth, Devon, Great Britain—was never served by a train after opening in 1864. A ferry across the Dart Estuary connected Dartmouth with the Kingswear station, where the trains stopped.

London-bound trains of the London & North Western Railway and the Great Western Railway left the station at Chester going in opposite directions.

Above: The beaux arts–style Union Station in Washington, D.C., was designed by the noted architect Daniel Burnham and was completed in 1907. Owned by the Washington Terminal Company, whose stockholders were the Pennsylvania and Baltimore & Ohio railroads, it was called "the perfect example of the city gate, designed in perfect harmony with the community for which it serves as the entrance."

◆ ◆ ◆

A number of large terminals have been converted to serve shoppers and tourists. Mid-size depots have become libraries, town halls, and even, in one case, a college of the arts (the Maryland Institute College of Art in Baltimore, formerly the Baltimore & Ohio's Mount Royal Station). Smaller rural depots have been converted to restaurants, antique shops, real estate offices, chamber of commerce offices, and museums. Many of the frame structures have been moved off railroad property and converted into private homes.

Washington's Union Station, the gateway to the capital of the United States, is still used for rail passengers, but a major portion of the vast facility has been converted to a shopping mall. Along the south shore of the Monangahela River in Pittsburgh, what was once the Pittsburgh & Lake Erie Railroad's sprawling facility—including freight houses and other structures—has been converted to a very successful shopping area. An elegant restaurant occupies the grand, faux marble-columned Edwardian waiting room, the restoration of which was paid for by a large grant from a local philanthropic foundation, while commercial financing underwrote the conversion of the train sheds. The Amtrak station in Pittsburgh moved into a remodeled baggage facility in Pittsburgh's Pennsylvania Station, with the depot's office tower converted to luxury apartments and its waiting area set aside for commercial use.

That so much effort and expense is frequently lavished on underused depots in cities and towns around the world is ample evidence of the importance that rail travel continues to hold in the human psyche.

Above: The Michigan Central depot in Detroit, Michigan, is topped by an office tower, which could either be used by the railroad or leased to outside tenants, reflecting the flexible and intensive use of small plots of land made necessary by the high costs of urban locations. Note the trolley in the foreground: urban stations needed to have public transit service to facilitate delivery of passengers to their final destinations. Left: The Musee d'Orsay in Paris exhibits an important collection of impressionist art in the former Gare d'Orsay, a depot designed by noted French architect Victor Laloux. The station, located on the Quai d'Orsay and serving the Orleans line, was opened for the Paris Exposition of 1900. It was the earliest station to use multiple levels to facilitate traffic, with an upper concourse over lower-level platforms. A single barrel vault roof spanned both levels and provided a prototype for urban stations around the world.

Epilogue

The cold dark waters of Puget Sound segue to rolling hillsides covered with the bright yellow blossoms of Scotch Broom, as Amtrak's Coast Starlight speeds south from Seattle, rolling off the miles to Los Angeles. The lounge car is half-filled with eager passengers, some consuming snack-bar food while others await the rasping announcement on the intercom: "Breakfast is now being served in the dining car." The women of a tour group chatter excitedly, whooping in surprise as a Union Pacific freight passes by with an explosive whoosh a few feet outside their window. An older man from Texas strikes up a conversation with a thirty-something couple from eastern Pennsylvania, and two young men with crew-cuts flirt shamelessly with a smiling dark-eyed woman.

It may not be the oft-lamented golden age of passenger trains, but this contemporary version satisfies the soul nonetheless. No one would confuse Amtrak's Superliner Sightseer Lounge Car with a classic Budd-built stainless steel dome, and welded rail has eliminated the hypnotic *clickety-clack* that characterized rail travel of the past, but the seats are comfortable and can be swiveled to face each other, the window glass wraps expansively up onto the ceiling, and the bar is open. Despite Amtrak's budgetary problems, rail travel in the United States can still be a gratifying experience.

After gliding through several miles of fern-carpeted mixed forest, occasionally interrupted by the ruins of abandoned houses or the rusting hulks of long-abandoned pick-up trucks, the rails suddenly break into the open, and we briefly parallel the concrete ribbon of Interstate 5. It is hard to resist a smug smile as the twin GE Dash 8 2B diesels bring the ten-car train past the laboring motor traffic. The automobile travelers may beat me to San Francisco by an hour or two, but I will be rested and well-fed, while they likely will be suffering from the rigors of both the highway and road food.

Unfortunately, the Starlight doesn't represent all Amtrak trains, and the U.S. government–controlled National Railroad Passenger Corporation suffers from a lack of dedicated funding. While some politicians recognize the efficiency of rail transportation, others continue to ratify funding for airports and highways while denying obvious sources of revenue, such as a share of gasoline taxes, to Amtrak. Indeed, the state of affairs in U.S. and Canadian rail travel is a microcosmic warning to rail systems around the world.

Other countries seem to understand the importance of passenger trains as a vital link in the transportation network, but the governments of the United States and Canada continue to justify allowing a decline in railroad services in the name of budget balancing. The argument is that most passenger trains worldwide require a subsidy to cover operational costs not recovered from fares. What this assessment fails to encompass is that highways and airports also require subsidies and that their operation has hidden costs to society in the form of, for instance, lost land-tax revenue, noise pollution, and unwieldy govermental regulatory beauracracies. Standard accounting practices (designed to express income and expenses for tax purposes) don't properly reflect these hidden costs or account for such intangibles as environmental damage.

Still, even though investment capital for the equipment and facilities necessary for service improvements is hard to come by in North America and represents a long-term investment, Amtrak has from the beginning

Amtrak imported several European train sets in the early 1990s for experimental purposes. In a return to the heyday of the early passenger service, the streamlined Talgo and Inter City Express (ICE) trains (pictured here) were exhibited to the public around the United States and operated on several routes as a prelude to a decision on the next generation of equipment. In another return to tradition, the Dreyfuss firm was hired to produce styling treatments for the new high-speed train sets, to be built to Amtrak's specifications.

HIGH-SPEED PASSENGER TRAINS

❖ ❖ ❖

Because traveling by rail is so convenient in cases where the departure and arrival cities are no more than a few hundred miles apart (note, for instance, the eastern U.S. "shuttle service," which connects New York City with several other important cities), train service can often compete successfully with airplane service. Since railroads usually stop at downtown terminals, they eliminate the time needed to travel to and from the airports; additionally, rail passengers don't need to arrive up to an hour ahead of departure time. As a result, net travel times between downtowns are often quite close whether by plane or by train.

Rail service has other advantages, too. Since trains are less affected by adverse weather, and are more conducive to relaxation or accomplishing a little work, many business travelers around the world take the train when appropriate. Unfortunately, outside of Europe, major cities of the world can be many hundreds of miles apart, rendering one-day business travel by rail impossible.

The answer to this problem is to field trains that are capable of reaching higher speeds on dedicated rights of way. The Japanese Shinkansen (Bullet Trains), the French TGV and Eurostar (the Chunnel train), the British HST (High Speed Train), and the Amtrak Metroliners have all proven the practicality of such ventures—passengers of many types, especially business travelers, ride them in substantial numbers.

The current state of affairs in the airline industry—overburdened and out-of-date airports, aging planes, and overcrowded air routes—clearly points to the need for an alternative. Unfortunately, however, the horren-dous construction and land-acquisition costs necessary to launch new rail lines has greatly limited the number of such ventures. And while some technical innovations—such as the tilting cars of Britain and Spain (which minimize problems on sharper curves) and improved electrification along many routes—have been proven, other high-speed rail concepts, such as maglev (for "magnetic levitation") technology (which is being perfected in Germany), remain in the future.

The French began the modern race for speed with the postwar Mistral; today, the TGVs operate efficiently at 125 mph (200kph) and are capable of 160 mph (256kph) along the Paris–Lyons route. In Japan, the Shinkansen New Tokaido line is heavily used, with trains averaging 101 mph (63kmh). And in the United States, the High Speed Ground Transportation Act paved the way for the speed advance; along the northeast corridor, the Metroliners that operate between Boston, New York, and Washington all travel at speeds above the century mark.

Also in the United States, Amtrak continues to experiment with proven European technology, and several private interests have initiated bold ventures with maglev concepts. Maglev technology uses powerful magnetic forces to float wheelless equipment a few inches above a guide-way and to propel the virtually frictionless train at very high speeds with great efficiency. It remains to be seen whether the great amounts of capital necessary for such a venture can be raised privately, or whether the government will risk making such an investment during the current atmosphere of fiscal restraint.

aggressively pursued the latest technology available, despite the funding difficulties. From the Rohr Turboliners to the Genesis locomotives and from Metroliners to Superliners to Viewliners, Amtrak has searched for economy with quality. Experiments with the European Talgo-Train and Inter City Express (ICE) trains, as well as the newest electric locomotives, may yet prove fruitful.

Even for the devout rail fan, though, certain fundamental questions remain. Is the passenger train an endangered species, to be protected at all costs? Does the railroad provide a truly valuable alternative to the problems of noisy, crowded jet planes and the numbing ennui of driving endless miles of interstate highway?

The answer to both remains clearly "yes" in many parts of the world—the success of Japan's Shinkansen and France's TGV, as well as countless commuter trains around the world, prove it. But even in the United States, there is adequate evidence that passenger trains can be made to work physically as well as aesthetically. Amtrak's new generation of equipment—the long-distance Superliners of the West and the high-speed Amfleet of the East—have all but eliminated the reliability problems of the fifty-year-old Heritage equipment handed down to Amtrak at its inception; the onboard staff is generally competent and cheerful; and the limited menu available in the dining car can be quite good. Maybe they'll eventually bring back fresh flowers on the table to complement the china, tablecloths, and metal flatware.

If travelers around the world—but especially in the United States—have the will and can find the means to support and subsidize their rail systems, and the next twenty-five years show the same improvement and growth as the past quarter century, then rail travel will remain the wondrous and soul-satisfying experience that it has always been.

Bibliography

Alexander, Edwin P. *Down at the Depot*. New York: Bramhall House, 1970.

Allen, Godfrey Freeman. *Luxury Trains of the World*. New York: Everest House, 1979.

Ball, Don. *The Pennsylvania Railroad: 1940s—1950s*. Chester, Vt.: Elm Tree Books, 1986.

Beebe, Lucius, and Charles Clegg. *The Trains We Rode,* Vol 2. Berkeley: Howell-North Books, 1966.

Brigmano, Mary, and Hax McCullough. *The Search for Safety: A History of Railroad Signals and the People Who Made Them*. Pittsburgh: Union Switch and Signal Division, American Standard Inc., 1981.

Carroll, Brian. *Australia's Railway Days*. Melbourne, Australia: MacMillan Company of Australia Pty Ltd., 1976.

Church, Robert J. *Snowbound: The Rescue of Train 101, The City of San Francisco*. Wilton, Calif.: Signature Press, 1995.

Ellis, Hamilton. *The Pictorial Encyclopedia of Railways,* 4th ed. Feltham, Middlesex, United Kingdom: The Hamlyn Publishing Group, Ltd., 1973.

Hollingsworth, J.B. *The Atlas of Train Travel*. New York: Elsevier-Dutton Publishing Co. Inc., 1980.

Johnston, Bob. "Amtrak at 25: Which Vision for Amtrak?" *Trains*, Vol. 56, No. 6, June 1996.

Le Massena, Robert A., et al. V*anishing Vistas* (collector's cards). Rocklin, Cal.: Richard E. Cox, various dates.

Lyle, Katie Letcher. *Scalded to Death by the Steam*. Chapel, N.C.: Algonquin Books, 1983.

Marshall, John. *The Guinness Railway Book*. Enfield, Middlesex, United Kingdom: Guinness Publishing, Ltd., 1989.

McGonigal, Robert S. "Silver Survivor." *Trains*, Vol. 55, No. 5, May 1995.

Nock, O.S. *Railways of Canada*. London, United Kingdom: Adam and Charles Black Ltd., 1973.

———. *Railways Then and Now: A World History*. New York: Crown Publishers, Inc., 1975.

Parks, Pat. *The Railroad that Died at Sea*. Brattleboro, Vt.: The Stephen Green Press, 1968.

Reed, Robert. *Train Wrecks*. Seattle: Superior Publishing Co., 1968.

Riley, C.J. *The Encyclopedia of Trains & Locomotives*. New York: Michael Friedman Publishing Group, Inc., 1994.

Signor, John. *The Coast Line*. Wilton, Calif.: Signature Press, 1995.

Staufer, Alvin, Bert Pennypacker, and Martin Flattley. *Pennsy Power*. Medina, Ohio: Staufer Railroad Books, 1962.

Turner, Charles W., with additions by Thomas W. Dixon, Jr., and Eugene L. Huddleston. *Chessie's Road*, 2nd ed. Alderson, W. Va.: The Chesapeake & Ohio Historical Society, Inc., 1986.

Welsh, Joseph M. *By Streamliner: New York to Florida*. Andover, Mass.: Andover Junction Publications, 1994.

Wheaton, Timothy. *Luxury Trains*. Edison, New Jersey: Book Sales, Inc., 1995.

Zimmerman, Karl R. *The Remarkable GG-1*. New York: Quadrant Press Review, 1977.

———. *Santa Fe Streamliners: The Chiefs and Their Tribesmen*. New York: Quandrant Press, Inc., 1987.

Photo Credits

AP/Wide World Photos: pp. 155 top, 155 bottom

Archive Photos: pp. 32 bottom, 33 bottom, 36, 42-43, 48, 60-61, 62 bottom, 63 top, 65 top, 65 bottom, 69, 82 top, 105 bottom, 132

Association of American Railroads: pp. 8-9 background; Illinois Central railroad: p. 147

Australian Information Service: ©Norman Plant: p. 19 top

©Christopher C. Bain: pp. 25, 43, 81, 109, 115, 141, 157

©karen l. barr: p. 169 bottom

©JOHN C. BENSON: p. 83

BROWN BROTHERS: pp. front endpaper, 17 top, 26 top, 37 top, 46 right, 116 bottom, 117 top, 117 bottom left, 146 bottom, 159, 165 bottom

California State Railroad Museum: pp. 98, 103 bottom, 105 top, 110 top, 110 bottom left, 110 bottom right, 111 top, 111 bottom, 112

Canadian Pacific Limited: pp. 15, 116 top

Corbis-Bettmann: pp. 10–11, 11, 13, 14, 24–25, 26 bottom, 33 top, 34, 37 bottom, 53, 58, 60, 76, 90 bottom, 131 bottom, 142 top, 143, 144 top, 146 top right, 156–157, 160–161, 166–167

Denver Public Library, Western History Department: pp. 87, 99, 107

Harold A. Edmonson Collection: pp. 27, 96–97; ©Harold A. Edmonson: pp. 9, 22, 38–39, 41 top, 41 bottom, 64, 77, 100, 101

FPG International Corp.: pp. 45, 54, 66–67, 74, 91, 117 bottom right, 131 top, 135 bottom right, 158 right, 163 top, 164 bottom right, 165 top, 167, 168–169, 169 top, back endpaper

©Steve Glischinski: pp. 1, 6–7, 35, 72, 108–109

©Scott A. Hartley: p. 49

Kansas State Historical Society, Topeka, KS: pp. 89 top, 89 bottom, 92 top, 92 bottom, 94, 96, 164 top, 164 bottom left

Library of Congress: pp. 140–141, 150

National Archives of Canada: pp. 114–115

National Railway Museum: pp. 12 top left, 23, 124–125, 128; Science and Society: pp. 126, 127

©James A. Neubauer: p. 68

North Wind Picture Archives: pp. 12 bottom, 16, 145

Shannon Phipps Collector: p. 21; Alexander Turnbull Library, Wellington, N.Z.: pp. 17 bottom, 18

Picture Collection, New York Public Library: pp. 130, 142 bottom, 151 left, 151 right, 154

Railroad Museum of Pennsylvania (PHMC): pp. 30, 32 top, 78, 102, 104, 170–171 background

©D. Randy Riggs: pp. 113, 163 bottom

C.J. Riley Collection: p. 52 bottom; C&O Historical Society Collection: p. 31

©ERNEST H. ROBL: pp. 136, 137, 138, 139

Smithsonian Institution: p. 47

Springer/Corbis-Bettmann: p. 59

Superstock: pp. 129 bottom, 135 bottom left

©Alan Tillotson: pp. 2–3, 58–59, 119, 121, 122–123, 162 left, 162 right, 170

UPI/Corbis-Bettmann: pp. 50, 51, 52 top, 55, 56, 62 top, 63 bottom, 71, 73, 75, 80–81, 82 bottom, 84, 85, 88, 90 top, 93, 103 top, 106, 129 top, 134, 135 top, 148, 149, 152

Index

Index